Exegeting Orality

"What difference does it make if the Exodus story is read from a page or performed on a stage? Is reading a Gospel like attending a Passion Play? Are authors and scribes the same as performers? Are readers and audiences more alike than they are different? Nick Acker distills the insights of two generations of scholarship on such questions and explores their importance for Christians today who approach the Bible as the word of God. Read this book, then hear anew the old, old stories."

—**Rafael Rodriguez**, professor of New Testament, Pittsburgh Theological Seminary

"The study of orality is making us think about the Bible in new ways reflecting its original social contexts from each Testament. *Exegeting Orality* is a worthwhile read because it surveys well where orality studies currently stand and proposes a series of suggestions about how the move to text interacted with oral tradition, not in opposition to it but alongside it. This book will help you get situated in a discussion that is becoming more prominent in biblical studies."

—**Darrell L. Bock**, senior research professor of New Testament studies, Dallas Theological Seminary

"Critical to faith are the ways in which human beings express the foundations of their belief, and even though not all readers of Nick Acker's book may share his particular faith, we can applaud his appreciation for the oral traditional qualities of Scripture and the implications of those qualities for cultural communities and their identities. Acker is to be commended for his bibliographic thoroughness and for his thoughtful review of the history of relevant scholarship in context."

—**Susan Niditch**, professor of religion, Amherst College

"It's obvious to modern people that the Bible is a book that we read (silently). Yet over the centuries, most people listened to it read by someone else, and the people who wrote the Bible expected that most people would hear it read in that way. So in their oral culture they wrote it with that expectation. So it's useful to have this book from which you will learn a lot about scholarly theories concerning orality."

—**JOHN GOLDINGAY**, senior professor of Old Testament, Fuller Seminary

"The Bible we study is a written text whether we read it in the original languages or in a modern translation. Nick Acker reminds us that these texts originated in an ancient oral culture and warns us about an uncritical application of modern textual assumptions as we interpret it. I recommend *Exegeting Orality* to all serious students of the Bible. This book will get you thinking through some of the most important issues of biblical interpretation."

—**TREMPER LONGMAN III**, professor emeritus of biblical studies, Westmont College

Exegeting Orality

*Interpreting the Inspired Words of Scripture
in Light of Their Oral Traditional Origins*

Nick Acker

Foreword by Paul R. Eddy

WIPF & STOCK · Eugene, Oregon

EXEGETING ORALITY
Interpreting the Inspired Words of Scripture in Light of Their Oral Traditional Origins

Copyright © 2024 Nick Acker. All rights reserved. Except for brief quotations in critical publications or reviews, no part of this book may be reproduced in any manner without prior written permission from the publisher. Write: Permissions, Wipf and Stock Publishers, 199 W. 8th Ave., Suite 3, Eugene, OR 97401.

Wipf & Stock
An Imprint of Wipf and Stock Publishers
199 W. 8th Ave., Suite 3
Eugene, OR 97401

www.wipfandstock.com

PAPERBACK ISBN: 978-1-62032-942-9
HARDCOVER ISBN: 978-1-4982-8770-8
EBOOK ISBN: 978-1-7252-4845-8

VERSION NUMBER 09/03/24

Some Scripture quotations are from the ESV® Bible (The Holy Bible, English Standard Version®), copyright © 2001 by Crossway, a publishing ministry of Good News Publishers. Used by permission. All rights reserved. You may not copy or download more than 500 consecutive verses of the ESV Bible or more than one half of any book of the ESV Bible.

Some Scripture quotations are taken from the Holy Bible, New International Version®, NIV®. Copyright © 1973, 1978, 1984, 2011 by Biblica, Inc.™ Used by permission. All rights reserved worldwide.

Other Scripture quotations are the author's translations.

Daniel Block's chart on the judges' pattern has been modified with permission from Lifeway Christian Resources.

This book is dedicated to my wife, Rebekah Mawumenyo.

Contents

List of Illustrations and Tables | ix
Foreword by Paul R. Eddy | xi
Preface | xv
Acknowledgments | xix
Abbreviations | xxi
Introduction | xxiii

Part 1: Orality, Textuality, and the Bible | 1

1. Summary of Studies in Orality and Textuality | 3
2. A History of the Application of Orality to Old Testament Studies | 23
3. Oral Tradition and the Textual Tradition of Habakkuk | 28
4. Inspiration and Authority of the Biblical Text | 36

Part 2: Exegeting Orality | 51

5. Concepts for Exegeting Orality | 53
6. The Book of Judges | 61
7. The Synoptic Tradition | 134
8. The Divine Proposal in John | 158
9. Romans 9–11 | 202
10. A Multiform Tradition and Performance | 226

Final Words: A Performance for our Modern Tradition of Exegesis | 257
Bibliography | 263

List of Illustrations and Tables

Patterns of the Judges | 66–67

Phrasings of Rom 11:25–27 | 222

Foreword

IT IS ONE OF the ironies of modern biblical studies. In the first few decades of the twentieth century, the form-critical theories of scholars such as Hermann Gunkel and Rudolph Bultmann were solidifying themselves within the discipline. At the heart of these theories were certain assumptions about the nature of human oral communication, assumptions that were deeply indebted to the intuitions and communication dynamics that characterized the post-Gutenberg, highly-literate world of modern scholarship. And now the irony: At the same time that the form-critical model of orality was spreading and captivating the academic study of the Bible, two Homeric scholars at Harvard, Milman Parry and his assistant, Albert Lord, were busy recording and analyzing live performances of traditional Serbo-Croatian oral epics—and, in the process, igniting a spark that has led to a revolution in our understanding of orality and oral tradition. In an important sense, the field of biblical studies is still in the process of catching up to this revolution.

It is an honor to write this foreword to Nick Acker's book, *Exegeting Orality*, which represents a distinctive contribution to the ongoing revolution in our understanding of the orally-oriented nature of the biblical texts. Simply put, Acker's work is both an academically robust, and admirably accessible, guide and contribution to the orality revolution that is currently underway within the field of biblical studies. The academic rigor of this book is rooted in Acker's 2022 PhD dissertation and is on display throughout the volume. From the opening chapters that offer a guided tour of the history and current status of orality research and its relevance to biblical studies, to the latter chapters providing concrete examples of the benefits that accompany the practice of "exegeting orality,"

Acker's thought is uniformly up to date and informed by the best minds working at the intersection of orality and biblical studies today. Beyond providing a reliable guide to the broad impact of new understandings of orality and performance criticism upon contemporary biblical studies, at least three aspects of Acker's work stand out as distinctive contributions to the field.

First, Acker applies an informed, orally sensitive hermeneutical lens to specific scriptural texts, and in the course of doing so, practically models the method he advances, while delivering significant exegetical insights. Acker applies his approach to a good range of biblical genres, including OT historical narrative (the book of Judges) and prophetic literature (Habakkuk), the tradition(s) contained within the Synoptic Gospels and the Gospel of John, and a Pauline epistle (Romans 9–11). An important observation emerges from Acker's theoretical work that has direct bearing on his practice of exegeting orality, one that is tied to an infamous problem in orality studies known as the "Great Divide." Put briefly, the Great Divide refers to the conviction—common in earlier orality studies—that orality and writing are mutually exclusive, even contradictory, phenomena. Acker rightly rejects a Great Divide approach to his subject matter. However, he also brings balance to this issue by pointing out that if there are no significant distinctions between orality and writing, then the very field of orality studies itself may be up for question. Acker explains that repetition is a significant characteristic of orality, one that serves to economically activate entire streams of tradition through metonymy (i.e., where the part signifies and brings to communal remembrance the whole). He then takes this observation in a practical direction when he identifies repetition via ring/echo composition as characteristic of an oral register and one that is present in many biblical texts. In doing so, Acker demonstrates the type of hermeneutical insights that can accompany the tracking of various modes of repetition within a text—from structuring devices (e.g., the judges cycle) and thematic patterns to repetition of words, names, phrases, and scenes. At this point, some might push back by arguing that such communicative techniques can be fully recognized and appreciated within the context of a straightforward literary approach to the biblical texts, apart from any concerns about orality. But Acker challenges this response by rightly noting that "proper interpretation of material stemming from oral cultures requires the consideration of aspects of oral traditional culture such as activation, communal memory, structural repetition, and performance" (p. 157). At the same time, Acker once again demonstrates a careful and balanced methodological approach when he warns against the unrestrained, speculative application of performance criticism to biblical texts that lack clear evidential support.

A second distinctive of this volume emerges from Acker's equal commitment to serious application of orality studies to the Bible, on one hand, and to core theological convictions of historic Christianity—including a high view of scripture and its divine inspiration—on the other. This dual commitment is seen in chapter nine, for example, where Acker exhibits the way in which consideration of orality can bring new light to a text embroiled in more than one theological controversy over the centuries (i.e., Rom 9–11). Acker also gives sustained attention to a theological issue that naturally emerges when we take seriously the pluriform nature of the biblical tradition and the related implications for the concept of a single "original" inspired text. To be clear, Acker recognizes the Bible as "the written word of God" (p. xv). As such, he takes seriously the inspiration, canonicity, and authority of the Christian scriptures. Yet Acker's theological commitment to a high view of Scripture does not prevent him from fully engaging the question of how our knowledge of the communicative dynamics at work in the orally dominant ancient world should impact our understanding of biblical inspiration and the textualization process. Acker perceptively writes, "As opposed to theories of inspiration that seek a series of inerrant autographs, the inspiration from God did not rest simply on individual authors or editors who penned the original text or any kind of a final form of the text. God's inspiration was communal.... The inspired word was a living tradition" (p. 44).

Finally, there is Acker's goal of making this book both accessible to, and practically useful for, those who are preaching, pastoring, and ministering within the context of the local church and beyond—an admirable goal that he clearly achieves. Nowhere is this achievement more apparent than in the final pages of the chapter on the Johannine theme of Jesus as the divine groom. Here, moving seamlessly from exegetical insights to words of pastoral encouragement, Acker offers a touching meditation on the profound depths of God's love. Acker finally ends his book by taking us back to the original garden of delight; to God's original loving purposes for humanity; to the fateful human quest for a type of "knowledge" that, in its desire for self-aggrandizement, ultimately destroys love relationship itself; and to the one who eventually comes to give his life so that humanity can intimately know, and fully be known by,

God. Ultimately, it is in service to this type of true, life-giving knowledge of and by God that Acker offers this book to us. It is a book that I wholeheartedly recommend.

    Paul Rhodes Eddy
    Professor of Biblical & Theological Studies
    Bethel University (St. Paul, MN)

Preface

THE BIBLE IS THE written word of God. Its content came into being in an oral/aural culture and is now received in written words. The Old Testament is the authoritative representation of Israel's testimony as the people of YHWH. The New Testament contains teachings of Jesus the Messiah who fulfilled Israel's testimony of YHWH. The Bible is the product of the Holy Spirit of God moving through the people of God. God spoke through priests, prophets, sages, apostles, scribes, "average" people, and apparently even a donkey. As the textual product of the word of God spoken into the world, the Bible is the authoritative standard as to how we should expect to experience and understand the current move of the Holy Spirit as our counselor, guide, and teacher of the truths of YHWH. Since the identity of the Bible is so weighty, it is important that we intentionally work to understand its true nature and to study and interpret it exactly as it is, not as our own culture desires it to be. Emerging theories of orality and textuality growing out of the fields of studies in orality may challenge some Western, modern, text-saturated views of Scripture, how to study it, and how to interpret and proclaim it.

In *Exegeting Orality* I summarize and expand upon the concepts of orality and textuality as discussed in my 2022 dissertation from B. H. Carroll Theological Institute. My goal is to offer an introduction to recent theories on orality and textuality (biblical performance criticism or media criticism), followed by a series of examples of applying those theories to the work of interpreting the Bible for the benefit of the believing community. Some material is taken and edited from my dissertation, especially the discussions of the nature of orality and textuality, as well as my suggestions for the application of theories of orality to topics concerning the Bible, such as its inspiration, authority, and exegesis.

Scholars who are familiar with the field will notice a seeming disparaging lack of technical terms, as well as a very large neglect of many currently emphasized nuances in the field and in the history of the field as I narrate it. I acknowledge these gaps. The purpose of *Exegeting Orality* is to organize the findings in the field(s) under discussion and provide an introduction to what is most immediately useful and, in my opinion, most enduringly relevant for the practicing, preaching, and ministering scholar/pastor. I steer the content of this book toward suggestions for exegesis rather sharply. Should a pastor have no desire to further delve into the field(s) of biblical performance criticism or media criticism, I believe that the following summary of theories on orality, textuality, oral tradition, and performance, along with the examples of their applications to biblical interpretation provided, will help ministers effectively apply the crucial implications of Scripture's oral traditional origins. Should one desire to begin to study the field in a more holistic way, in addition to the works of other scholars I refer to throughout my work, I suggest beginning with Peter Perry's article, "Biblical Performance Criticism: Survey and Prospects," available freely online,[1] and Rafael Rodriguez's work discussed below in the introduction.

In the preface of my dissertation that explored the book of Habakkuk in light of these theories, I said the following: the work that follows is an attempt at an interdisciplinary approach to the study of the Hebrew Bible.[2] The disciplines I will attempt to engage are nuanced, complicated, and emerging. Studies in orality are multiform and developing at a staggering pace, and I have but dipped my toes into the field of textual criticism. I hope that my understanding of the experts cited in this work and my applications of their theories to the manuscripts of Habakkuk discussed below are proficient enough to offer a study that will benefit

1. https://www.mdpi.com/2077-1444/10/2/117/pdf; accessed through https://www.biblicalperformancecriticism.org

2. Terminology for the literature under review will follow the common vernacular of a Protestant Christian understanding of the Tanak and New Testament, though with an understanding of the critical issues for using those terms. Unless specifically outlined, phrases such as "Hebrew Bible" and "Old Testament" will be used to discuss the same set of writings without making a point concerning the manuscripts or book order. Indeed, the intention of using such a general vocabulary is to acknowledge the broad critical discussions on the shape, purpose, and meaning of the literature and so, hopefully, leave room for conclusions to be made on the literature at-large and not on a certain selection of perspectives on them.

both fields and most importantly, lead to a deeper understanding, appreciation, and application of the truths and purposes of the amazing library frequently referred to as the Bible.

To all of the above I will add a note concerning my favorite aspect of an oral traditional approach to the canon of Scripture: Oral traditional material is not communicated for data transfer, but each performance represents ancient understandings of the community's identity in order to re-activate that identity in the hearts and minds of the community in new ways. Through performance, the community re-experiences its identity and purpose with all of its past historical realities activated in the immediate present circumstance. The word is not proclaimed to be received merely as knowledge to be analyzed, discussed, and argued over but instead to be lived out as a communal identity. The Bible is not simply a text to be studied; it is a tradition of identity that is to be re-proclaimed and reenacted in the community of faith.

May the Spirit of the living God use this work to lead Christ's church, as well as others who may be open to his words, to experience the biblical traditions as our communal identity, and may we actualize that ancient identity today for his glory and our joy.

Acknowledgments

WE ARE COMPOSITES. EACH of us carry generations of DNA, and our neurological networks are shaped by unique paths through countless interactions and experiences with others. Any good that comes from this work is undoubtedly due to the Spirit's gracious guidance, steering me through a multitude of interactions, despite my often poor navigational skills.

I am grateful for my parents who raised me in the faith and gave me freedom, direction, and support in my educational pursuits. I am grateful for my wife's parents for their unending grace and encouraging lives.

I live with voices of various influential people in my head. Chris Stapper says, "Don't be so hard on yourself." Doug Jackson always asks, "Can you say that more creatively? How does it fit into your relationship with Jesus?" Geoff Smith pokes, "Yeah, but is that really what Jesus said? Is that what the text really means?" Mark Rotramel directs, "So what? What do you do with that?" Karen Bullock says, "You need to cite that." William Kappen challenges, "Are you being too black and white? Is this really relevant for relational faith and practice?" John Holt encouraged me to think beyond the limits I had set for myself. I hope this work does their voices justice.

I am grateful for Ron Lyles and how he graciously guided me to let go of what I wanted the Old Testament to be so that I could begin a pursuit for the Old Testament that Jesus fulfilled. I am grateful for Timothy Pierce for launching me into my doctoral studies and for Rick Johnson for carrying me across the finish line. Stark College and Seminary and B. H. Carroll Theological Seminary have been safe havens for my educational and formational pursuits.

Susan Niditch has demonstrated such incredible kindness as I have pursued the application of studies in orality and media to teaching and preaching. From phone conversations on teaching the book of Judges to so many answered emails and encouraging words after reading portions of this work, she only always encouraged me. Ray Person also gave generous hours to email correspondence and reading portions of my dissertation, providing direction, and sharing some of his thoughts and research. Peter Perry redirected my studies to engage Rafael Rodriguez's work, and Rodriguez has been incredibly generous with his time and encouragement as well. Darrell Bock's email correspondence was very instructional, opening new questions for future study.

I am so very grateful for everyone who read drafts and gave guidance and wrote blurbs for the book. Even those who could not read early versions due to time and commitment issues responded kindly and with encouragement. There are so many fingerprints on the thoughts in this work, and without all the encouragements along the way, I am not certain I would have persevered the process. The fellowship around this work has been a beautiful experience.

Thank you, Wipf & Stock, for publishing this work.

Most of all I want to thank Paul Eddy. His work opened my mind to certain nuances of oral tradition, and his correspondence at the beginning of my doctoral studies set the trajectory for my focus on oral tradition and the Old Testament. He provided much of the bibliography found in this work back in 2015. He then so graciously guided me into and through this publication process.

Rebekah, Zoe, Liam, and Baxley. You guys are my joy.

As composite relational creatures, we pray that we can be faithful tradents, performing the best of the traditions we have received. I pray this performance is true to the best of what I have received from so many.

Abbreviations

BDB
Brown, Francis, S. R. Driver, and Charles A. Briggs, eds. *The New Brown, Driver, and Briggs Hebrew and English Lexicon of the Old Testament*. 1906. Reprint. Lafayette, IN: Associated Publishers & Authors, 1981.

HALOT
Köhler, Ludwig, Walter Baumgartner, M. E. J. Richardson, and Johann Jakob Stamm, eds. *The Hebrew and Aramaic Lexicon of the Old Testament*. 2 vols. Leiden, The Netherlands: E. J. Brill, 1994.

Introduction

THE BIBLE IS A funny thing. On one hand, it is believed by the majority of the largest religion in the world to be a holy collection of writings that can instruct us in the way of loving God and others and finding purpose in life and eternal salvation. On the other hand, it has been abused, even to the extent of justifying human slavery. Among those who testify that the Bible is holy and profitable for intimacy with God and others, many often find themselves divided, sometimes bitterly, over perspectives of its interpretation and application.

People of faith have been engaging the content of the Bible for many thousands of years. A few manuscripts of the Bible date from around the third century BCE—the earliest of the Dead Sea Scrolls. Most scholars believe that even before the words were written down, the content of what was eventually written existed among the community in oral form. The "Song of Deborah" (Judg 5) is often considered to be some of the earliest content contained in the Bible, due to its oral register and ancient style.[1] At any rate, while the believing community has been utilizing the written words for thousands of years, much of its authoritative content, such as the Song of Deborah (in one form or another), has defined the community for longer than we can accurately account.

This raises the specific issue of the interaction of the oral and written forms of the content, and, curiously, biblical studies seem to be lagging behind in the study and application of the issue of orality and its interaction with the written word.

---

1. Niditch, *Judges*, 67–82.

The Bible is a product of a predominantly oral culture.[2] Recent studies of the epigraphical evidence argue that while "the beginning of a literary tradition in Israel and Judah in the ninth and tenth century [BCE] is certainly not impossible,"[3] evidence of scribal education can be argued from the consistency of Old Hebrew only from the ninth and early eighth centuries.[4] Therefore, large-scale scribal presence and the environment needed for the production of long texts for Israel may not have existed until the late ninth or eighth centuries.[5]

Of course Ugaritic and Ebla texts demonstrate that extensive writing was not unknown to the Levant from very early dates, but, as Brian B. Schmidt stated, "It is at the same time both obvious and profound that literacy in the ancient Near Eastern and Mediterranean theaters emerged in a predominantly oral world."[6] Even when the written word is prevalent in oral cultures, it does not overtake the oral dimensions of the culture.[7] This means that the traditions preserved in the Bible were not written for individual readers to read silently. Likely, the authors wrote them for performers to perform (not theatrical performance, but at the very least public readings) and audiences to experience in a public arena.[8]

The application of concepts of oral tradition to biblical studies has been discussed since at least the Reformation,[9] and Hermann Gunkel brought the discussion to the forefront of Old Testament studies at the

---

2. For a discussion on this topic focusing on the New Testament, see Rodriguez, *Oral Tradition*, 1–10.

3. Lemaire, "Levantine Literacy," 34.

4. Rollston, "Scribal Curriculum," 86.

5. Schmidt, "Memorializing Conflict, 126–27.

6. Schmidt, "Introduction," 1.

7. The presence of an oral register in the textual traditions stemming from oral cultures is a major aspect of this study. For a brief discussion on this perspective from a work that utilizes the concept for its ongoing thesis, see Carr, *Formation*, 5–6; see also Person, *Deuteronomic*, 43–51, and 75–76; Horsley, "Oral Tradition in New Testament Studies," 34–35; Rodriguez, *Oral Tradition*; and Niditch, "Oral Tradition and Biblical Scholarship," 43–44; The concluding words of Niditch's book, *Oral World*, 134: "To study Israelite literature is to examine the place of written words in an essentially oral world and to explore the ways in which the capacity to read and write in turn informs and shapes orally rooted products of the imagination."

8. For an argument for the texts operating as a means of memory aid for performance, see Miller, "The Performance of Oral Tradition," 175–96; see also Harvey, "Orality and Its Implications," 99–109.

9. Culley, "Oral Tradition and Biblical Studies," 32.

Introduction

turn of the twentieth century.[10] Gunkel's work led to the formation of form criticism, which has had a lasting effect on both Old and New Testament scholarship.[11] Interestingly, as large of an impact as Gunkel's work has had on biblical studies, his views on orality were based on questionable presuppositions.

Susan Niditch claimed Gunkel was "influenced by the Brothers Grimm's own artificial portrait of the German folk" and "by Axel Olrik's 1908 study 'Epic Laws of Folklore.'"[12] Olrik later determined that his own "epic laws did not apply to all oral narrative genres in the same way and to the same extent."[13] Robert C. Culley said Gunkel did not "indicate how he arrived at his approach to biblical literature or where he came by his perception of oral tradition, although he acknowledges a general debt to Herder."[14]

Theories concerning orality have been, and will remain, an aspect of biblical studies. At least to some degree, one's understanding of the function of the oral nature of ancient Israel will affect one's approach to the study of the text. Since the concept of orality has already had such a lasting effect on biblical studies while often leaning on unsupported theories,[15] and since the concept of orality will continue to impact biblical studies, it is important that current studies in orality be applied to the study of biblical texts to correct the application of any faulty theories and to ensure that future applications of orality are as true as possible. Many

---

10. Culley, "Oral Tradition and Biblical Studies," 33: "The fullest discussion of oral tradition by Gunkel may be found in the introduction to his commentary on Genesis."

11. In 1998, John H. Hayes could write that Gunkel's "work remains foundational for practically all contemporary psalms research," Hayes, "Songs of Israel," 157; and Gunkel's views are still discussed in current studies of orality: see: Polak, "Oral Substratum," 220; and Sanders, "Empirical Models for Pentateuchal Criticism," 285.

12. Niditch, *Oral World*, 2. Olrik influenced Gunkel while Gunkel worked on his third edition of his commentary on Genesis—Holbek, "Introduction," xxiii.

13. Holbek, "Introduction," xxiii.

14. Culley, "Oral Tradition and Biblical Studies," 33. Culley also pointed out that Gunkel's theories were impressive and "based on a sensitive reading of the texts along with a rather general notion of oral tradition and oral culture, perhaps owing much to Herder," 35. The present author in no way means to be overly critical of Gunkel. Some of his discussion comes close to some current perspectives on orality, such as the communal memory he hints at on page lvi of his introduction to *Genesis*.

15. Besides the discussion of Gunkel above, see: Horsley, "Oral Tradition in New," 34–36; Kelber, "Oral Tradition in Bible," 40–42; and Niditch, "Oral Tradition and Biblical Scholarship," 43–44. They assess the state of the application of orality in biblical studies up to 2003.

scholars are seeking to explore the growing understanding of orality and how it applies to biblical studies.[16]

The term "orality" carries various definitions.[17] For my use of the term, I will be focusing on the concepts of oral traditional cultures and how they vary from the modern, Western (Occidental), post-Gutenberg cultures that have led in biblical studies over the past two or three hundred years. Oral traditions vary from modern, Western cultures in many ways, and oral traditional cultures themselves vary considerably from each other.

I hope to highlight general tendencies of oral traditional cultures and how they often vary from the text-saturated culture mentioned above, in order to direct the community of faith toward a more accurate understanding of the Bible's identity and how it should be interpreted and received. I continue to use the term "orality" since many pastors and scholars may still attach the word to form criticism and other outdated theories. I hope to divorce the terms "oral" and "orality" from those old approaches. But let the reader understand, the use of these terms and their various definitions are of great interest in the field. I have intentionally bypassed a thorough discussion of issues behind my use of these terms.

In 2003, after seventeen years of publication, the journal *Oral Tradition* produced two volumes that sought to serve as a synopsis of the current state of studies in orality.[18] In the introduction to the volumes, John Miles Foley said that oral tradition is "in numerous practical ways anything but a unified field."[19] Many of the over eighty contributions, representing fieldwork and study across diverse arenas, discussed either the difficulty of defining *oral tradition* or else defined it a bit differently.[20] What was lamented twenty years ago remains true today. While it

---

16. For a small sampling of further arguments for and discussion of the application of findings in oral tradition to biblical studies, see Culley, "Oral Tradition and Biblical Studies," 30–65; Niditch, *Oral World*; Eddy and Boyd, *Jesus Legend*, especially pages 237–306; Carr, *Formation*; Kelber, "Oral Tradition in Bible," and the collection of works edited by Schmidt, *Contextualizing Israel's Sacred Writings*. For an excellent summary and introduction to the study of orality and the New Testament, see Rodriguez, *Oral Tradition*.

17. See Rodriguez's discomfort with the word in *Oral Tradition*, 6–7.

18. *Oral Tradition* is now managed through Harvard University.

19. Foley, "Editor's Column," 1.

20. See, for instance, Ruth Finnegan's discomfort with both the words "oral" and "tradition," "Oral Tradition," 84; Thomas Hale's stance is that the field is "defined by what it is not—it is oral, not written, but the barrier between the two remains rather fluid and artificial," "Oral Tradition," 91.

may be impossible to systematize orality into a consistent model for all oral traditional cultures, what may be agreed upon generally is that oral tradition embodies communication constructs distinct from text-based modern Western communication. Oral traditional cultures emphasize the communal experience of information through auditory and visual performance, contrasting with the more modern experience of individuals reading and interpreting texts. I will discuss the concept of oral tradition further in chapter 1.

Two significant effects arising from the integration of recent orality studies into biblical analysis hold relevance for interpreting, proclaiming, and applying the Bible. First, the growing data on how oral cultures actually function are calling into question the conclusions and applications of old theories of orality (such as form criticism) in reference to the biblical text and story. Second, old paradigms of approaching the Bible, which did not consider orality much at all, are undergoing transformation. For instance, in the field of textual criticism, instead of tracing variants within manuscript evidence to find the original text/tradition, room exists to understand many different scenarios that may lie behind the text. Gary D. Martin said:

> We have to conceive of an entire range of possibilities in the interface between oral and written: written texts may have derived entirely from previous oral forms; written texts may have been shaped by oral traditions; written texts may have originated as written compositions without an oral predecessor. We may not know which scenario, or which combination of them, lies behind a particular text.[21]

The tradition may have existed most purely within the hearts and minds of the community regardless of any textual witnesses, and so multiform texts could have concurrently represented the tradition that was embedded authoritatively within the communal memory of the community at large. Also, as will be discussed further below, the full communal tradition contains not only memory of narratives and performances of material but traditions of interpretation and meanings of words, themes, scenes, etc. The tradition is larger than any performance or text could ever contain, because the tradition at large is required to interpret any singular performance—whether delivered orally or in written form.

---

21. Martin, *Multiple Originals*, 68.

Thus, not only are dynamics of the scholarly opinion of oral cultures shifting, but these shifts are revealing how assumptions of other critical areas of study may have been tainted by an unanalyzed cultural appropriation of a text/literate-saturated Western culture into the study of texts preserved by cultures that functioned within communication constructs much closer to those of oral/aural cultures.[22] Therefore, studies of the literature of the Bible are broadening to include a range of possibilities that could not be expected from within past constructs. This range of possibilities will not only affect critical scholarship but also the interpretation and proclamation of the message of the Bible by the faith community.

My purpose in *Exegeting Orality* is closely aligned with Rafael Rodriguez's work, *Oral Tradition and the New Testament: A Guide for the Perplexed*. Rodriguez provides an excellent introduction for students of biblical criticism into the field of oral studies, or as he identifies it, *media criticism*. I highly recommend Rodriguez's work, though this book will diverge from it in some ways.

First, I hope the current work will be more palatable for pastors and teachers who may not desire to wade as deep into the field and jargon of biblical media criticism. I want pastors and teachers to be able to pick up this book and immediately apply the concepts to their studies, sermon/lesson prep, and proclamation.[23] I believe that the recent findings stemming from studies on orality and textuality have much to say about the nature of Scripture, its interpretation, and its proclamation, and I believe the church stands to benefit from a clergy and body who are informed and growing in their knowledge of these concepts.

Second, as my doctoral studies focused on the Old Testament, I will begin my discussion on orality as it relates to the Old Testament, though

---

22. While arguing for a comparative approach of Israel's surrounding cultures to the study of the Bible, Carr said, "Models of textuality and education developed through a careful comparative approach are much more likely to be helpful than the anachronistic models of textuality and reading we often unconsciously presuppose on the basis of contemporary experiences." Carr, *Writing on the Tablet*, 14. T. M. West offers a good discussion of biblical scholarship's anachronistic models of textuality in his dissertation "Art of Biblical Performance," iii–vi; also pertinent are Douglas A. Knight's words: "Too often modern scholars have sought documentary sources, oral traditions, and literary editors from the [viewpoint] of our own literate world or our romanticized fantasy of antiquity." Knight, Foreword, x.

23. That is not to say that Rodriguez's work is unpalatable but to make an apology for my choice to avoid certain technical terms and discussions of certain critical issues in the field of orality, textuality, memory, media criticism, biblical performance criticism, and media studies.

I will offer significant discussion on the activation of the Old Testament tradition in many New Testament passages.

Finally, I will diverge from what I understand from Rodriguez's argument for a strict focus on what he calls the *contextual approach* to oral tradition and the New Testament, and I will argue that some aspects of what he calls the *morphological approach* are applicable and that their application does not require an admission, whether implied or otherwise, to a theory of a great divide between orality and literacy.

Exegeting Orality is divided into two main parts. The first part delves into the concepts of orality and textuality. I start in chapter one by exploring the field of oral tradition and discussing some recent theories that have emerged from it. I then outline a practical working definition of oral traditions and their interactions with the written word, focusing on the contrast between oral traditional cultures and the Western text-saturated culture that has influenced the modern critical study of the Bible. In chapter two I review the application of theories of orality to biblical studies, from Hermann Gunkel to the present. In chapter three I summarize my work on the Habakkuk tradition in order to demonstrate the validity of applying recent theories of orality and textuality to the biblical tradition. Chapter four explores the identity of the Bible and concepts of inspiration in light of these theories.

In the second major section I attempt to apply these theories to the interpretation of various biblical books and sections of the Bible. Chapter five summarizes concepts of orality that should be considered when exegeting Scripture. Chapter six surveys the book of Judges, while chapter seven surveys the book of Mark, the passion predictions of the synoptic tradition, and Luke 13:10—14:35. Chapter eight demonstrates the matrimonial themes of the parallel passages found in John 2:1—4:54 and John 19:24b—20:31. Chapter nine engages the difficult section of Rom 9–11. Chapter ten explores other possibilities of exegeting orality, and I conclude with some final words for the church in her faithful reenactment of the ancient tradition.

Part 1

Orality, Textuality, and the Bible

1

Summary of Studies in Orality and Textuality

IN THE FOLLOWING DISCUSSION of the literature on orality and ancient texts, I do not attempt to outline the entire field of orality. Instead, I endeavor to provide an accurate summary of certain important distinctions between oral traditional cultures and the text-saturated Western culture in which so much study of the biblical text has been conducted over the past 250 years or so. For a brief and accurate depiction of the growth of the field, one could look to the introductory chapter of the 2018 dissertation of T. M. West, "The Art of Biblical Performance."[1] As mentioned above, for an incredibly informative and helpful introduction into the vocabulary, theory, and application of orality to biblical studies with special emphasis on the New Testament, see Rafael Rodriguez's *Oral Tradition and the New Testament: A Guide for the Perplexed*. Also relevant is Peter Parry's article, "Biblical Performance Criticism: Survey and Prospects," also cited above. Finally, for a current perspective on the growth of the field as it relates to the historical reliability of the early Jesus tradition one

---

1. West, "Art of Biblical Performance," 2–46. West's dissertation is also available through GlossaHouse's Dissertation Series. For a critical look at the potentially anachronistic history of biblical studies, specifically as it relates to the concepts of scribe and prophet, one could look to Floyd, "'Write the Revelation,'" 103–43.

should not overlook Paul Rhodes Eddy's article, "The Historicity of the Early Oral Jesus Tradition: Reflections on the 'Reliability Wars.'"[2]

Relevant to my purposes, the rest of this chapter is divided into four areas that move from a broad to a successively narrower focus: Context of Orality, Defining Orality, Summation of Oral Traditions, and Oral Traditions and Written Texts.

Context of Orality

Communication is not merely verbal. In her book *Where Is Language?* Ruth Finnegan referred to the process of writing down certain performances of oral cultures as "[an attempt] to capture the magic of live story-telling, in the cage of linear print."[3] Expressing her conclusions and sentiments from a lifetime of fieldwork and study of subjects such as language and orality, Finnegan made the case that the *language* used for human communication goes well beyond words, whether spoken or written. Along with verbal language are "facial expression, gesture, bodily orientation, spatial indications, movement, touch, images, and a variegated range of material objects, from scepters, flags or guns to meaningful apparel, stethoscopes and pulpits."[4]

Even focusing merely "on the auditory dimensions of speech," one must account for "intonation, tempo, dialect, rhythm, volume, timbre, emphasis and all the near-infinite modulations of the speaking—and singing—voice."[5] Finally, one could mention the powerful communicative effects of "sobs, laughs, [and] silence."[6] Though much of Finnegan's work engaged cultures and performances very different than those of ancient Israel, it is still certainly true that the texts preserved within the Bible were originally heard by the vast majority through performances of voice, action, and emotion, and not mainly through the media of the written word.[7]

---

2. Eddy, "Historicity."

3. Finnegan, *Where Is Language*, 55; see also Taylor McConnell's discussion of the recording of oral traditions, "Oral Cultures and Literate Research," 350.

4. Finnegan, *Where Is Language*, 77.

5. Finnegan, *Where Is Language*, 77.

6. Finnegan, *Where Is Language*, 82. Emphasis on the power of these communication tools is added.

7. As discussed below.

The work of Albert Lord and Milman Parry, on the oral traditions of Serbo-Croatia and the oral register of Homeric literature (circa 1960), ushered in a new season of studies in orality.[8] Scholars of other ancient literatures began to investigate whether or not they could apply the theories from Lord/Parry to their own corpus of study. While these studies produced initial fruit in other fields, oral traditions were soon found to be much more diverse than Lord had anticipated.[9] As the field of studies in oral tradition broadened, the field of biblical studies was slow to engage it. Even recently Brian B. Schmidt lamented that the implications of the predominantly oral nature of the culture in which the Bible was birthed has "made only sporadic and gradual inroads into the modern study of early Israelite society, the Hebrew Bible and the relevance of orality and literacy for the actual historical composition of biblical literature."[10]

Defining Orality

Oral Tradition's 2003 two-volume synopsis of oral studies, discussed above, gave various definitions for oral tradition.[11] Beverly Stoeltje said, "The full range of prose and poetry, when communicated primarily through oral performance for an audience familiar with the genre, constitutes a large body of oral tradition."[12] Stoeltje highlighted the content and performance aspect of oral tradition, but she also mentioned, almost in passing, the fact that the audience already is assumed to be familiar with the content. Tradents (or performers of oral traditional material) do not give performances of elements of oral traditions to inform the community of the tradition but to remind the community of their familiar tradition in creative ways for specific contexts. The data is already known

---

8. Niditch, *Oral World*, 8–9; Carr, *Formation*, 13–14; and West, "Art of Biblical Performance," 5.

9. See for instance Foley, "Plenitude and Diversity," 103–6.

10. Schmidt, "Introduction," 1.

11. I fully acknowledge the difficulty of the words *oral, orality, oral tradition*, etc., as Rodriguez discusses in *Oral Tradition*, 6–8. To restate my purposes: while I appreciate and understand his avoidance of the term "orality," as this work is meant to operate as an introduction to concepts of orality and oral tradition, I will continue to use these terms to apply to cultures like those behind the Old and New Testament—cultures in which the majority received important traditional material primarily through oral/aural means and largely did not have access to or the ability to engage in reading the material for themselves.

12. Stoeltje, "Global and the Local," 93.

by the community. The performer simply casts the content in the light that the community requires in the moment so that the community can embody the shared identity defined by the body of canonical tradition. Furthermore, the community also commands traditional knowledge of certain connotations of words, themes, scenes, and other material that allows them to interpret each unique performance. Oral traditions do not look for an "original text" of their traditions. They expect a level of fluidity and freedom in each performance.

Bonnie D. Irwin said, "Oral narrative tradition means the process by which stories are composed and performed for an audience."[13] Irwin highlighted the performance aspect of oral tradition, and it is interesting that she defined oral tradition not by the nature of the content but as an ongoing *process*. Oral tradition can have a level of fluidity and multiformity, as performances and texts of traditions interact with the living community in an ongoing creative process. The tradition is stable and secured from unrestrained transformation in that the entire community holds the tradition in their hearts and minds, but the tradition is also able to conform to speak to the community's shifting contexts. This is very different than the models of much of modern biblical study applied in the past.

For instance, as opposed to the concept of *fluidity and stability* discussed just above, textual critics have often operated under a matrix of *stability with variation*. In other words, the tradition, especially as it is found in written format, is expected by the textual critic to be reproduced almost verbatim, though some variation is expected due to human error or theological bent. The concept of *fluidity and stability*, in which oral traditions more often operate, expects fluidity in the presentation of the tradition, though with an overall trend of stability due to the communal preservation of the received tradition.

In his article "The Ancient Israelite Scribe as Performer," Raymond F. Person Jr. offered a potent example from Foley of an interview of an oral traditional bard:

> Nikola: Let's consider this: "Vino pije licki Mustajbeze" ("Mustajbeg of Lika was drinking wine"). Is this a single word?
> Mujo: Yes.
> N: But how? It can't be one: "Vino pije licki Mustajbeze."

---

13. Irwin, "Frame Tales and Oral Tradition," 125.

M:	In writing it can't be one.
N:	There are four words here.
M:	It can't be one in writing. But here, let's say we're at my house and I pick up the gusle [a traditional single-stringed instrument]—"Pije vino licki Mustajbeze"—that's a single word on the gusle for me.
N:	And the second word?
M:	And the second word—"Na Ribniku u pjanoj mehani" ("At Ribnik in a drinking tavern")—there.[14]

Our text-based, Western, scientific, exact-data-driven culture looks at the phrase "Vino pije licki Mustajbeze," and we say, "That is four words." The oral traditional culture from which this phrase was birthed says, "It is one word." Then the oral traditional culture says that "one word" differently—"Pije vino licki Mustajbeze"—and they call it the *same* word. Modern textual criticism would see this as a variant. Desiring an inspired textual stability with variation only due to human error, we would say, "The scribe accidentally inverted the words 'vino,' and 'pije.'" We miss that the culture that produced this variation saw the entire phrase all as the same singular word, even in the multiform examples given above. Oral cultures do not produce texts within the matrix of stability with variation due to human error but within the matrix of an expected fluidity within a stability defined by the community's cultural identity.

Chan Park simply said, "Oral tradition is a living community."[15] Park's definition dealt with the community itself, not merely its content and process. An oral tradition is tied to a community. The tradition is not merely a set of stories and poems and interpretive customs taught for knowledge consumption or performed for entertainment. The tradition often carries the identity of the community in such a way that Park can say the tradition *is* the living community.

Thomas A. DuBois said, "In my understanding, oral tradition refers on the one hand to concrete players and objects observable in oral performance, and, on the other hand, to a murky yet essential body of knowledge that underlies every aspect of the performance as created, enacted, and interpreted."[16] Dubois's phrase, "a murky yet essential body of knowledge," speaks to the fluidity of the tradition with the term "murky"

---

14. Person, "Ancient Israelite Scribe," 603; Foley, "Editing Oral Epic Texts," 92n11.
15. Park, "Korean *P'ansori* Narrative," 241.
16. Dubois, "Oral Tradition," 255.

and to the stability of the tradition with the phrase "essential body of knowledge." While he did not use the term "community," he certainly conjured the necessity of community when he spoke of a "body of knowledge." After all, where would this body of knowledge be stored in an oral culture? The body of knowledge is stored in the hearts and minds of the community.

William Schneider's definition was a bit more thorough and will help transition into a more substantive discussion of the generalities of oral tradition:

> Oral tradition is characterized by three qualities: (1) It is shared orally among people who, to varying degrees, hold common understandings of their histories and cultures. (Some people share in multiple histories and cultures.) (2) The knowledge that comes from oral tradition is learned and subject to common and yet ever-evolving understandings of what constitutes performance and its contents. (Included here is consideration of how stories are told, the roles of storytellers and audiences, the purposes and settings for tellings, and the use of symbols and metaphor to convey what people want to be understood.) (3) Oral traditions are told over time in recognizably similar ways but with variations of detail and emphasis subject to the circumstances of each performance and the liberties taken by the speakers.[17]

The work of Paul Rhodes Eddy and Gregory A. Boyd, *The Jesus Legend: A Case for the Historical Reliability of the Synoptic Jesus Tradition*, echoed the definitions of orality listed above. Eddy and Boyd provided a very helpful introduction to oral tradition for biblical scholars who may not have researched the matter beyond form criticism stemming from Hermann Gunkel and Rudolf Bultmann. In fact, Eddy and Boyd discussed oral traditions as a polemic against many conclusions of scholarship following Bultmann.

Eddy and Boyd argued concerning oral narratives, "Oral performances are almost always composed of a longer narrative plot line together with various smaller units that compose the bulk of the story in any given performance."[18] If the narrative is told at length, it is often

---

17. Schneider, "Search for Wisdom," 268.

18. See Eddy's discussion of Lauri Honko's contribution to our understanding of long oral narratives in oral traditions: Eddy, "Historicity," 157–59; Eddy and Boyd, *Jesus Legend*, 253.

told through smaller narrative units that can be edited, lengthened, shortened, or rearranged to meet the needs of any given performance. A "collective memory of the community"[19] is so prevalent that bards or tradents normally do not tell the entire epic in one sitting, but they only need to tell a part of the narrative that, in turn, calls to mind within the community the narrative as a whole.[20] This argues against form criticism's views that oral traditions begin as small units, which are later arranged or evolve into larger narratives.[21]

Information in oral cultures is not dictated for rote memory retention, but the content of the tradition forms the identity of the community, even as the community shapes the content through performance and enactment. Information is performed in order to be shared and experienced as the information draws the community into itself within longstanding traditions of tribal identity. This sort of experiential collective memory attaches itself deep into the psyche of the individual, making memory a natural phenomenon and not merely a mental practice.

Ella P. Mitchell wrote of her experience in Nigeria when she saw "young children capable of quoting at length from their culture's collection of proverbial wisdom ... even [providing] interpretation."[22] When she asked them when they had learned all of this information, they had no answer.[23] This sort of *natural memorization* can lead to astounding

---

19. Person, "Problem," 224.

20. Foley calls the idea of "calling to mind the whole from the part" "metonymy." The idea that different concepts from the collective memory of the community can be "activated" through any given performance comes from Egbert Bakker. See Eddy and Boyd, *Jesus Legend*, 257, and the discussion in chapter five of this work. See also Person, "Problem," 223–24 and 233–37. Foley discussed a "metonymic referentiality," or "traditional referentiality," referring to the idea that even a full representation of a tale or epic could not exhaust the full tradition embedded within the culture and so would only be a referent to that culture. West, "Art of Biblical Performance," 15–20.

21. Gunkel said, "Only later did collectors gather several such legends or did authors form larger literary constructions from them. The process also applied to Hebrew popular legends." Gunkel, *Genesis*, xxvii–viii; see Kelber, "Oral Tradition," 40–42, and Niditch, "Oral Tradition and Biblical Scholarship," 43–44, for brief discussions on some ways form criticism is being found wanting by studies in orality. See also Elizabeth Oyler's contribution that highlights how her field of the study of Japanese oral culture should have moved beyond "the general assumption that shorter tales, composed by itinerant performers, were strung together into a longer work that was finally committed to paper," due to the empirical evidence to the contrary, but the field is still impacted by old paradigms. Oyler, "Heike in Japan," 18.

22. Mitchell, "Oral Tradition," 94.

23. Mitchell, "Oral Tradition," 94.

feats of retention. Mitchell reported that certain diviners can call to mind at need 4,096 tales and that this sort of memory is not absolutely abnormal throughout Africa.[24] This astounding memory retention does not mean every tradent who calls to mind a tale and performs it will do so with the exact same words.[25] A fluidity in performance is expected while also being held together by the culturally expected boundaries of the traditions, as well as a common collection of vocabulary and formulae from which the performer can draw.[26] Eddy said, "Flexibility, fluidity, and variation play a significant role within the verbal dynamics of orally dominant cultures. But such dynamics are only sensibly enacted within the conserving conceptual parameters of a stable, communally shared tradition that functions as the 'enabling referent,' the permanent anchor of each and every one of its own performative variations."[27]

The collective memory of the community acts as a sort of mental text or canon in the heart of the people. Tradents or bards, the normative mode of oral traditional delivery,[28] may demonstrate creativity in their performance of the traditions, but the core of the traditions remain the same.[29] Indeed, through their collective memory, the entire community holds the tradent accountable to the tradition and even corrects him/her if they feel it necessary.[30] Eddy and Boyd pointed out that some oral scholars have argued that since oral cultures do distinguish between factual and fictional history,[31] and since the community holds the traditions in trust, oral history should be held in higher esteem than it has in the past.[32] However, it must be noted that while oral cultures tend to preserve

---

24. Mitchell, "Oral Tradition," 98.

25. See for instance, David M. Carr's discussion on memory retention based on studies in fields dealing with memory in *Writing on the Tablet*, 7, and *Formation*, 13–18; see also Person's discussion of the concept of *word* in "Ancient Israelite Scribe," especially 603–9.

26. See discussion of "theme bank" or "word bank" below.

27. Eddy, "Historicity," 157. For a discussion of the idea of an "enabling referent," see the context just before this citation—Eddy, "Historicity," 156. Also, see the discussion of metonymy just above and on note 20 and note 39 below as I acknowledge other terms I have left out of this work.

28. Eddy and Boyd, *Jesus Legend*, 265.

29. Person, *Deuteronomic History*, 69–74.

30. Eddy and Boyd, *Jesus Legend*, 262.

31. Eddy, "Historicity," 153–54; Miller, "Performance," 190; and Eddy and Boyd, *Jesus Legend*, 260–61.

32. Eddy, "Historicity"; Eddy and Boyd, *Jesus Legend*, 263.

the core of their traditions, they allow fluidity in detail[33] and do not focus on perfect chronology.[34]

Summary of Oral Tradition[35]

Oral traditions tend to be carried by some sort of culturally official tradition-bearer through performance. The longstanding identity of the community shapes the content, even as its shared canon of content continuously shapes the community. This content may contain narratives, poems, wisdom sayings, law codes, genealogies, or even traditions of interpretation of various traditional units.[36] Within the community, a metanarrative and a collective memory of tradition often is communicated through smaller units that can be performed creatively for the situation at hand, and the collective memory of the tradition at large is required for a full interpretation of the performance.

The entire metanarrative does not need to be performed to be "actualized" by the community. Smaller units of tradition, even specific words or phrases, can call to mind other aspects of the community's tradition.[37] The tradition at large is so culturally and contextually specific, and so fluid in meaning and application, that even a full telling of the story could not exhaust the tradition as it is embedded within the minds and hearts of the entire community.

Since the overall tradition is held in trust by the community at-large, it is often guarded with high degrees of preservation, though with fluidity of language and certain details. The parts of tradition considered

---

33. Person, *Deuteronomic History*, 66, 69–74; and Carr, *Formation*, 36.

34. Eddy and Boyd, *Jesus Legend*, 263; and Miller, "Performance," 190.

35. The following summary is given fully aware of Foley's warnings of avoiding "both the discredited binary of orality versus literacy and parochial descriptions based on a small selection of examples" (Foley, "Plenitude and Diversity," 117). However, the investigation of this work requires some generalization, and it is hoped that the following summary takes heed of Foley as he continued—A responsible model for approaching the diversity of the field of orality "must instead highlight the fundamental parameters of composition, performance, and reception" (Foley, "Plenitude and Diversity," 117). The entirety of Foley's article (103–18) should be consulted to avoid receiving the following summary as a conclusive model for all aspects of oral traditional cultures and their interaction with written texts.

36. See Shem Miller's discussion of the interaction of orality and textuality in law codes in *Dead Sea Media*, 98–106. Additionally, Miller discusses some aspects of shared oral interpretations of written texts, 89–90.

37. See Niditch's synthesis of Foley's idea of "metonymy," *Oral World*, 11.

to be historical are preserved by the community as true history, though not necessarily with modern/Western cultural priorities of exactitude of detail and chronology. Small units and genres may be called "forms," but they are not the source of the overall tradition. Instead, they act to communicate and/or activate the tradition in any given performance.

The "growth" of the tradition does not flow in a linear direction. Instead, it flows back-and-forth in a multidirectional, organic sort of growth from one performance to the next. While not all oral traditional cultures are exactly the same, I argue that the generally accepted description of orality discussed above might be categorized by three principles [38]: (1) fluidity and stability of tradition; (2) collective memory and the ability of "activation" through tradent performance; and (3) the absorption of textuality into the oral register[39] of a culture, which will be discussed below.

Oral Tradition and the Written Text

The third principle that helps to categorize traditions stemming from an oral register concerns the presence of written texts within an oral traditional culture. Simply put, the third principle is that textuality does not interrupt the oral traditional nature of the culture as if some sort of "great divide" is present between orality and literacy.[40] Indeed, as one begins to study the texts of certain cultures, a broad range of issues can emerge. In his book, *Orality, Textuality, & the Homeric Epics: An Interdisciplinary*

38. Also helpful is to review the "Four common, cross-cultural phenomena" of oral tradition in Eddy, "Historicity," 155–63.

39. Those already initiated into the field of orality, oral tradition, biblical performance criticism, and media criticism will certainly have recognized in this discussion concepts related to Foley's ideas of *Immanent Art* and *traditional referentiality,* Kelber's idea of *biosphere* (terms to which Rodriguez introduces students in chapter two of *Oral Tradition*), as well as other concepts that could be located with technical labels from various authors. As discussed in the preface, I am intentionally avoiding these terms in the attempt to offer a general picture of oral tradition, how it differs from the expectations of traditional scholarship and exegesis, and a beginning point for pastors, teachers, and scholars to open their minds to a different way to approach the text without getting bogged down in technical jargon. I do acknowledge the importance of shared and exact vocabulary, and I continue to point readers to Rodriguez for his excellent introduction to these terms. At this point, "oral register" is meant to identify the cultural realities and expectations within a community that shares information along the lines of oral traditional cultures discussed so far.

40. See note 7 in the introduction above and Eddy and Boyd, *Jesus Legend*, 293–94. Rodriguez emphasizes the lack of the "Great Divide" throughout *Oral Tradition*.

Study of Oral Texts, Dictated Texts, and Wild Texts, Jonathan L. Ready exemplified the complicated nature of written texts stemming from oral traditional cultures as he discussed the various theories concerning the definition of "Homeric text," as well as the seemingly fluid definitions of "orality" and "textuality." In doing so, Ready noted just how complicated things can get as a "nuanced understanding of textuality" can be added to a "nuanced understanding of orality."[41]

The shift required when studying texts stemming from an oral register is not a matter of simply shifting from a text-based model toward an oral-traditional model in which every variant and issue of the tradition is easily explained through some oral-cultural metric that can be applied to all texts of all cultures. Robert D. Miller wrote,

> We are concerned here with more than the literature's emergence, but with its performance in a culture that was not merely "primarily oral" but oral-and-written. Written texts circulated in spoken form by recitation long after they were committed to writing. And those recited forms begat oral forms that were not in writing, or were not put in writing for some time afterwards. Oral texts that circulated from bard to audience or bard to bard could be recorded in writing, could be consulted by writers, and could be consulted by bards of other stories.[42]

A nuanced interplay exists between text and performance, between literacy and orality, which must be considered in the study of the ancient biblical traditions.

While textual criticism has demonstrated that ancient texts were certainly copied from each other, the modern examination of "the Dead Sea Scrolls proved the antiquity of some [variant readings] and how textual plurality was a characteristic of the Qumran library itself."[43] Scholars are coming to grips with the fact that early scribes, including those of the early biblical tradition, operated within a metric closer to the fluidity and stability of oral traditional cultures than the modern notion of an expected stability with variation due to human error. Ancient scribes clearly needed a working memory of the texts even in order to be able to read them, this memory was an aspect of their oral culture, and this oral

---

41. Ready, *Orality*, 2. Rodriguez also discusses the murky definition of orality, *Oral Tradition*, 6–8.
42. Miller, "Performance," 182.
43. Person, "Text Criticism," 204.

memory shows up in the copies of manuscripts of these oral traditions that were committed to writing.

David Carr argued that early Greek manuscripts were in all caps with no spaces so that they "were constructed for reading by people who had already mastered the relevant text."[44] Similarly, early alphabet systems such as Hebrew had no vowels, which demanded an understanding of the tradition in order to vocalize its texts. Carr pointed out, "One early manuscript for the Hebrew prophets does not even record the complete words of each verse. Instead, only the first word is given, along with the first letter of each succeeding word."[45] The literacy required to read the defining texts of cultures such as the traditions standing behind the Bible goes far beyond the ability to write one's name or pronounce words and understand syntax. A "literacy" of the tradition itself was a requirement—a literacy defined by the culture's specific dynamics of their oral traditions. Clearly, the text of the Bible emerged in an oral context, and scholars are working to understand the interplay between the oral traditional nature of the cultures and the texts these cultures left behind.

For instance, Susan Niditch identified signs that a text may have developed within an oral register. She discussed how the presence of intentional repetitions, formulaic language, and patterns of content are well-documented in oral cultures and likely identify traditions stemming from an oral register.[46] She discussed how evidence of the presumed actualization of the larger tradition by the presentation of a smaller traditional unit, as discussed above, also locates a text within an oral register.[47]

Niditch provided biblical examples of the features she discussed. As far as repetition is concerned, Niditch presented the framing language pattern of the creation account in Gen 1:1—2:4, along with the discussion of patterns of repeated dialogue, such as Isaac's plans to give his blessing to Esau in Gen 27. Another example of repetition in the Hebrew Bible is found in the use of *Leitwörter* (key words), such as "to eat" and

---

44. Carr, *Writing on the Tablet*, 4.

45. As cited by Carr, *Writing on the Tablet*, 5; from Würthwein, *Text*, 170–71.

46. Niditch, *Oral World*, 8–38. As I will explain more, I think that Niditch's approach of acknowledging the well-documented saturation of elements of repetition, formulaic language, and patterns of content within texts stemming from an oral register can be applied to the interpretation of the biblical texts without implying the "Great Divide Theory." I also readily acknowledge the importance of what Rodriguez calls a "contextual approach" to interpreting the biblical texts with orality in mind: Rodriguez, *Oral Tradition*, 55–85.

47. Niditch, *Oral World*, 11–12.

"to kill" in Gen 27.[48] Formulaic language is found in the Hebrew Bible often in "noun-epithets," such as *'ăbîr ya'ăqōb* or "the Mighty One of Jacob."[49] Longer formulas are represented in the cases of people in a court calling for help from "advisors and assistants" represented by a "chain of wisemen [that] can include any number of wizards, magicians, advisors, officials, and other members of the royal entourage (for example, Gen 41:8; Exod 7:11; Jer 50:35; Dan 1:20; 2:2)."[50] This formula brings "into context the aura of the foreign court and the notion of contest between those in power and those who are in a more marginal political position but who are backed by God."[51]

Thus, formulaic context is utilized to actualize the underlying traditional themes and identity within the community at large. This discussion is similar to the patterns of content found in recurring places, themes, genres, and other contexts, such as the "victory-enthronement pattern" found in Scripture and the ancient Near East, upon which Niditch has elaborated.[52] As can be seen in this brief overview, Niditch provided a rich context of the comparison of oral tradition and the Hebrew text for scholars to investigate.

Following Niditch, David M. Carr has utilized studies in orality, textuality, and memory to add another empirical element to source and redaction criticism.[53] In Carr's publication, *The Formation of the Hebrew Bible: A New Reconstruction*, he made a case that ancient texts were often used as memory aids for performance in oral traditions.[54] Again, while this does not lead to a shift from a clear textual metric to a mere oral-cultural metric of studying the texts, the copying of the texts plainly reflects more than a simple textual tradition. This is not a mere case of word-for-word preservation with various errors—not a case of *stability with variation* as discussed above. More of an oral cultural mindset exists behind the process, including an acceptance of more textual fluidity and

---

48. Niditch, *Oral World*, 13–14.
49. Niditch, *Oral World*, 15–17.
50. Niditch, *Oral World*, 17.
51. Niditch, *Oral World*, 18.
52. Niditch, *Oral World*, 20–24.

53. Raymond F. Person Jr. and Robert Rezetko have called his work one of "the two most significant publications that explicitly explore empirical models in an effort to refine source and redaction criticism within plausible limits." Person and Rezetko, "Introduction," 14.

54. Carr, *Formation*, 5.

what Carr referred to as "memory variants" among manuscripts.[55] Carr utilized the findings concerning how manuscripts in oral cultures grow to offer a modest attempt of a model of textual reconstruction for the Hebrew Bible that challenges older consensuses of source and redaction criticism.

Raymond F. Person Jr. used oral-written transmission models to study Samuel and Chronicles in *The Deuteronomic History and the Book of Chronicles: Scribal Works in an Oral World* and in his articles in *Contextualizing Israel's Sacred Writings* and *Empirical Models Challenging Biblical Criticism*.[56] Ian Young made a case for the option of a shared oral tradition as an explanation of the variant textual witnesses of the Old Greek and Masoretic text of chapter 5 of Daniel.[57] Shem Miller explored the interaction of orality and textuality (and memory) in the Dead Sea Scrolls in *Dead Sea Media: Orality, Textuality, and Memory in the Scrolls from the Judean Desert*.

The application of the studies of medieval and ancient Eastern texts explored in these works demonstrate the theory that the presence of the written word within oral traditions does not convert the culture to an Occidental, text-based culture.[58] Instead, the orality of the culture absorbs the written word. Text acts as a memory aid for performance, which in turn influences the oral traditions, and the performances and memory of tradents instigate the formation of new texts. A complex, multidirectional impact exists of text upon tradition and tradition upon text.

---

55. Carr, *Formation*, 17–18, 34–35, and 41–42. T. M. West identifies a distinction Carr makes: "More recently [Carr] further nuanced the traditional binary of orality and literacy by arguing for memory as a 'third pole' of the transmission process that is related to yet distinct from the other two, and in some ways is the essential link between them. '[T]hese different forms of variation point to *three* not *two* major poles in ancient textual transmission: the written text, the oral performance reception dimension, *and the medium of memory*. Furthermore, in many contexts, these three poles are integrally interrelated.' . . . emphasis original." West, "Art of Biblical Performance," 35, citing Carr, "Orality, Textuality, and Memory," 168–69. However, an important distinction should be made between the concepts of memory in a literate Western society and an oral traditional culture. Memorization is often a *practice* yearning for *exactitude* in the Western mind, but the *natural memorization* within a culture of fluidity and stability as discussed above is a very different concept. A *communal memory* exists in oral traditional cultures and is supported through a shared vocabulary of words, phrases, themes, scenes, etc.

56. Person, "Text Criticism," 197–215. Others cited previously—Person, "Problem"; and Person, *Deuteronomic History*.

57. Young, "Original Problem," 271–301.

58. While these works focus on conclusions related to the Hebrew Bible, they discuss and employ findings from studies from other works from other cultures.

Summary of Studies in Orality and Textuality

Fluidity marks the textual traditions within oral cultures as even scribes can see their productions as creative performances, and solidification of the text into a received or "canonical" form occurs late in the process as the performances are divorced from their defining cultural traditions.[59] For these reasons, the presence of meaningful variants (variants that shift the meaning in an intentional way) and memory variants (such as replacing a word with its synonym) among manuscripts may very well demonstrate that a textual tradition was developing within an oral register. Variations such as these provide a multiformity of tradition found in the texts—a fluidity—that is typical of oral traditions. Even so, oral traditional cultures maintain a level of stability in their traditions. While producing unique performances of the tradition, these meaningful variants nonetheless will remain true to the tradition as a whole as it is held within the hearts and minds of the community.

As an example of fluidity and stability, oral cultures often have a sort of word bank, or theme bank, which performers can draw from in order to compose a presentation of the tradition on the spot, as well as to conjure up the desired emotions and identities of the community.[60] The bank, as well as the interpretive tradition of the culture, provides a level of stability in which tradents can create unique performances. Carr presented a list of comparable proverbs as potential examples of the presence of a word bank and the memory variants that can be produced by such a bank.[61]

The comparison of Prov 16:2—כָּל־דַּרְכֵי־אִישׁ זַךְ בְּעֵינָיו וְתֹכֵן רוּחוֹת יְהוָה, "All the ways of a man are pure in his eyes, but YHWH weighs spirits," with Prov 21:2—כָּל־דֶּרֶךְ־אִישׁ יָשָׁר בְּעֵינָיו וְתֹכֵן לִבּוֹת יְהוָה, "Every way of a man is right in his eyes, but YHWH weighs hearts" (Carr's translations), serves here as one of the more than fifteen examples referenced by him from the book of Proverbs. In this example, one can see what very well may represent memory variants between each line in these two proverbs. They are not visual errors of replacing similar letters or dropping words but rather variations in saying the same sort of thing

---

59. Besides the works already cited, for instance in notes 7 and 8 in the introduction, see also, Carr's discussion on this sort of variation in "Orality, Textuality, and Memory," 161–73; and Carr, *Writing on the Tablet*. Person explores how ancient texts from a more oral tradition, like those of Homer, began with a more fluid tradition and grew into a more fixed and received state, "Text Criticism as a Lens," 198–207; and Carr, *Formation*, chapters two to three, and the introduction to chapter four.

60. Niditch, *Oral World*, 13.

61. Carr, *Formation*, 25–34.

with different vocabulary and syntax, likely drawing from a common traditional bank of words and phrases. After reviewing the evidence from Proverbs, Carr said:

> This range of instances of proverbs with parallels concentrated in one line may testify to how the tissue of proverbial sayings were not just transmitted as wholes, but that their parts almost served like lexemes in an internalized wisdom vocabulary, one composed of sayings, lines and phrases—along with words particularly attached to learning. Those who had memorized this vocabulary could recombine elements from it in the process of forming new sayings.[62]

What Carr and others are finding in the text of the Old Testament seems to represent what studies in orality demonstrate concerning oral traditions.

One could argue that these sorts of variants may simply represent the literary or theological slants of the scribes. For instance, the community at Qumran interpreted the הַכַּשְׂדִּים (the Chaldeans) of Hab 1:6 as הכתיאים (the Kittim or "Westerners"), though they did not modify the text of Habakkuk in this case.[63] The Qumran pesher scroll of Habakkuk demonstrates that certain communities may have their own interpretations of the text, and so any meaningful variant from manuscript to manuscript could just as easily be explained by a scribe who simply wanted to insert his perspective into the tradition.

Scholars such as Rafael Rodiguez have questioned the value of identifying structural elements from within the text that are common in oral traditional literature. Rodriguez emphasized the reality that examples of repetition discovered in oral traditional material can also be seen in texts from more literate cultures. Critiquing Joanna Dewey's approach to the book of Mark, Rodriguez argues that "if [certain literary features, such as chiasms ('ring structures'), repetition, parataxis, and others] are not necessarily and essentially oral, then conclusions based on their alleged orality begin to unravel."[64] Therefore, Rodriguez places little value on identifying such structures as marks of literature stemming from oral traditions as well as utilizing them within exegetical methods specifically targeting the biblical text as it relates to orality.

---

62. Carr, *Formation*, 29.
63. Cook, "Commentary," 80–81.
64. Rodriguez, *Oral Tradition*, 61.

However, while one could certainly overreach by identifying every repetition as a mark of orality and every textual tradition containing a memory variant as the product of an oral traditional culture, one can also dismiss the demonstrable presence of these features within literature stemming from oral traditional cultures and so overlook conclusions and interpretive aids available by acknowledging their likely presence in such texts.

After all, even Rodriguez admits an "impressive display of these features in actual oral traditions in the modern world."[65] But for some reason he is adamant that "even if anthropologists could demonstrate that *every* oral tradition is paratactic, visually robust, and repetitious, that would not establish a *causal* connection between the tradition's medium of communication—its 'orality' and the features in question."[66] Rodriguez argues that "if written language can naturally and organically exhibit the features media critics ascribe to oral language, then the basis for ascribing them to orality vanishes."[67] In other words, if all measurable oral traditional cultures have such features, there is no causal connection of those features to oral traditional cultures, and if any feature can also be found in more textual cultures, then it cannot be identified as "oral" and therefore loses its value as a tool for exegesis.

Interestingly, the approach Rodriguez does promote, the contextual approach, rests on the repetition of the extended tradition in various performances—the concept of *activation* discussed above and further below. Essentially, the greater tradition of the culture is the context through which any text left behind by that tradition should be interpreted. An author or performer depends on the meanings of terms, scenes, and other concepts and performances for the audience's ability to interpret the current performance. However, this feature is widely featured in modern textual works. Orwell's *Animal Farm* requires a world of understood referents for an understanding audience. While Rodriguez admits that traditional performers can operate with levels of creativity, he does not seem to acknowledge that aspects of this contextual approach can be found in texts stemming from written traditions as well. He argues, "Traditional works exhibit a greater degree of inherent meaning in comparison with increasingly literary or creative works of verbal art."[68]

65. Rodriguez, *Oral Tradition*, 70–71.
66. Rodriguez, *Oral Tradition*, 70–71.
67. Rodriguez, *Oral Tradition*, 69.
68. Rodriguez, *Oral Tradition*, 75.

Following his logical critique of the morphological approach, it seems that if the contextual aspect of a text can be located outside of an oral traditional culture, the feature loses any direct connection to orality. Should he not argue that, even if anthropologists could demonstrate that *every* oral tradition exhibits a greater degree of inherent meaning in comparison with increasingly literary or creative works of verbal art, that would not establish a *causal* connection between the tradition's medium of communication—its "orality"—and the features in question?

Rodriguez's approach to the application of oral traditional studies to biblical interpretation seems much too narrow. As an example, I could argue that since certain doctrinal beliefs such as believer's baptism and the priesthood of the believer can be found in many different denominations, we cannot categorize them as strictly Baptist. While that may be true, I will still expect to find those doctrinal approaches in almost every Baptist institution I attend. While we cannot identify some features as "only oral," we can still expect to find these features that have been "impressively" located with oral traditional cultures. Every suggested scenario of repetition and activation will then stand or fall upon its own merits.

Again, the presence of certain types of variants and structural features is not absolute proof that the textual tradition was formed within an oral register. However, their presence reflects what studies in orality suggest are frequently reflected in a textual tradition that sprung from an oral register.

The Egyptian Execration texts[69] and the Mari and Nuzi texts[70] do not prove the historicity of the patriarchal narratives, but they do provide evidence that the patriarchal narratives fit within the cultural milieu of the Middle Bronze II period. Similarly, as discussed in Niditch's work above, aspects of oral registers and meaningful and memory variants that produce a textual tradition of fluidity and stability, as discussed in Carr's work above, do not prove an oral register behind a textual tradition, but they have been shown to be expected within a textual tradition stemming from an oral culture.

Students, interpreters, and teachers and preachers of the Bible would do well to expect to find these sorts of features in the various media of Scripture. Scholars like Rodriguez do well to avoid engaging in ancient texts as if a great divide separated orality and textuality, but it is also

---

69. Kitchen, *On the Reliability*, 333–35.
70. Lasor, Hubbard, and Bush, *Old Testament Survey*, 42–43.

important to acknowledge general differences between oral traditional cultures and text-saturated cultures—at least the text-saturated Occidental culture of the past two or three hundred years. These differences are significant for understanding and interpreting the preserved texts of an oral traditional culture. Rodriguez already acknowledges such differences with his contextual approach, and we would do well to broaden Rodriguez's approach to some degree in light of the impressive display of other forms of repetition in oral traditional cultures.[71]

Concluding Remarks on Oral Tradition and the Written Text

The Occidental textual bias of biblical criticism and the unsupported approaches to orality stemming from Gunkel are being called into question. Oral tradition is a cultural phenomenon that has impacted our understanding of the origins, preservation, and application of the text of the Bible, and work is being conducted to understand just how oral traditional cultures operate and how textuality functions in cultures situated within an oral register. This work is ongoing, as scholars continue to investigate how texts were seen, used, and reproduced in cultures where traditions comparable in varying degrees to those studied in oral cultures were preserved in writing.

For instance, performance criticism is a growing methodology in biblical studies,[72] and Raymond F. Person Jr. is producing works devoted to text-critical variants from the perspective of scribal memory,[73] currently focusing on providing a clear cognitive-linguistic model from conversation analysis for how word selection can work in textual transmission in

---

71. Readers may discern a great gap in this discussion—specifically, what was the process that led to a "received text" or "final form" of a text, and when did that process begin and end as it relates to the tradition of Christian Scripture? I will briefly address this issue in chapter four. However, the growth of our understanding of this process is ongoing, and my purposes are to discuss issues of exegesis and proclamation more than to summarize every current issue in the field. This is certainly an area that needs attention as the discussion of orality and the Bible moves forward. Person, "Text Criticism," and Carr, *Formation*, address this issue in various places and to varying degrees.

72. As can be seen in West's dissertation, "Art of Biblical Performance."

73. Person was incredibly generous to share chapters of some of his forthcoming works and direct this study toward the works of Jonathan Ready and Shem Miller, with whom Person has been conversing concerning these issues.

traditions that have textual plurality and textual fluidity as a characteristic.[74] This new approach to orality and textuality is also working itself out into cognate fields, as can be seen in the works of Paul Delnero in Sumerian texts and Chloé Raggazoli on New Kingdom Egyptian texts.[75]

Recent studies in orality and textuality claim to demonstrate that the history of the textual traditions of many ancient documents, including those of the Bible, are not explained best merely through a written-textual-oriented approach, but rather through a nuanced interplay of orality and textuality. They also suggest the inaccuracy of older models of orality applied to the study of the Bible. What follows is a brief overview of the history of the application of orality to the study of the Old Testament.

---

74. Some language of this description comes directly from email correspondence with Person.

75. Delnero, *Textual Criticism*; Chloé Raggazoli, *Scribes*. In his generous correspondence, David M. Carr suggested these scholars.

2

A History of the Application of Orality to Old Testament Studies

THE FOLLOWING SUMMARY MAINLY draws from Robert C. Culley's 1986 article in the first edition of *Oral Tradition* and from T. M. West's recent dissertation, "The Art of Biblical Performance," both of which are already cited above. Culley outlines his summary: Up to the time of Gunkel, From Gunkel to the Sixties, and From 1963 to the Present. West is less chronological, outlining his summary: Hermann Gunkel; Milman Parry and Albert Lord; The Scandinavian School; Orality vs. Literacy: Walter Ong, Jack Goody, and the Character of Oral Cultures; John Miles Foley; Susan Niditch and the Oral World of Ancient Israel; and Recent Developments in Orality and the Hebrew Bible. A definite overlap occurs in the emphasis placed on Gunkel, the Scandinavian School, Parry and Lord's impact, and the shift away from the great divide between orality and literacy.

Gunkel

When one thinks of oral traditions in the field of Old Testament studies, Hermann Gunkel and form criticism most naturally come to mind as the entry point.[1] Gunkel's approach to Genesis brought a different focus

---

1. West, "Art of Biblical Performance," 3; Culley, "Oral Tradition and Biblical Studies," 32.

to the text than the reigning paradigm of the time, governed by Julius Wellhausen's presentation of the documentary hypothesis. This new approach looked not at the literary history of the Hebrew Bible but at the pre-literary stage of oral forms.[2] Gunkel "deemed his task to be that of uncovering the original oral form" of the oral sagas behind the text of the Old Testament "through an examination of the various types of literary composition in the Hebrew Scriptures in terms of his particular methodology."[3]

These forms were analyzed under the rubric of the *Sitz im Leben des Volkes*—the life-setting of the community that would give rise to and/or be served by the form or genre in question.[4] These oral traditional forms or genres were relatively small legends and sagas that could be told in a family setting around a campfire or by "a class of storytellers, well-versed in the traditional narratives, who travelled the country and appeared at festivals."[5] Thus, Gunkel even envisioned an aspect of official performance.

While scholarship has moved away from Gunkel's view of a legendary and naïve oral stage of ancient Hebrew tradition that was totally distinct from a later literary stage, he began a trajectory in Old Testament studies that considered the importance of orality. From Gunkel's approach arose the category of biblical studies known as form criticism. Scholars like Hugo Gressmann, Albrecht Alt, Martin Noth, and Gerhard von Rad, whose works have had lasting effects on Old Testament studies, utilized form criticism, as well as influential New Testament scholars such as Rudolf Bultmann.

Scandinavian School

In 1935, H. S. Nyberg began to argue against the approach to oral traditions that stood behind form criticism.[6] He was convinced that written texts, being regulated mostly for more practical purposes than the epic histories or cult-legends, were not as pervasive in ancient Israel as other

---

2. Harrison, *Introduction*, 35; note the divide between orality and literacy.
3. Harrison, *Introduction*, 36.
4. Harrison, *Introduction*, 35; West, "Art of Biblical Performance," 3; Culley, "Oral Tradition and Biblical Studies," 33.
5. Culley, "Oral Tradition and Biblical Studies," 34.
6. Culley, "Oral Tradition and Biblical Studies," 36.

scholars had argued.⁷ Even when traditions were physically recorded, their main mode of transmission was still oral, and "in large part the traditions of Israel achieved a written form after the Babylonian Exile of the fifth century BCE."⁸ Nyberg argued that "texts from ancient times should not be read like the written literature with which we are familiar because such texts are only supports for an oral tradition which remained dominant."⁹

Ivan Engnell supported Nyberg's assessments and "rejected the theory of literary documents in the Pentateuch (Wellhausen's J, E, D, and P) as well as similar documentary analysis for other parts of the Bible" under an oral traditional approach called the traditio-historical method.¹⁰ Engnell and Nyberg held that oral traditions could reliably preserve the traditions, albeit with some fluidity.¹¹ In his 1954 work, *Oral Tradition*, Eduard Nielsen discussed and engaged Nyberg and Engnell's work in English.¹² For those who followed this school's thought, "the presence of writing and the existence of writing technology [did] not necessitate the end of oral tradition."¹³ The school did see the shift to writing as the beginning of a new system where greater consistency and permanence were possible, as was the text's potency of being "divorced from the living community's memory and therefore cut off from its interpretive tradition."¹⁴

Parry and Lord's Impact

In 1960, Albert Lord published *The Singer of Tales*, in which he built upon the work of Milman Parry in the field of orality. Lord investigated Parry's theory that formulaic language lay behind oral communication by analyzing the oral traditions of Serbo-Croatia. He then applied his findings to the Homeric literature, concluding that the literature shared aspects of orality that he described as formulaic, metrical, and conclusive at the end

---

7. Culley, "Oral Tradition and Biblical Studies," 36; West, "Art of Biblical Performance," 7.
8. Culley, "Oral Tradition and Biblical Studies," 37.
9. Culley, "Oral Tradition and Biblical Studies," 37.
10. Culley, "Oral Tradition and Biblical Studies," 37.
11. Culley, "Oral Tradition and Biblical Studies," 37.
12. Nielsen, *Oral Tradition*.
13. West, "Art of Biblical Performance," 8.
14. West, "Art of Biblical Performance," 8–9.

of each line.[15] The few biblical scholars who did pursue this new conception of comparative orality were to be disappointed.[16] Later, orality was revealed to be more nuanced than Lord and his early followers perceived. The great divide that was imagined between orality and literacy was reinforced by oral scholars such as Walter Ong and Jack Goody.[17]

Richard Horsley said, "Because the written text is deemed sacred ... it may be understandable that oral tradition in the broader sense assumed in other fields poses a considerable threat to New Testament (biblical) scholars."[18] Werner H. Kelber explained that modern biblical scholarship has not grown past the study of the technology of the fifteenth and sixteenth centuries—the print Bible, and "for this reason, the historical, critical scholarship of the Bible has risked laboring under a cultural anachronism, projecting modernity's communications culture upon the ancient media world."[19] As expected, the exception Kelber noted is form criticism, though he confessed, "Today, form criticism is besieged with multiple problems, the most significant of which is its complicity with post-Gutenberg assumptions about ancient dynamics of communication."[20]

These observations echo the lament of Brian B. Schmidt, already cited above, that the implications of the fact "that literacy in the ancient Near Eastern and Mediterranean theaters emerged in a predominantly oral world ... have made only sporadic and gradual inroads into the modern study of Israelite society, the Hebrew Bible and the relevance of orality and literacy for the actual historical composition of biblical literature."[21] Thus, while Milman Parry and Albert Lord ushered in a new approach to orality and texts suspected to be birthed from oral tradition, comparably little was done to apply those concepts to the area of biblical studies.

---

15. Niditch, "Hebrew Bible and Oral Literature," 3–4.
16. Niditch, "Hebrew Bible and Oral Literature," 6.
17. West, "Art of Biblical Performance," 9.
18. Horsley, "Oral Tradition," 34.
19. Kelber, "Oral Tradition," 40.
20. Kelber, "Oral Tradition," 40.
21. Schmidt, "Introduction," 1.

A History of the Application of Orality to Old Testament Studies

John Miles Foley and Susan Niditch

The notion of a great divide between orality and literacy was challenged by John Miles Foley who, in many ways, "[acknowledged] an ongoing relationship of influence between texts and performances in a single culture."[22] Foley established the journal *Oral Tradition* in 1986 and edited it until shortly before his death in 2012.[23] *Oral Tradition* provided an arena in which scholars of different language areas and disciplines could "inform specialists of parallel developments in their own and different areas, to build and maintain bridges among disciplines in order to promote the healthy growth of the field as a whole."[24] Much of what was summarized concerning oral cultures earlier in this chapter had its roots in the theories of Foley,[25] and the collaboration of field work and literary studies and other disciplines often facilitated through *Oral Tradition*.

Niditch was a catalytic link between Old Testament scholarship and the work in the field of orality, as Foley represented. David Carr said Niditch "has been foremost in introducing considerations of orality, including the work of Milman Parry, Gregory Nagy, and other classicists into biblical studies, along with many other creative and original contributions to the field."[26] Thus, this discussion of the history of the application of orality to Old Testament studies has come full circle to the summary material in chapter one, in which some of Niditch's contributions, as well as the approaches of many scholars who have followed in her footsteps, have been summarized.

---

22. Schmidt, "Introduction," 15.
23. West, "Art of Biblical Performance," 15.
24. Foley, "Introduction," 7.
25. For a summary of some of Foley's largest contributions, see West, "Art of Biblical Performance," 15–25.
26. Carr, "Orality, Textuality, and Memory," 161n1.

3

Oral Tradition and the Textual Tradition of Habakkuk

My dissertation investigated a selection of the textual tradition of Habakkuk within the theoretical models discussed above in order to determine if the tradition of Habakkuk demonstrates elements of an oral register according to these theories. Habakkuk contains unique features that make it an interesting subject for the study of orality. In Hab 2:2, the prophet is told to "write the vision and make it clear on tablets in order that he might run reading it."[1] This command could imply prophecies or visions were not normally written down. Further, the implication could be that the act of recording the vision instilled it with a sense of assurance, permanency, and even authority. Finally, it implies the ability of the prophet to write and for a "runner" to read. All of these features are aspects of study within the interplay of orality and textuality. Chapter 3 of Habakkuk has liturgical notation similar to that of Ps 7, suggesting performance. It was also "used in the liturgies of both Eastern and Western Christianity as a morning canticle, and it is the *haphtarah* for Pentecost in Judaism."[2]

---

1. All biblical citations are my own translations unless otherwise marked.
2. Harper, *Responding*, 19. Harper indicated that such use of Hab 3 could be dated "before AD 70" or even as early as "the second century BC." Harper, *Responding*, 27.

My studies of the witnesses to the textual tradition of Habakkuk discovered dynamics of orality as discussed above, therefore, confidence in these theories and the warrant for their application to the biblical corpus can be strengthened. The evidence for orality in the Habakkuk tradition emerged from the variants found among the Masoretic Tradition (MT), Codex Vaticanus, 1QpHab, Or 2211, Mur XII, and 8HevXII, as well as in the early scribal/translation/interpretive period, as represented by ms 86, ms 7a1, and Codex Amiatinus. The analysis of the manuscripts mentioned above discovered signs of fluidity and stability, metonymy/activation (signs of a shared communal knowledge of the traditional narrative and content including a tradition of meaning and/or tradition of interpretation), as well as other signs of an oral register.

Again, I acknowledge that these features are not exclusive to texts that have their origin in oral traditional cultures, but I maintain that their prevalence in the verbal art of such cultures should not be ignored. The presence of these features do not "prove" that the biblical material stemmed from an oral register, but in the case that the material does stem from an oral register similar to what I have been discussing, the presence of at least some of these features might be expected.

My dissertation pursued the following question: is the available data of the biblical tradition best represented from within the broader matrix which is now growing out of an ever-increasing understanding of orality and its interaction with the written word, and what are the implications of these theories on biblical study, interpretation, and proclamation? Specifically, my dissertation added to this exploration of orality and biblical studies by analyzing a number of relevant textual witnesses of Habakkuk in order to determine whether the preserved tradition of the prophet can be located within a register more closely aligned with recent theories of orality.

I compared the texts of a number of ancient witnesses to the tradition of Habakkuk in order to determine whether the data from Habakkuk's textual tradition can be situated within the theories of orality and textuality discussed above. The analyzed textual witnesses of Habakkuk included the Masoretic Text (MT), as represented in Biblia Hebraica Stuttgartensia; the Septuagint (LXX), as represented by Codex Vaticanus (B); the Qumran pesher scroll of Habakkuk (1QpHab); the Hebrew scroll of the Minor Prophets found at Wadi Murabba'at (Mur XII); the Greek scroll of the Minor Prophets found at Nahal Hever (8HevXIIgr), the Barberini Greek version of Hab 3 (Ms 86 [Vat. Barberini gr. 549]);[3] Targum Jonathan as represented by Or 2211; the Peshitta as represented by Ms 7a1; and the Vulgate as represented by Codex Amiatinus.

Individual manuscripts of Habakkuk, as opposed to eclectic or critical texts, were chosen as specific witnesses to the textual tradition because scholars have demonstrated that individual scribes may have seen themselves as performers of the text in varying likeness to the bearers of oral tradition.[4] Most manuscripts were meant to stand as valid representatives of the faith tradition,[5] and a consensus is growing that the fluidity found among these manuscripts did not invalidate them as true witnesses to the tradition as some modern textual critics have assumed. Susan Niditch said it this way:

> As a student of the place of manuscripts in largely oral worlds, I am less inclined to reconstruct a whole text, to build it, however judiciously, from the limited number of available manuscripts. I worry about the artificiality of such a process and believe it more true to life to assume that there were always multiple versions of the tradition before the Common Era. One can never know if a reconstructed text ever lived in a community, nor can one recover an original version, if there is such a thing. With a vital interest in religions as lived, I would like to know that an extant manuscript was meaningful to a group. Variation among manuscript traditions, however, is of lively interest and important to the study of literary and religious tradition, for these various texts may reflect different ways in which communities of Jews and Christians understood the tradition. Scripture was heard in different words, and the medium was important to the message.[6]

As represented by the Leningrad Codex, the Masoretic Tradition was chosen since it is the standard text for English translations. Codex Vaticanus was selected for its important witness to the LXX. The Qumran pesher scroll was chosen because of its importance in textual criticism of Habakkuk, as well as for the perspective the community had on the

---

3. In choosing these manuscripts, the following were consulted initially: Mathews, "Performing Habakkuk," 91–92; and Bruce, "Habakkuk," 835–36.

4. Person, "Ancient Israelite Scribe," 601–9; and Person, *Deuteronomic History*, 170–72.

5. For instance, the Qumran community carried different versions of various works. Niditch says, "The attitude is typical of a traditional world in which variant texts are deemed valid and authentic." Niditch, "Hebrew Bible," 15.

6. Niditch, "Hebrew Bible," 15.

message of the Habakkuk tradition. Mur XII was chosen since it is an important secondary witness to the MT tradition dating much earlier than the Leningrad Codex and mainly for its alternative presentation of Hab 3:10.[7] 8HevXIIgr stands as an early and important link between the LXX and a form of the Hebrew resembling the MT.[8] The Barberini Greek version of Hab 3, as Bruce said, is the most important independent Greek representation of Hab 3.[9] Codex Amiatinus was chosen for its early representation of the Latin Vulgate, and Or 2211 was chosen as it was the base text for Alexander Sperber's edition of the Targum of the Latter Prophets.[10] Manuscript 7a1 was chosen for its important witness to the Peshitta.[11]

After providing the overview of orality and textuality above, I gave a brief summary of the critical issues surrounding the book of Habakkuk, including a summary of the discourse analysis of Habakkuk by David J. Fuller. Fuller's analysis provided a convincing argument for taking the Masoretic Tradition of Habakkuk as a whole performance of the tradition in order to compare the MT to the other versions. Chapter three offered a brief overview of the manuscripts under investigation, and then chapter four, the bulk of the work, analyzed the versions of the Habakkuk tradition to see if the interplay between orality and textuality may offer explanations for the variations. I also analyzed the language and presentation of the tradition at-large to determine if markers of an oral register can be identified, and if the manuscripts, in both their stability and fluidity, can represent a common broader tradition.

My dissertation discovered that the versions do seem to expect freedom to produce fluid performances while retaining an important measure of stability, and signs of collective memory and the ability of activation are apparent. The versions do not represent a rigid copying or translation process of a singular set of inspired words that left every difficult passage or graphic variant lingering and disconnected to the version's overall presentation of the tradition.

---

7. Ian Young has demonstrated that the Mur XII scroll has only one variation every 222 words, representing a very stable tradition of the MT. Young, "Stabilization," (for the date of the texts found at Murabbaʿat, 365).

8. Greenspoon, Review, 137–40.

9. Bruce, "Habakkuk," 836.

10. Cathcart and Gordon, *Targum*, xi.

11. Emidio Vergani says it "is the earliest of the three most important complete manuscripts of the Peshitta: 7al, 8al, 9al." Vergani, "Introduction," xi.

Instead, almost every variation represented creative moves to deliver unique yet mostly consistent representatives of the tradition. The versions demonstrate a tradition of translation, interpretation, pursuit of meaning, and performance from one presentation to the next as if they were creative variations of performance of what would be understood as a singular communal tradition. It was as if each manuscript had acted as a tradent or bard, singing a unique "song" easily recognizable as "Habakkuk."

As to fluidity and stability in the tradition: Vaticanus utilized unique choice words in Hab 1:2–4 that emphasized the communal breaking of God's covenant and which also set up for its major shift in emphasis in verse 9. Using the key words of "end" and "ungodly," Vaticanus presented a performance with different emphases than the MT. The performance carried the hearer along with Habakkuk as the prophet grew in faith in God's global sovereignty and even a promise of atonement. This growing faith resulted in the prophet viewing the coming of the Babylonian judgment as a fulfilment of God's promises, which actually brought confidence to the prophet of the fulfilment of future promises, such as the promised vision with all its hope and the coming atonement of God's people. Habakkuk can rejoice in God even in the face of war-induced famine because it is all a sign of the strength of his God who has promised salvation.

The Barberini version of Hab 3 varied from the other performances as it presented God's move of judgment against the singer's enemy as a sudden and devastating event. The concluding words of the psalm declare, "Having been swift, it ceased." In contrast to Vaticanus, Barb promises the suffering of God's people to be short and his victory over her enemies sudden.

At Hab 1:6, Ms 7a1 explicitly equated the insolence of the Babylonians with the insolence of the Judeans, reflecting other creative choices of the translation from Hab 1:2–4. The performance of the Syriac in this manuscript, therefore, emphasizes the need of God's people for YHWH's compassion as he judges the nations.

As to the other versions: Amiatinus seemed to play more with the eternal nature of YHWH, and the paraphrastic interpretation of the Targum in 2211 emphasized Torah obedience. Not enough was present in the Nahal Hever scroll to determine major shifts except that, just like 1QpHab, it seemed to largely follow the Masoretic tradition.

The variations in the versions usually drew out nuances that could be located within the MT but also, in a few places, carried the tradition to fairly unique expressions—such as Vaticanus's *atonement* and Barb's *swift* ending of the people's suffering. No singular performance seemed to even try to encapsulate the Habakkuk tradition as a whole. I will discuss the various interpretations of the version further in chapter ten.

There also seemed to be a communal memory represented by the manuscripts, first discussed in light of apparent traditions of interpretation of the Habakkuk tradition. This tradition of interpretation was seen especially in the similarities between the paraphrase of Targum Jonathan and the pesher of 1QpHab. The shared interpretive approaches demonstrate an oral traditional understanding of the text that a single performance could not fully represent. As one example, the Targum mentions robbery at Hab 2:11, which is absent from the Hebrew text of Habakkuk, and the pesher of 1QpHab mentions robbery in the commentary of the same verse. While there is no indication for a reader of the MT to assume a connection to robbery at 2:11, apparently there was some connection in the ancient interpretive tradition.

Similar to this interpretive tradition demonstrated to exist behind the book of Habakkuk, the Qumran community that engaged the pesharim shared a narrative tradition of the Teacher of Righteousness and his adversaries. Knowledge of this narrative was necessary for proper interpretation. No names are given in the commentary of the Habakkuk pesher connecting to the historical events of the teacher. The community is assumed to already be familiar with the story of the Teacher of Righteousness.

While the pesher's interpretations of the text certainly pointed to aspects well beyond the intent of the prophet Habakkuk, pointing to historical events well after Habakkuk's time, the interpretations still had to connect to the text through themes, phrases, and catchwords. In all of its fluidity of interpretation, it was bound to the tradition of Habakkuk, even as the text's meaning was derived from traditional themes, phrases, and catchwords applied to the community's current historical situation.

This demonstrates at least three layers of essential tradition for the community of the pesher. First, the tradition of the book of Habakkuk existed, the fluidity and stability of which has already been discussed. Second, the tradition of interpreting the book of Habakkuk existed, as seen in the connection of the pesher's commentary and the targum's paraphrase. Third, a narrative tradition of the community's founder existed, a tradition required to interpret the community's texts. Any performance, whether written or oral, was held captive within these layers of tradition. Other signs of a shared tradition of interpreting Habakkuk were also discussed.

Also apparent in the variations between the textual representatives of the Habakkuk tradition were signs of activation in which a word or phrase from the text activated elements of the extended shared tradition. This was clearly seen, for example, in Hab 1:3 where the phrase רִיב וּמָדוֹן activated elements of judges and bribes for the translators of the LXX and the Peshitta discussed further in chapter five of this work. Many other signs of activation were given, including the memory variant found in the assimilation of Ps 77 in Mur XII's presentation of Hab 3:10. Finally, other signs of orality in the tradition of Habakkuk were discussed, including the echo/ring-composition of the five woe oracles in Hab 2 (also discussed further in chapter five).

The Habakkuk tradition, as investigated within the manuscripts described above, seems to fit solidly within the matrix of orality and textuality growing out of recent studies in the field. The ancient community did not value the Habakkuk tradition only within a certain written form of a Hebrew text. Instead, the witnesses to the tradition—as seen in Hebrew texts like Mur XII and the citations in 1QpHab; in the early interpretive traditions of Targum Jonathan, the pesher scroll, and the versions; in early translations such as the LXX, the Barberini version of Hab 3, and the scroll from Nahal Hever; and in later translations such as the Peshitta and Vulgate—all have significant intersection with the growing theories of orality and textuality.

The tradition of Habakkuk existed in a fluid form, so the LXX could significantly restructure the flow of performance, even while the Nahal Hever scroll was also utilized as a Greek witness to the tradition that was much closer to the Masoretic Text. Yet the tradition was seemingly held to a level of stability so that the pesher scroll was constrained to the text even when it was tempted to shift the text toward its interpretations.

The versions demonstrate the ability of activation within the community, as words, phrases, and scenes called to mind broader aspects of the tradition, and in that when a broader part of the tradition was activated, the versions often realigned. The later editions, the Peshitta and Vulgate as seen in Ms 7a1 and Codex Amiatinus, follow trends of expansion and elimination seen in other ancient writings stemming from oral cultures.

Within the tradition itself, signs of orality can be seen in the discussion of the writing down of the vision for proclamation and in the echo/ring composition of the woe oracles. The tradition of Habakkuk certainly seems to be defined by much more than a textuality but by a textuality embedded within an oral traditional culture with strong connections to recent theories of orality and textuality.

Since the tradition of Habakkuk demonstrates the tendencies of orality as discussed above and below, my dissertation adds to the confidence biblical scholars can have in applying these theories of orality to biblical studies, to biblical exegesis, and to the proclamation of the biblical message. Finally, issues of inspiration, exegesis, and proclamation of Scripture were discussed in light of receiving the biblical text within these matrices of orality and textuality. These themes are taken up in the current work in the following chapter.

4

Inspiration and Authority of the Biblical Text

Second Samuel 18:24–25 says, "And David was sitting between the two gates as the watchman went up to the roof of the gate along the wall and lifted his eyes and saw a man running alone. The watchman cried out and announced it to the king. The king said, 'If he is alone there is good news in his mouth.'" Habakkuk 2:2 says, "Write the vision, and make it clear on tablets so that the one reading it might run." The one who runs to read brings a message to perform. The current community of faith desires to run with the text to read it and deliver its message.

Biblical studies have been slow to apply recent studies in orality. This is an interesting trend since biblical studies already apply theories of orality that are often outdated to influential areas such as form criticism. The explanation for this aversion to recent studies in orality may be honorable—those who study the Bible often place great faith in the words as written. As Horsely pointed out, the text itself is often deemed sacred and inspired, and so moving away from an original text may imply for some a moving away from the inspired words of God.[1] This need not be so.

Recent studies in orality may be demonstrating this sort of text-focused theory of biblical inspiration could represent an anachronistic projection of recent Occidental thought onto the methodology of God. The

---

1. Horsley, "Oral Tradition in New Testament Studies," 34.

important witnesses of the textual tradition of Habakkuk investigated in my work seem to support emerging theories of orality and textuality that would insist the written biblical manuscripts operated as a part of the oral traditional milieu of the ancient believing community. These theories oppose the warrant for a pursuit of an original and inspired written text (for most of the Old Testament material and possibly much of the New Testament as well) and point to other implications regarding how the texts should be handled.

Many of the resources I have cited represent scholars who are applying emerging theories of orality and textuality toward correcting older critical models, such as form, source, redaction, and textual criticism, and their work is greatly needed. However, theories of orality and textuality do not simply affect critical models of biblical studies. Since they affect the very nature of the text's identity and purpose, they affect our understanding of inspiration as well as the process of interpretation of the text's meaning, which should have an impact on the proclamation and application of the texts within the current believing community. Those desiring to interpret the Bible and run with its message—a message that is to be performed and proclaimed—must be mindful of the oral origins of the content of the text.

This must be a modest endeavor. The traditions stored in the biblical texts certainly fall within a category which Foley called "voices from the past."[2] Such texts "are oral traditions that because of the accidents of time and place reach today's prospective audience only in textual form." While it is certain these texts stemmed from a culture that operated within oral-traditional metrics, the specific diversity of the orality of those cultures cannot now be unearthed entirely. Foley said, "We must be judicious, since it is dangerous, unnecessary, and misleading to proceed beyond the limits of our available knowledge—to base research on hypothetical scenarios of origin and transmission that cannot be proven."[3]

---

2. For the following discussion of "voices of the past," see Foley, "Plenitude and Diversity," 108–9. I disagree with Rodriguez (*Oral Tradition*, 102) in the need to identify some of the New Testament works, such as Paul's writings, as "voiced texts." Perhaps they were originally composed as "voiced texts," but, as we do not have access to the specifics of their oral delivery methods, etc., and since they are essentially products of both the oral traditions of the Old Testament and the early Christian oral culture, they should be considered "voices from the past." Perhaps a compromise is possible—we can receive them at best as "voiced texts from the past."

3. Foley, "Plenitude and Diversity," 108.

What should the believing community do? Since she cannot retrieve the exact matrices of orality that gave birth to her holy writings, should she simply despair of ever understanding the tradition and so continue to approach the text with no regard to aspects of orality? Foley continued,

> Since modern fieldwork has shown that textuality and oral traditions not only co-exist but interact, and since the chief criterion of how verbal art works is the language or register within which it morphs and through which it communicates, the role of textuality is certainly no reason to deny oral traditional roots. Better to remain agnostic about scenarios for which we have no primary, irrefutable evidence, and *at the same time to take full account of the oral traditional structure and expressivity of such works.*[4]

Therefore, while exact conclusions on every metric of the orality of ancient Israel and the infant church cannot be attained, the oral origins of the texts should still be considered. At least, general aspects of orality and textuality should be applied to contemporary interpretation and proclamation of the tradition represented in the biblical texts. This should include both an understanding of the broad interpretive traditions as well as structural tendencies of repetition within the performance.

The current community of faith that claims to find its identity in the biblical tradition has mainly just the biblical texts as a representative of the tradition. No video or audio recordings exist of ancient performances of the tradition. Almost all that remains of the tradition and its message to humanity are the text and its readers. Should the message of the text be proclaimed, the readers, just as in Hab 2:2, must be able to "run" with the text in order to deliver it. In light of the orality behind the text of the Bible, how should the reader run? This chapter will explore how the application of the theories of orality and textuality discussed thus far may affect issues of inspiration of the biblical texts. The next chapter will focus on how to interpret texts stemming from an oral register.

It is important to emphasize that changing one's perspective on the nature of the Bible in this way does not necessitate the rejection of one's commitment to the inspiration and authority of the Bible. As required by the views investigated in this work, the move away from a singular authoritative text need not diminish the authority and reverence of the biblical corpus. However, these theories evoke certain questions. If any

---

4. Foley, "Plenitude and Diversity," 109 (emphasis added). While Rodriguez utilizes Foley's categories and discussion in *Oral Tradition*, he does not acknowledge that Foley suggested that we take full account of the oral traditional *structure* of such works.

given text does not fully represent the biblical tradition, what then is the Bible, and how can one still hold to a theory of inspiration?

Inspiration and Epistemology[5]

Inspiration is more than a dogmatic religious belief about ancient writings. Dorothy Sayers said, "It is a lie to say that dogma does not matter; it matters enormously. It is fatal to let people suppose that Christianity is only a mode of feeling; it is vitally necessary to insist that it is first and foremost a rational explanation of the universe."[6] A belief in the inspiration of Scripture drastically affects one's rational approach to the universe. One's thoughts on inspiration and epistemology are indivisible. Inspiration applies to the concept of special revelation, which suggests a realm of knowledge unattainable without divine initiative. Therefore, should someone accept the reality of inspiration her epistemology would include, and likely require, a level of divine revelation for fuller understanding of the universe. Should one reject the reality of inspiration, this rejection would become an aspect of that person's epistemology.

Since epistemology is an expansive field of investigation far beyond the scope for this chapter (or for one book) to cover, only the perspective of epistemology assumed by this work will be presented briefly as the basis for my approach of applying the growing conception of orality to biblical exegesis, with only a little interaction with the historic philosophical discussion of the topic of epistemology.

The view assumed in this work holds that a working epistemology requires immaterial authority, specifically the God of Christian Scripture, for internal consistency. The immaterial realities, such as logic, value, and induction, which render the universe as intelligible, cannot be assumed with consistency unless one also assumes God. As a case study of the inconsistency evident within a mere materialistic epistemology, one could investigate the perspective represented by the following quotations of Friedrich Nietzsche:

---

5. While the current author certainly does not agree with Cornelius Van Til, R. J. Rushdoony, and Gregory Bahnsen on every application of Scripture, their perspective on epistemology is certainly influential in the following discussion. For reference, one might see Cornelius Van Til, *Defense of the Faith*; Greg L. Bahnsen, *Always Ready*; and R. J. Rushdoony, *One and the Many*.

6. Dorothy Sayers, *Letters*, 49.

> In some remote corner of the universe, poured out and glittering in innumerable solar systems, there once was a star on which clever animals invented knowledge. That was the haughtiest and most mendacious minute of "world history"—yet only a minute. After nature had drawn a few breaths the star grew cold, and the clever animals had to die. One might invent such a fable and still not have illustrated sufficiently how wretched, how shadowy and flighty, how aimless and arbitrary, the human intellect appears in nature. There have been eternities when it did not exist; and when it is done for again, nothing will have happened.[7]

On one hand, Nietzsche seemed to understand some of the implications of his epistemological standards. In a material universe, void of God, humanity is but a blip of organized matter upon an eternal timeline of meaninglessness—her intellect but an incredibly miniscule moment of a certain mixture of chemical reactions.

On the other hand, Nietzsche continued in his *intellectual evaluation* of the vanity of human intellect. If he had been consistent concerning humanity's vain intellect, which stems from his epistemological standards, he would not have written intellectually about his vain intellect. The godless worldview presented by the quotation is internally inconsistent as it leaves no room for authoritative logic, intellect, or value and yet utilizes logic toward an intellectual evaluation of the absence of value of human intellect.

Nietzsche even ridiculed the use of words. He identified every word as "a nerve stimulus, first transposed into an image—first metaphor. The image, in turn, imitated by a sound—second metaphor...."[8] According to Nietzsche, words are, at best, second-hand metaphors of nerve stimuli that flighty human minds attempt to piece together into concepts that only reflect the vanity of human intellect. Thus, "truths are illusions about which one has forgotten that this is what they are; metaphors which are worn out and without sensuous power; coins which have lost their pictures and now matter only as metal, no longer as coins."[9]

C. S. Lewis said, "An open mind, in questions that are not ultimate, is useful. But an open mind about the ultimate foundations either of Theoretical or of Practical Reason is idiocy. If a man's mind is open on these

---

7. Kaufmann, *Portable Nietzsche*, 42.
8. Kaufmann, *Portable Nietzsche*, 46.
9. Kaufmann, *Portable Nietzsche*, 47.

things, let his mouth at least be shut. He can say nothing to the purpose."[10] In Nietzsche's case, perhaps Lewis would say, "If someone, while discussing the problem of truth, also rejects the potency of words while utilizing words to argue against the ultimacy of truth, and above all, this person wants his writings of words about the vanity of truth to be read as true, then for the love of God let him make his point without words and spare humanity the time and hypocrisy and save a tree."

A consistent epistemology cannot find its source in the human mind alone and remain consistent. Nietzsche was not the first philosopher to stumble in this respect. Faced with the opposing rationalistic systems of Descartes, Spinoza, and Leibniz and the skeptical deconstruction of empiricism by Hume, Immanuel Kant suggested a transcendental approach to epistemology to bridge the gap.[11] Whereas Hume demonstrated that the vital knowledge category of cause and effect is never truly experienced and is therefore unknowable and unprovable, Kant argued that the mind imposes categories of knowledge such as cause and effect upon experience because these categories are preconditions for the intelligibility of the world. Humans cannot even discuss thought unless the mind imposes the category of "thought-ness" upon itself.

In this argument, Kant presented a case for elements of reality that transcend rationality. In other words, rationality is impossible without these transcendent preconditions. Kant's move toward transcendentalism was genius, but the centering of his transcendent argument within the human mind betrayed the fact that he too was slave to what was then the prevailing philosophical bias toward humanistic reason.

Kant was correct. Transcendental properties are necessary to make the universe intelligible, but Kant was wrong in identifying the transcendent preconditions for the intelligibility of the universe in the human mind. No human mind is transcendent because every human mind is different, finite, and mutable.[12]

---

10. Lewis, *Abolition of Man*, 48.

11. The following discussion on epistemology is based on thirty audio lectures on apologetics from Greg L. Bahnsen, accessed with permission at the now extinct website, www.bahnsenuniversity.com. Similar lectures can be accessed from the Covenant Media Foundation: https://www.cmfnow.com/mp3/apologetics.

12. This, of course, assumes the philosophy of monistic naturalism or materialism. Dualistic naturalists may claim that immaterial realities, such as logic, do exist, but they have the philosophical impossibility to explain how the immaterial realm interacts with the material realm. They also have no way of explaining which "gave birth" to the other or how the immaterial realm could produce something material and vice versa.

However, if one approaches epistemology through the lens of Christian Scripture, one will assume that God is the transcendent one who created all things in the beginning. Because God is truth and no lie abides in him,[13] one can claim logic to exist—God's nature requires some assertions to be true, and therefore others to be false. His nature also assumes a proper way of life that includes abiding in the truth. Therefore, within a worldview with the Christian God as its source, reasoning between what is true and false may be expected and should be pursued. Logic and value can be assumed due to the nature of God.

When a follower of Christ utilizes knowledge and logic, they are operating consistently within their presuppositions concerning the transcendental reality of the universe. The biblical worldview is consistent. Those who do not assume God's transcendence might also assume that truth exists and that it should be pursued, but, as in the examples discussed above, those assumptions cannot be supported consistently from within their worldview—no basis exists for appealing to logic, value, or induction in a godless worldview. As represented in Scripture, God is the precondition for the intelligibility of the universe.[14]

This discussion is not meant to be an apologetic for the theory of epistemology and inspiration that I hold, and it would certainly spark spirited debate in many circles. At any rate, these are my views on epistemology. Even as I have come to believe that God's word was not delivered to us through older models of verbal plenary inspiration of written autographs, I still believe in the authority and inspiration of Scripture. God, as the foundation and fountain of love, truth, value, and induction, has revealed himself to humanity. His revelation of himself is recorded in the Old and New Testaments and perfectly personified in the incarnation—the life, death, and resurrection of Jesus the Messiah. The Bible is the standard for faith and practice for all who follow him.

Orality and Inspired Text

The theories of orality and textuality discussed in this work argue that any specific written text will not be the singular exhaustive and authoritative

---

13. John 14:6; 17:17; Prov 30:5; Deut 32:4; Num 23:19; Heb 6:18.

14. This section on a biblical epistemology is clearly too short to be convincing to skeptics, nor does it justify the specificity of the *Christian* God of Scripture, but hopefully it is sufficient to describe the view of inspiration and epistemology behind this present work.

representative of a tradition steeped in orality. For instance, the book of Habakkuk seems to have been multiform, perhaps from its inception and into the time of the translation of the Vulgate. Habakkuk has been witnessed to and received in many forms and many languages, with significant variation even within the same languages. Yet still, only one "book" of Habakkuk exists. The oldest remaining texts seem to reflect that the ancient community of faith did not pursue an "original text" but rather allowed for multiformity while still receiving a "singular" tradition.

What then is "the book of Habakkuk"? The book of Habakkuk is the tradition of the revelation from YHWH through Habakkuk to the believing community that was preserved through multiform-inspired performances within the cultural and traditional realities of the community. The inspiration itself was acknowledged by the believing community through communal traditional understandings of YHWH and his interaction with the community throughout their extended shared traditions—it was received into the traditional canon situated within the community's collective heart and mind.

The specific scenario that delivered the textual witnesses of that canonized tradition to the modern era is largely lost to the believing community. As mentioned above, no recordings of performances exist other than the manuscripts as they are now received. The tradition of Habakkuk exists today almost only in ancient print. In addition to the textual performances of the book of Habakkuk themselves, I demonstrated in my dissertation that some of the lost traditions of interpretation might be recovered by comparative approaches, such as comparing the interpretations of 1QpHab and Targum Jonathan.

Insights can also certainly be gained through comparing written texts from other ancient communities, as well as by studying various works of ancient art and other relevant archaeological artifacts. However, it still stands that what remains of the performance tradition of Habakkuk exists almost exclusively within words written down on media. What is true of Habakkuk is also true of the Bible as a whole. Different books and portions of Scripture may have various textual representatives and media for comparison, but the biblical tradition is available to the modern community of faith mainly through the written text. Yet, it is still important that the believing community "take full account of the oral traditional structure and expressivity of such works."[15]

---

15. Foley, "Plenitude and Diversity," 109.

As opposed to theories of inspiration that seek a series of inerrant autographs, the inspiration from God did not rest simply on individual authors or editors who penned the original text or any kind of a final form of the text. God's inspiration was communal. He moved through a community of faith and established his holy word in its very cultural and historical identity. He created for himself a people and imbedded his inspired word among them as a holistic oral traditional "text" that was written on the hearts and minds of the community of faith. The inspired word was a living tradition.

The texts that remain bear witness to this inspired word. One might argue that receiving the inspired word of God as a living tradition embedded within God's community of faith is more representative of the character of the communal triune God than the more recent approach of expecting an authoritative, original, and holy series of written words. Perhaps God is not a modern Occidental author who wrote theological theses, scientific explanations, and historical accounts through individual authors and editors. Perhaps God has always been working toward establishing a relationship with humanity and writing his word—the tradition of the history and understanding of his relational move—on the hearts of his people and not merely upon stone or page.

The notion of an inspired multiform tradition of performance, and interpretive constructs which are now received in residual texts, opens doors to many necessary areas of study. For instance, when was a textual performance at such variance that it was not accepted as a faithful representation of the community's traditions? Why did the reception of authoritative texts end with the corpus now received? What was the process of the solidification of the tradition so that no other performances, textual or otherwise, are accepted as equally authoritative?

It is evident that certain textual performances, like the Septuagint, were widely accepted by the early Christian community, including well-educated Jewish Christians such as Paul. However, other textual representations found at Qumran may have only been embraced by certain sectarian groups.

Even focusing on the Masoretic Text alone, many issues are worth investigating. Are the vowel markings inspired? What of the oral traditional nature of the *ketiv* and *qere* and the *tiqqunê soferim* (correction of the scribes)? Additionally, one could argue that the version of the accepted text has continued evolving into modern times, as Protestants generally use a canon closer to the Masoretic canon compared to Eastern and Oriental Orthodox and Catholic traditions.

A study of the solidification of the Old Testament tradition would certainly vary from that of the New Testament. Carr has discussed at length possibilities of the growth of the Old Testament tradition in *The Formation of the Hebrew Bible*. This process spanned thousands of years and represented a people's growing understanding of their identity before their God. Part of their traditional understanding included YHWH's guidance toward the establishment of a certain nation in a specific land. The New Testament tradition launched out from the tradition of the Old Testament through the life, teachings, and resurrection of the Jewish Messiah. The Jesus tradition was catapulted out on a global scale into a global community, and so it relied on specific faithful re-tellings and texts in very different ways. Some variations in the performances of the Gospels, such as the repositioning of John 8:1–11 in the textual witnesses and the issue of the short/long ending in Mark, seem to indicate some fluidity in their reception, even as the scarcity of such examples of this kind of variation speaks to the highly stable nature of the tradition.[16]

In exploring how the believing community transitioned from an oral performance tradition to a reliance on solidified written texts, we must be careful not to impose modern assumptions of linear development. The shift from aural reception to textual reception did not necessarily follow a straightforward, progressive path. The word of God did not transition from an oral stage of variation and gist to a "received" Word in textual form (the capitalized "Word" implying a more divine product). The text that remains is representative of the Word that was embedded into the community (I would say the text is the *residue* of the revelatory tradition, but the connotations of the word "residue" belittles the text and misrepresents what I really mean).

The text bears witness to a relational move of YHWH to his people. We can be tempted to chase after notions of an original text or original performance or some kind of linear growth according to our modern metrics of exactitude, so that we can feel a sense of control over the text. If we can understand the process in a systematic way we can imagine a

---

16. I am very grateful to Darrell Bock's email correspondence that revealed this great gap in my discussion of this subject. Bock also pointed to issues such as the D tradition in Acts, not fully reflective of Luke's efforts but relevant to such discussion and further reflection. Other issues he pointed out may not have been adequately addressed here, and he may disagree with me on several points. This is indeed an emerging field of study!

control over the text. If we can feel a control over texts, we can nail down more secure data points. We want to know that we can always get the same output from the input we supply. I am concerned that this kind of desire for control over God's words may reflect the sin of the garden—deciding for ourselves what is good and evil so that we can be like God on our own terms. It can be scary to feel like we are losing some control over the text. But relationships are not about control. They are about faith. Relationships are always harder than the control that religion sometimes offers through the letter.

For us to even receive the inspired relational message standing behind the text, we need to explore as much as we can of the greater tradition embedded within the hearts and minds of the tradition's community. That certainly requires the study of historical/linguistic contexts, but it also means stepping into the traditional mindset of activation, including the reception and interpretations of things like type scenes and keywords and interpretive frameworks—as will be discussed below.

The historical development that led to our reliance on solidified manuscripts as the authoritative tradents of our faith may simply reflect the community's growing disconnection from the tradition's cultural, sociological, and ideological roots. The texts are solidified for us now because there are no living tradents of the revelatory tradition embedded in the sociocultural environment of the ancient tradition to give creative performances that carry the same kind of lasting authority as the performances represented by the texts the oral tradition left behind.

That begs the question—why does God not give that kind of revelatory inspiration now?

In answering this question, we must first point out that to say that the inspired word of God was the living tradition of the community does not justify an approach to inspiration that would equate the authority of ongoing church tradition with the texts of the Bible. The gospel of Jesus the Messiah spread like wildfire, so that within twenty years of the resurrection, there were congregations in Rome to which Paul could write. As the community of faith expanded rapidly beyond its geographical and cultural center, it was in danger of outrunning the historical and interpretive traditions that gave it birth. This is likely the reason the writings of the New Testament became so precious—they were tied to the living tradition of Christ through his apostles, the tradents of the Messiah's teachings. The apostolic voice was held in trust through their performances which circulated in written form. While the tradition of the Gospels may certainly reflect a more oral-traditional development (though much different than the Old Testament traditions), certain works in the New Testament seem to have had some sort of "original text." For instance, Paul dictated a letter to Rome and sent it to be performed by Phoebe to that specific congregation.[17]

This outrunning of tradition could also stand as an explanation for some of the struggles the early church had with various heresies and doctrinal debates. In the midst of the struggles that emerged from a move away from the geographical and cultural center of the inspired tradition, it was largely the texts that held the community to the ancient traditions—the writings stemming from the apostles which bore witness to Christ's performances and interpretations of the ancient Israelite tradition.[18]

No current member of the church can proclaim a new tradition that carries equal authority as the ancient tradition to which the biblical texts bear witness. The historical teachings of Jesus were carried by the apostles and preserved in the New Testament. There are no teachings of the historical Jesus of which we can be certain except those preserved by his tradent-apostles. The inspired tradition that now remains for the church is the witness of the texts as they stand written.

Clearly, a full discussion of these issues is beyond the scope of this work in which I focus on the application of theories that seem to be the most agreed upon in the field of oral tradition and most relevant for pastors, teachers, and scholars toward the goal of exegesis and proclamation. While further investigations into these questions are needed, it has been thoroughly argued in this work that, regardless of the gaps in our knowledge of specific scenarios of certain processes, the inspired word of God was the living tradition of the community. Although limitations in our research constrain how we can apply this principle to biblical

---

17. We are not sure of what Phoebe's performance was like—did she stop and explain certain issues and/or add asides from her time spent with Paul in drafting the letter? And even though Romans likely had some kind of "original text," it still represents an oral traditional performance in that it activates the greater biblical traditions for rhetorical purposes.

18. The ancient community's use of the texts certainly does not reflect the modern, Western, text-based use of the text for apologetic ends. What can be observed is a phenomenon of written oral tradition, as the tradition of the apostles is appealed to for orthodoxy, and the tradition is reflected through quotations and references to their message and writings. A common traditional vocabulary (apparent in the New Testament itself as well) may be seen as one reads over the creeds and the writings of the apostolic fathers. For instance, see Irenaeus's rhetoric and vocabulary in *Against Heresies*, Book 1, chapters 8–10 (easily obtainable online).

interpretation, the available evidence suggests that some level of application is feasible and desirable.

God's ongoing providence in producing and preserving the Bible includes his move of creating a living tradition (the greater tradition behind what we call the Old Testament) among his established people that bore his word to humanity and pointed to Christ. It also includes his "filling full" of those traditions in Christ (as reported in the New Testament), his work in all oral performers and editors of the writings, and the efforts of the community to recognize which traditions represented by the surviving texts rank as canonical. The authoritative tradition must be mined from an appropriate approach to the texts. An appropriate approach to this textual witness of an oral tradition must consider aspects of orality.

Jesus and Scripture

Earlier I began discussing something like the following question: Why does God not give new inspiration for new canonical performances of new material? We could add: What does *canon* even mean in light of oral traditional matrices of communication? These questions certainly require future research and discussion.

For the purposes of this work, I will suggest that the final word on the inspiration and canon of Christian Scripture, as understood within the matrices of orality and textuality, should be spoken as it relates to Christ. The present Christian community of faith testifies to have encountered, both as individuals and within local expressions of the community at-large, the person of Jesus Christ through the Holy Spirit. Due to those experiences, to the epistemological reasons discussed above, and to historical investigations as represented in works such as Eddy and Boyd's *The Jesus Legend*, Christians believe in the historicity of Jesus as represented in the New Testament, and they believe the New Testament preserves the teachings of Jesus through his followers. Jesus claimed to fulfill the traditions of the Old Testament.

Jesus emerged in a world in which oral performance prevailed, and he performed aspects of the communal tradition of the Old Testament in seemingly new ways that he insisted and demonstrated were in line with the ancient traditions. In Matt 5:17 he definitively declared, "Do not suppose that I came to destroy the Law or the Prophets. I did not come to destroy but to fulfill." In the narrative found in Luke 24:13–49, it is clear that Jesus considered the Old Testament to be Scripture that spoke of him (see also John 5:39) and which he fulfilled and saturated with its intended meaning. Therefore, the Christian, as described above, believes that in whatever form Jesus received the Old Testament, he saw it as Scripture and as a witness of his identity and purpose.

From the Christian tradition, the canon is the Old Testament as Jesus received it, and the New Testament writings bearing the apostolic authority—representing the very teachings of Christ. Everything revolves around Jesus—the Word made flesh.

We have Moses and the Prophets; let us listen to them (Luke 16:29). Indeed, we have the fulfillment of the Law and the Prophets (Matt 5:17). We have the teachings of the one upon the bosom of the Father who has exemplified him (John 1:18). The incarnated fullness of God's purpose and identity revealed himself to us in the person of Jesus of Nazareth, and he left behind tradents—his apostles—to proclaim his identity to us. Their testimony stands as the prophetic word that is more sure than a personal experience of the transfiguration (2 Pet 1:19).[19] Even more than that, he has given us his very Spirit to lead us into all truth according to his word (John 14:15–26).

There is no further revelation needed. The fullness has been revealed in Christ. All that remains is for us to abide in the Spirit he left behind, so that we can interpret for today the meaning of the revelation we have in Jesus from Nazareth. The texts left behind, as defined by the performance of the Jesus tradition, are our tradents of the tradition of God's move to reveal himself to us through Christ of whom the Law, Prophets, and Writings spoke.

As the Christian comes to the texts that now represent the preserved traditions of the Old and New Testaments, she must do the work to discover what these texts actually represented at the time of their writing instead of presuming that the Scriptures should reflect more current assumptions of textuality.

---

19. Notice that 2 Peter also refers to Paul's writings as Scripture in 2 Pet 3:16.

Part 2

Exegeting Orality

THE FOLLOWING DISCUSSION IS given as an addition to the works already discussed above; especially relevant are Niditch's suggestions from *Oral World and Written Word* concerning signs of an oral register in the biblical corpus.

On one hand, a view of the Bible that accepts the emerging theories of orality and textuality will vary radically from the approaches to the text by most post-Renaissance scholars. So much regarding the formation and purpose of the written text is viewed differently. On the other hand, this shift really requires nothing new. The shift in perspective does not necessarily change the methodology of biblical studies as a whole; it just requires new proficiencies, new tools, and new investigations. The overall methodology remains—one must study to determine the nature of the Bible, what it meant to the community that produced it, what it meant to the communities that followed, and what it means to the current community of faith.

New investigations that take orality into account are required, as is the application and practice of new tools stemming from a growing understanding of oral traditions in general and of the oral traditions of the ancient biblical world. What follows in chapter five are some suggestions on how to engage and perform the text with these more accurate conceptualizations of the cultures behind the Bible in mind. The following chapters will offer examples of how a heightened expectation of occurrences repetition and an understanding of how they are employed can aid in exegeting the texts.

5

Concepts for Exegeting Orality

Repetition

IN HIS ARTICLE "On the Theoretical Foundations of Orality and Literacy," Emevwo Biakolo criticized the work of Eric Havelock and Walter Ong for their approach to literacy and orality that supposed a great divide between the two.[1] Biakolo's article argues against the dichotomic nature of Occidental anthropological studies, which pits aspects of culture against each other—such as orality and literacy, scientific and religious, and savage and civilized.[2] Biakolo concluded, "The insidious manner in which these sanctified prejudices are deployed in different discourses within the human sciences is one more proof that Western attempts to understand the Other seem to be useful only insofar as they shed light on the peculiar mentality of those who engage in such inquiries."[3]

However, Biakolo offered an estimation of the defining feature of oral literature similar to Havelock.[4] Biakolo said, "Of all the features of oral

---

1. Biakolo, "On the Theoretical Foundations," 42–65.

2. Floyd agreed with Biakolo's estimation and offered a historical overview of how the Western mind arrived at such a prejudiced approach to the study of other cultures, "'Write the Revelation,'" 106–22.

3. Biakolo, "On the Theoretical Foundations," 62.

4. Havelock had an interesting take on the great divide. He certainly supported it, but he also felt like textuality could be absorbed into the orality of a culture—at least within ancient Greece. Due to what he thought was unique in Greece, in that the

poetry, the one held to be most distinctive by many scholars is repetition."[5] He did not limit this feature of repetition to poetry alone but said that it is "an aesthetic touchstone of oral art in general."[6] He expanded:

> More than this, many of those stylistic features which are recognizably *oral*, for example, formulae and parallelism, are merely instances of repetition, which in principle and practice range from simple lexical or phrasal recurrences to more structurally elaborate forms, including repeated motifs of theme, character and action and even of the binary forms of (psycho) logical life, as structuralists have argued.[7]

Of course, some of these features of repetition are often found in modern cultures that are enriched in literacy. The difference seems to be the prevalence of such features. However, Biakolo joins with Finnegan (and others such as Rodriguez) in warning against the attempt to draw clear and consistent lines between oral and written literature.[8]

While I certainly acknowledge that any given piece of literature, whether stemming from a more "oral" or "literate" society, may vary in the literary features that dominate, the most general statements of trends must be allowed. It does not follow logically that just because literature stemming from more textualized cultures may also use similar features of repetition as oral traditional cultures that scholars and exegetes should completely ignore the prevalence of repetition in oral traditional literature. Cultures that mainly share information orally and aurally do utilize written texts differently than largely literate Western cultures. Many aspects of biblical studies have been driven by general assumptions concerning oral tradition, such as the works of Gunkel and form critics.

---

alphabet was birthed from within the society and literacy grew gradually within it, he said, "What was expected at first from alphabetized scripts as they became available was not a literate 'literature' but an extending series of written versions of oral storage" (Havelock, "Oral Composition," 185); he also said, "It is a mistake to suppose, as G. S. Kirk and others have argued we should, that once the Homeric poems were written down the results for the creative oral process became a negative" (Havelock, "Oral Composition," 186). Thus, at least with the literature he examined in the article cited above, Havelock operated within some sort of a paradigm of an orality that had absorbed textuality into its communication constructs.

5. Biakolo, "On the Theoretical Foundations," 60.
6. Biakolo, "On the Theoretical Foundations," 60.
7. Biakolo, "On the Theoretical Foundations," 60–61.
8. Biakolo, "On the Theoretical Foundations," 60–61.

Some categorization is necessary to evaluate past assumptions, as well as to give context for current and future study.

Generally, studies of texts stemming from oral traditional cultures demonstrate a high level of repetition that, though with qualification, even Biakolo can acknowledge. Scholarship that approaches the field of oral tradition in such a way that assumes a great divide between orality and literacy has been largely discredited. However, if there were no divide or difference between oral traditional cultures and highly literate Western cultures at all, then the field would not exist. There would be nothing to discuss or apply in our understanding of oral traditional cultures or to textual works stemming from them such as the biblical corpus. There are features of oral traditional cultures that diverge in some degree from the modern Western text-saturated culture that has been dominating biblical studies for the past two centuries, and these features are worthy of investigation and application toward exegesis. We should not throw out the baby with the bathwater. Even scholars such as Havelock, who supported the great divide theory, may have some things to teach us about tendencies of oral traditional material.

Havelock explained the oral narrative will "avoid sheer surprise and novel inventions," and instead, "the basic method for assisting the memory to retain a series of distinct meanings is to frame the first of them in a way which will suggest or forecast a later meaning which will recall the first without being identical with it."[9] Like a tapestry, the oral performance will present an idea and then carry it along through the "echo" of similar stories, themes, or other devices.

John D. Harvey discussed what he called "ring-composition." He said, "Ring-composition is the technique in which a speaker or writer 'returns to a previous point in the discussion, either concluding or resuming the train of thought.' The framing is done with sentences, and the extent of the section framed varies from a few lines to many pages."[10] Ring-composition seems somewhat similar to Havelock's concept of the "echo principle."[11]

I discovered a clear example of a ring-composition and echo principle in Habakkuk. Besides the clear ongoing *echo* of the broadening of Habakkuk's landscape of human suffering and God's sovereignty, a specific

---

9. Havelock, "Oral Composition," 183; Eddy and Boyd, *Jesus Legend*, 358.

10. Harvey, "Orality and Its Implications," 104–5; Harvey, *Listening to the Text*, 103; and Eddy and Boyd, *Jesus Legend*, 58.

11. Havelock, "Oral Composition," 183; Eddy and Boyd, *Jesus Legend*, 358.

interaction of these aspects of orality and Fuller's discourse analysis of Habakkuk emerged within the woe oracles of Hab 2.

While the manuscripts I analyzed do not agree in dividing the text at 2:6b, they do align more closely as the woe approaches, which may argue for some sort of traditional division (or awareness) at this point. At the very least, the presence of the woe oracle marks off a comparably stable section of the tradition for the versions I studied.

Fuller found that "oracles 1–3 and 4–5 exhibited movement of progressively less focus on the evildoer, placing him in an increasingly passive position, while also showing greater interest in the scope of the earth as a whole and idolatry,"[12] while also finding that in the fourth oracle, the evildoer returns only to be "completely wiped out by violence and devastation."[13] Interestingly, along with the reemergence of the evildoer's centrality in the fourth woe, a statement recurs from the first woe: מִדְּמֵי אָדָם וַחֲמַס־אֶרֶץ קִרְיָה וְכָל־יֹשְׁבֵי בָהּ.

Therefore, utilizing something similar to ring-composition and the echo principle, the Habakkuk tradition presents five woes, the first of which likely connects one who *increases what is not his* (2:6) to the person in the previous section who *enlarges his throat like Sheol* and *is never satisfied* (2:4–5). This first woe concludes with the statement cited in Hebrew above, "For the blood of man and violence of the land, the city and all who dwell in it." Two woes follow, both having a theme of *building*, which shift to focus more on the power and strength of God, while presenting the evildoer as being increasingly passive. Indeed, in the third woe, the evildoer is only mentioned in the first line, in only 33 percent of the woe's clauses.[14] The rest of the woe speaks of the futility of human activity in light of the knowledge of YHWH, which will eventually fill the earth as water covers the sea. Suddenly, in the fourth woe, the evildoer is represented in the mode of 100 percent of the clauses—just like in the first woe.[15] Just like the first woe, this fourth woe ends with, "For the blood of man and violence of the land, the city and all who dwell in it."

Utilizing something like ring-composition and the echo principle, techniques which often present as literary features in oral compositions, the tradition of Habakkuk brings the evildoer back to the forefront, declaring the violence enacted on others will come back upon him—an

---

12. Fuller, *Discourse Analysis*, 205.
13. Fuller, *Discourse Analysis*, 202–3.
14. Fuller, *Discourse Analysis*, 177.
15. Fuller, *Discourse Analysis*, 184 and 163 respectively.

echo of the first woe: "You plundered many nations. The remnants of the people will plunder you." The fifth woe, the only woe with some sort of introduction,[16] wraps up the entire discussion of the evildoer and God's sovereignty with a woe concerning idolatry. As to the overall interpretation of this oral traditional feature, this must be an intentional move that argues that all that has gone before can now be summarized in a woe concerning idolatry and a call for all to stand silent before YHWH.

The echo/ring-composition of the woe oracles in the MT demonstrates the overall function of the woes. They serve to point out the nature of the idolatry of unbelieving and hostile nations such as Babylon. Essentially, humanity can choose one of two options: (1) Be silent before YHWH as his glory fills the entire earth—worship and follow him alone; or (2) Choose to worship idols—whether those idols manifest as literal idols or as idols of self, power, wealth, safety, drunkenness, or worldly lusts. In the midst of legitimate persecution, those who follow YHWH can rest assured that the end of those who reject YHWH will exhaust themselves for nothing. Idolaters will wither away and become just like their breathless idols, who are unable to give true aid.

One may come to this conclusion without labelling the structure as an echo/ring-composition—or without even considering orality at all. However, the tendency of oral traditional cultures to utilize repetition in general, and the presence of this type of structure in particular, adds to the confidence of this interpretation and may lead students of the biblical text to discover other repetitions that may have been overlooked. Also, the structure and flow of the echo/ring composition has an aesthetic value. I find the artistry of the presentation beautiful and delightful.

There is a real danger of over-applying the pursuit of repetition when studying the Bible. It is possible to paint with a brush of overgeneralization and find connections and repetitions that may not actually exist. Each instance of supposed repetition should be carefully examined based on our best understanding of the oral traditions of the biblical cultures. Additionally, the merits of the inter-contextual connections believed to demonstrate each specific case of repetition should be evaluated. Truth is often found on the razor's edge between two untrue approaches. We can deny the prevalence of repetition in orally derived literature, or we can try to find repetition behind every bush. By God's grace, may we discover the elements of repetition he inspired in the holy tradition originally

---

16. Unless one counts the first part of YHWH's speech, especially 2:6a, as an introduction.

imbedded within hearts and minds of his people and that come to us now in the written texts of Scripture.

Repetition as Activation

In oral traditional cultures, communal knowledge is reflected, in that the community has a shared understanding of traditions of interpreting the culture's performances. Communal knowledge is also demonstrated, in that when a performer mentions one small part of one traditional unit, the entire traditional unit can be activated in the mind of the community. Words, phrases, themes, scenes, and formulas are chosen purposefully to conjure other aspects of the tradition. The part can stand to represent the whole or conjure other parts of the whole for the sake of understanding the present performance.

Egbert J. Bakker discussed the concept of "activation," in which old knowledge that may be lying dormant or inactive in the mind can be activated through performance of the tradition. He said,

> The reactivation of the epic in performance creates a strong overarching sense of involvement in which the entire community participates, by the simple fact that the re-enacted, reactivated epic world and its heroic and dramatic features are in everyone's mind during the performance, a collective psychic state for which there is ample evidence in classical sources.[17]

Bakker also discussed how the re-mentioning of aspects of the tradition not only activates the tradition for the community but works to preserve the tradition for the community.[18] Thus, for instance, the refrain of the exodus throughout the Old Testament—in the covenant language in Deuteronomy and Joshua, in the prayers and songs of the Psalms, and in the hopes in the prophets—both *activates* and *preserves* themes of YHWH's faithfulness and power to deliver. The analysis of the manuscripts in my dissertation demonstrated that this process of activation can be seen in the textual tradition of Habakkuk.

For example, in Hab 1:3, the LXX (G) and Peshitta (S) share something like, "Judgment was before me, but the judge received a bribe." This varies greatly from MT's (M), "And it was that strife and contention arise." 1QpHab (Q) and 8HevXIIgr (H) are missing at this point, but Targum

---

17. Bakker, "Activation and Preservation," 11.
18. Bakker, "Activation and Preservation," 13–15.

Jonathan (T) does not agree in discussing judgment or a receiving judge. On the other hand, the Vulgate (V) mentions justice but not the receiving judge—"Justice is done, but the opposition is more powerful."

A text-based approach will certainly theorize various potential *Vorlage*, but an oral traditional approach offers another possibility. The Hebrew word רִיב has strong connection in the greater textual tradition to the judicial system. For instance, Deut 17:8 says, "If there is a difficult matter of judgment among you concerning blood for blood, judgment for judgment, or plague for plague—matters of *strife* in your gates; then rise and go to the place which the LORD your God will choose." A *dispute* or *matter of strife* is a matter requiring judgment—Deut 19:17; 21:5, 25:1; 1 Sam 24:16; 2 Sam 15:2; 15:4; Jer 11:20; 25:31; Ezek 44:24; and so forth. The word is even translated with a form of κρίσις in Exod 23:3 and 23:6 LXX. In Isa 1:23, the word is used in a similar context, as in Hab 1:3 (G and S), in which the lack of justice is connected to receiving bribes.

Therefore, the translator of G likely saw a word that activated elements of the tradition at large lying dormant in his mind, and he offered a translational performance well within the traditional understanding of the term. S certainly seems to have utilized G in its creation of its performance of the tradition, as did V. V's trend toward expansion included a tendency to eliminate elements of the tradition to conform different performances of the tradition to each other. V acknowledges the judicial connection in the tradition, but then utilizes its normal translational choice for רִיב to translate מָדוֹן and return to a presentation closer to M, thus eliminating the receiving judge from its performance.

The simple usage of the term רִיב conjured elements of judgment from the tradition at large, and the versions displayed an attachment to the broader tradition because of the word's presence. Most certainly this term activated elements of judges and bribes for the translators of the LXX and perhaps also for the translators of the Peshitta.

As will be demonstrated below, biblical authors utilize activation for rhetorical and inspirational purposes by situating the audience's hearts and/or minds within contexts of the broader tradition through words, phrases, and scenes. The greater tradition stands as a backdrop for the current performance. This backdrop can function as an emphasis on a current point or event, as a rhetorical contrast to a current line of thought or action, and even as an interpretive guide for the flow of an argument.

In the following section I will offer some exegetical remarks and suggestions on the book of Judges (chapter 6); the Gospel of Mark, the passion predictions found in the Synoptic Gospels, and Luke 13–14 (chapter 7); John 2–4 and 19:25—20:31 (chapter 8); and Rom 9–11 (chapter 9) based upon the presence of structural repetition within the works themselves, while also demonstrating the importance of activation (activation is a sort of repetition—it rehearses through allusion what the mind has already embraced through past performances). In reference to the book of Judges I will attempt a thorough exegetical commentary, taking into account the inner repetitions of the book of Judges itself, both in terms of internal structure and echoes, along with elements of activation of the greater Old Testament tradition. The "greater Old Testament tradition" includes elements from different chronological time frames: (1) the traditional elements that stand before and during the chronological time period of the judges as well as (2) the traditional elements existing in the exilic/post-exilic time period, in which the particular performance of the book of Judges in our possession was shaped. Regarding the Gospel of Mark, I will demonstrate the use of repetition for structuring and interpreting complete books of the Bible. The discussions on the passion predictions will engage repetition and activation from within the tradition of the Synoptic Gospels. Other examples of interpretation, such as my take on John 2–4 and 19:25—20:31; Luke 13–14; and Rom 9–11 will demonstrate the use of repetition and activation in order to interpret smaller units within a book of the Bible.

After these examples of exegeting orality through repetition, I will give examples of interpreting the multiform textual tradition of the Bible by reviewing the interpretation of multiple textual representations of Habakkuk, followed by a look at the use of Hab 2:3–4 in Heb 10:37–38. Finally, I will discuss interpretive issues in regard to performing the textual tradition today.

6

The Book of Judges[1]

THE BOOK OF JUDGES offers an excellent introduction to interpreting oral repetition for structure and meaning since its repetitive framework is explicitly stated in the book, and the general framework is broadly accepted. Judges 2:11–23 describes the pattern the book will follow: 1) the people of Israel rebel and serve other gods; 2) YHWH raises up a nation against the people and the people suffer; 3) the people cry out to YHWH; 4) YHWH raises up a judge to deliver the people; 5) the judge dies, and the people act even worse than before. As the audience moves into the large central section of Judg 3:7—16:31, they expect to see this repeated pattern spiraling downward into worse and worse idolatry. Before

---

1. Readers will find I rely heavily on Daniel Block's excellent commentary on Judges from *The New American Commentary* (Block, *Judges*). Block's influence on my understanding of Judges should be noted often, even when citation is unnecessary. I would also like to acknowledge Susan Niditch's commentary on the book of Judges (including her interesting translations) that she wrote with oral tradition in mind. Niditch's interpretive approach varies somewhat from my own, and she did not often improve upon Block's background material and literary analysis. Thus, I will refer to Block throughout this chapter and refer to Niditch's work only sparingly. This is no negative critique upon Niditch. Block simply displays considerable skill at communicating the applicable background material, and he demonstrates a mastery of drawing out interpretive frameworks from the literary features of Judges for the current Christian faith community. Block's commentary demonstrates the fact that a media critical approach to a text like Judges (an approach that considers the realities of oral traditional cultures) would never replace many current exegetical approaches but rather often act to supplement and direct them.

moving into this central section, I will further introduce the frame of reference of the book of Judges by discussing the purpose and structure of the introduction, 1:1—3:6. Then I will discuss the overall patterned flow of the book and offer a general outline of Judges. After an extensive discussion of the large central section of three rounds of major judges, I will conclude the chapter by examining the performance of the closing scenes of Judg 17–21.

Judges 1:1—3:6: A Satirical Introduction

Judges is a well-organized satirical performance of the great tragedy of Israel's tendency to adulterate herself to other gods and foreign customs—to abandon the covenant of YHWH. It drips with sarcasm and satirical wit. Perhaps the most blatant example of satire can be found in Jotham's scathing parable of the trees' pursuit for a king in Judg 9. This taunt song contrasts Abimelech with noble trees of purpose and provision, comparing him instead with bramble. The song calls for the trees to find shade in the bramble-king they had elected. However, should the motives behind their choice for king be less than honorable, fire will come forth from the bramble and consume them. The thought of trees seeking shade in bramble only to be burnt down by fire shot forth from the bramble reflects quite a humorous bit of sarcastic criticism. Abimelech lives up to the allegory.

Other examples of satire and sarcasm are not hard to find. Near the end of the book we meet a man named Micah, whose full name likely meant, "Who is like YHWH?" Micah builds idols for his household and sets up a false priesthood in his home! The person named, "Who is like YHWH" has no problem replacing YHWH with empty idols! As another example, in the Jephthah cycle YHWH speaks to the people of Israel with a sarcastic taunt reminiscent of Elijah's call to the priests of Baal to make sure their god was not using the bathroom (1 Kgs 18:27). YHWH says in Judg 10:14, "Go and cry out to the gods whom you have chosen; let them save you in the time of your distress."[2]

The entire episode of Ehud exudes satire. Block said, "With effective employment of ambiguity, irony, satire, hyperbole, and caricature, [the book of Judges] sketches a literary cartoon that pokes fun at the

---

2. Unless otherwise noted, all citations of Scripture in this chapter will come from the ESV.

Moabites and brings glory to God."[3] Eglon, the obese man whose name means "little-calf,"[4] is displayed like a fattened calf ready for slaughter[5] and seems to be as stupid as he is fat. His guards are presented as equally ditsy, and some of the vocabulary could carry double meanings—the root of the word in verse 29 that describes the men of Moab as stout men can also mean "to make fat" and is used in places like Isa 6:10, where it speaks of fattening the heart or mind. Eglon and his henchmen are presented as a bunch of big, dumb oafs. While we note that the performance of Judges is poking fun at Moab, we must not forget the larger theme of Judges—Israel's growing apostasy. Israel suffered under these big dumb oafs for eighteen years! Because of the Canaanization of Israel, they were brought lower than Eglon and his court of dumb henchmen!

Further examples abound, such as Israel's need for Jael's female, deceptive, tent-peg assassination, as well as Samson's constant breaking of his Nazarite identity. The book also offers two instances of chronological surprise in the final chapters. After a long narration of the many judges who, all together, brought about hundreds of years of rest for the land (Judg 3:7—16:31), the book of Judges recalls the names of two men involved in the final episodes of the book. These final episodes are meant as a final summary of just how horrible things got in the time of the judges. The men, Jonathan son of Gershom and Phineas son of Eleazar, were the grandsons of Moses and Aaron respectively! The worst of the atrocities illustrated by this downward spiral of idolatry occurred within one generation of Joshua. Phineas was even alive and active in the book of Numbers!

And finally, not the least of livid satire is found in that the only time Israel actually uniformly assembles (almost) as a nation against Canaanite evil is when they gather against their brother—the tribe of Benjamin. Therefore, when received as an exilic or postexilic performance, Judges presents itself as a satirical prophetic word concerning the catalysts of Israel's exile.

In the first verses of the book, Judah is called forth to lead the tribes in conquering the Canaanites, but the tribe immediately requests help from Simeon. In the first recorded campaign, Judah and Simeon conquer the king, Adonai-Bezek, who laments the turning tides of his power. Adonai-Bezek laments that he has become like the seventy kings he had

---

3. Block, *Judges*, 156.
4. HALOT, 785.
5. Block, *Judges*, 158.

conquered. The conquering king has become the conquered king. From the time of the performance of Judges (exile and after), this is exactly what has happened to the southern kingdom of Judah and to the northern kingdom in which Simeon participated. Adonai-Bezek even dies at Jerusalem, the place where Israel's kings were finally defeated. These allusions would work as a sort of chronological activation in reverse, utilizing the community's ancient traditions to activate their current experience.

In 1:8 Jerusalem was supposedly captured, struck by the sword, and set on fire by Judah. The only problem with this statement is that every other part of Israel's tradition, even the book of Judges itself, in 1:21 and chapters 19–21, makes it quite clear that Jerusalem was not conquered until David took the city with his own personal militia. Joshua 15:63 says, "As for the Jebusites, the inhabitants of Jerusalem, the children of Judah could not drive them out: but the Jebusites dwell with the children of Judah at Jerusalem unto this day." This claim of Jerusalem's sacking is biting sarcasm—reports at which anyone within the tradition would scoff. Judah and Simeon, now conquered in exile, are jestingly presented as the conquerors of a king-conqueror. Judah is said to have conquered Jerusalem just after the death of Joshua, except they actually did not. Judges 1:10 says that Judah conquered the Canaanites at Hebron, but Josh 10:36–37 makes it clear that Joshua and all of Israel with him took the city. While it is possible that the oral tradition simply carried multiform traditions concerning the conquering of these cities, it is equally possible, and I believe probable, that the performance of Judges activates the tradition of failed conquest in derisive jest.

Verses 11–15 describe how two of Judah's heroes, Caleb and Othniel, both failed to look after their families leaving Achsah to fend for herself—the theme of the mistreatment of women that will continue through the book. The Philistine cities of Gaza, Ashkelon, and Ekron were apparently conquered by Judah according to the sarcastic introduction of Judges, and yet they remained Philistine strongholds into the days of Samson and beyond. Again, while the incongruity between these various reports may simply reflect a more oral traditional perspective on history, requiring less rigidity of accurate details and chronology, I believe the contradictory reports to be intentional efforts to draw upon the traditions of the community for rhetorical effect. The audience is being set up to receive a performance that critiques her history through sarcasm, satire, and activation. The larger traditional understanding of Israel and Judah's history is required to properly interpret this introduction to Judges.

The only valid story of conquest that resembles the days of Joshua comes from 1:22–26, and it concerns the northern tribes of Joseph! And even in this story one Canaanite city is merely replaced with a new one.

We can imagine an oral performance of this section of Judges as it lands upon the ears of a crowd recovering from exile, an audience who knows the true failure of the conquest in these reports. The performer mentions Judah and Simeon as king conquerors, and the audience knows they currently stand as conquered kings. The performer proclaims false victory after false victory to the response of moans and eyerolls from the audience. Eventually, as the performance piles incongruity upon incongruity, the audience catches on. Perhaps a few even chuckle. They now understand what this performance is going to say—just like our ancestors, we failed to trust in YHWH and maintain covenant. This has been a part of our communal identity. Everything that follows will be interpreted through this matrix established by the performance's introduction.

The Overall Pattern of Judges

The book of Judges begins with the mocking summary description of Judah and Israel (1:1—3:6), and it ends with tribal idolatry, Benjamin's sin, and a civil war (17:1—21:25). Therefore, Judges begins with satire concerning the nation's failure and concludes with an equally satirical, episodic summary of her failure. Centered in this depiction of failure is the downward spiral of all Israel. Even without kings to lead her astray, she descends into total covenant rejection and civil war.

The central section of Judges (3:7—16:31) offers three rounds of "major" judges with each round introduced by a series of "minor" judges. The first round is introduced with three minor judges,[6] the second round with two minor judges, and the final round with three. The first two minor judges of the first round (Othniel and Ehud) contain much more information than the other minor judges since the tradition utilizes their

---

6. It could easily be debated that Othniel and Ehud should be classified as "major" judges since they establish the pattern that the other major judges follow, and all the other "minor" judges follow a separate pattern. Indeed, that would create an attractive deteriorating repetition of major and minor judges (M-M-m-M-M-m-m-m-M-m-m-m-M; where M = major judge and m = minor judge). That scheme may be preferable to my categorization of Othniel and Ehud as minor judges. I maintain my categorization due to the brevity of the two judges, especially Othniel, and because the minor judges operate as introductions and transitions to the major judges, which is the major role of the Othniel and Ehud cycles.

stories to establish a pattern for the presentation of the major judges. Also, these first three introductory judges (through later repetition) work to summarize and connect much of the book. The other minor judges, including Shamgar, the third minor judge in the first round of minor judges, have a different pattern they follow.

The following table is taken from Daniel Block's commentary from *The New American Commentary* and then modified for my approach.[7] Notice the pattern set by Othniel and Ehud. This is the pattern the major judges follow to varying degrees. The shaded columns represent the other minor judges that follow their own pattern. Each pattern contains six judges. Othniel and Ehud are the only minor judges to follow the pattern they set.

Formulaic Element	Othniel (m)	Ehud (m)	*(Shamgar) Barak (M)	Gideon (M)	*(Tola/Jair) Jephthah (M)	*(Ibzan/Elon/Abdon) Samson (M)
"The sons of Israel did evil in the sight of the LORD." (2:11–13)	√	√	√	√	√	√
"The LORD gave/sold them into the hands of [Oppressor]." (2:14)	√	√	√	√	√	√
"The sons of Israel cried out to the LORD." (2:15b, 18b)	√	√	√	√	√	
"The LORD raised up a deliverer." (2:16, 18a)	√	√				

7. Block, *Judges*, 146–47. Block does not indicate that the LORD handed the enemy into Jephthah's hand though he did (11:32). I corrected that oversight in my chart. I also indicate with an asterisk the minor judge that precedes the major judge (listed above the name of the major judge).

Formulaic Element	Othniel (m)	Ehud (m)	*(Shamgar) Barak (M)	Gideon (M)	*(Tola/Jair) Jephthah (M)	*(Ibzan/Elon/Abdon) Samson (M)
"The LORD gave [Oppressor] into the hands of the deliverer." (2:18a)	√	√			√	
"He land had rest for [X] years."	√	√	√	√		

Formulaic Element	*Shamgar (m)	*Tola (m)	Jair (m)	*Ibzan (m)	Elon (m)	Abdon (m)
"There arose [X]."		√	√			
"To save Israel."	√	√				
"[X] judged Israel for [Y] years."		√	√	√	√	√
[Biographical information]		√	√	√		√
Judge died.		√	√	√	√	√

m = minor judge
M = major judge
Secondary judge pattern

As demonstrated in the charts above, only Othniel and Ehud follow the pattern that they establish. After them, the pattern deteriorates, as does the faithfulness of the "nation" and her judges to YHWH and his covenant. The other introductory judges (Tola, Jair, Ibzan, Elon, and Abdon) have their own deteriorating pattern (shaded in gray). Interestingly, Shamgar only has one aspect of his presentation that is similar to either pattern, and it is a reflection of the pattern set by Tola and the introductory judges that follow him.

The tradition uses layers of repetition to structure this presentation and direct the audience toward a desired interpretive framework—the deterioration of Israelite society through Canaanization and idolatry. Following is my outline of Judges.

I. Introduction: Setting the Scene: 1:1—3:6
   a. Incomplete Conquest and its Consequence 1:1—2:5
      i. False Hope in Judah and Simeon: 1:1—1:26
         1. The Cycle of Human Power/(From King to Conquered): 1:1–7
         2. False Victory Reports 1: Jerusalem and Hebron: 1:8–10
         3. Upsetting the Power Structures and Setting the Stage for the Judges: 1:11–15
         4. False Victory Reports 2: Philistine Cities and Hebron: 1:16–21
         5. An (Almost) Actual Victory Report from the North: 1:22–26
         6. Incomplete Conquest of the North: 1:27–36
      ii. Consequence of Incomplete Conquest: 2:1–5
   b. The Cycle of the Consequence Described 2:6—3:6
II. The Cycle—Three Rounds of Major Judges: 3:7—16:31
   a. Round 1—Deborah/Barak and Gideon/Abimelech: 3:7—9:57
      i. Minor Judges Introduction
         1. Othniel: 3:7–11
         2. Ehud: 3:12–30
         3. Shamgar: 3:31
      ii. Major Judges
         1. Deborah/Barak: 4:1—5:31
         2. Gideon/Abimelech: 6:1—9:57
   b. Round 2—Jephthah: 10:1—12:7
      i. Minor Judges Introduction
         1. Tola: 10:1–2
         2. Jair: 10:3–5
      ii. Major Judge
         1. Jephthah: 10:6—12:7

  c. Round 3—Samson: 12:8—16:31

    i. Minor Judges Introduction

     1. Ibzan: 12:8-10

     2. Elon: 12:11-12

     3. Abdon: 12:13-15

    ii. Major Judge

     1. Samson: 13:1—16:31

III. The Chiastic Chaos of Canceling Covenant: 17—21

  a. Religious Ruin: 17:1—18:31

  b. Societal Ruin: 19:1—21:25

The Cycle—Three Rounds of Major Judges: 3:7—16:31

Round 1—Deborah/Barak and Gideon/Abimelech: 3:7—9:57

Minor Judge—Othniel 3:7-11

The first judge mentioned is Othniel who was actually introduced in the book in 1:11–15. Othniel is the first introductory judge in the book. Interestingly, this first judge battles a king of "double wickedness" (Cushan-rishathaim) from אֲרַם נַהֲרַיִם—*Aram Two Rivers*. The first judge battled a double wickedness from an area described in terms resembling Mesopotamia, which means "between rivers." This is quite the coincidence for the second book in the Former Prophets since these books represent God's word concerning the reasons why YHWH brought Assyria and Babylon (two wicked nations) from Mesopotamia to send Israel into exile.

  Othniel's enemy activates the greater tradition of Israel's failures, which eventually lead to exile. Once again, this introductory story connects the community's experience of exile to the community's ancient traditions. This story demands that the audience experience the performance as a part of the tragic narrative that flows toward that great move of YHWH's discipline—the exile.

  We learn that this first Israelite judge, representing the tribe of Judah, is actually a Kenizzite (3:9; 11), and while he was heroic enough to capture a city for Caleb, he was not willing to lead his household in receiving an acceptable portion of land (1:14–15). Indeed, Caleb, the great hero of the wilderness scouting troop of Num 13, seems to have shortchanged his family in regard to the land he gave to his personal hero (Othniel) and daughter (Achsah), so that Achsah must fend for herself against a stingy father and before a suddenly passive husband. In reference to Achsah's role in her family, the presentation of the Othniel tradition sets another precedent of the book of Judges—the centrality of women who are often mistreated or placed in roles outside of the norm for ancient Israel.

Minor Judge—Ehud 3:12–30

The tradition of Ehud, the second introductory judge, cannot fully be interpreted until after the final saga of the book (Judg 19–21). Ehud is a Benjaminite who was "bound of the right hand." This may have been a practice of the Benjaminites of binding the right hand to increase the dexterity of the left (see 1 Chr 12:2).[8] At any rate, this phrase is only found here in Ehud's story (3:15) and at Judg 20:16. In the second use of the phrase, it describes a special group of seven hundred Benjaminite warriors who joined their Benjaminite brothers in battling the rest of Israel in the bloody civil war that was instigated by the city-wide gang rape of a Levite's concubine—the saga that wraps up the book of Judges. The group of Benjaminites who raped the Levite's concubine had originally wanted to rape the Levite himself. This special troop of "left-handed" Benjaminites helped defend those who wanted to rape a man but settled for his defenseless concubine. They raped her to death.

Also relevant to the interpretation of this judge's activities are some of the words of Samson. Samson referred to his wife as a "heifer" in 14:18. The Hebrew word for "heifer" is *eglāh* (עֶגְלָה), which is very close to the name Eglon, since the Moabite's name means "little calf."[9] In Judg 15:1, Samson desires to go into his wife's room to consummate their relationship—literally, "go to my wife [in] her room" (אָבֹאָה אֶל־אִשְׁתִּי הֶחָדְרָה). Ehud, a Benjaminite, connected in his "left-handedness" to those who would defend the group of gang rapists who first sought to rape a male Levite, went to the upper chamber of Eglon—literally, "Ehud went to him as he was sitting in the cool upper room" (וְאֵהוּד ׀ בָּא אֵלָיו וְהוּא־יֹשֵׁב בַּעֲלִיַּת הַמְּקֵרָה). While different words are usually used for *room* between these

---

8. "Halpern has suggested that, like the Spartans, Benjaminites literally bound the right arms of young future warriors to train them to use the left in battle" (Halpern, "Resourceful Israelite Historian," 35), quoted in Niditch, *Judges*, 57.

9. HALOT, 785.

two stories, Judg 3:24 does refer to Eglon's cool room as a חֶדֶר, the same word used for Samson's heifer-wife's room.

The sexual innuendos of the Ehud cycle have been well rehearsed, and the cycle's connection (through the repetition of words, phrases, and themes) to the sexual desire of Samson and to the Benjamite rapists suggest a negative interpretation of this judge. Though these first two judges are utilized to establish a pattern for other judges to follow (or not), and though the first judges seem to be better than those that follow, the performer has planted seeds of doubt upon the righteousness of these early "heroes" through the oral artistry of repetition—seeds that will bloom to maturity through the telling of the following episodes of the book.

Minor Judge—Shamgar 3:31

When Shamgar is briefly mentioned after these two extended introductory judges, a general picture of the pattern of the book is established. The first two introductory judges set precedents of repetition for the structure the traditions of the major judges, and they also speak to the negative interpretation of the tradition. The way in which Othniel and Ehud's activities are described establishes a pattern of the raising up of judges by YHWH (a pattern which later deteriorates), forecasts themes such as the effect of the Canaanization of Israel on women and the pedigree of the Israelite judges, and even works to project forward to the final illustration of the state of a covenant-less Israel with the shady story of Ehud the left-handed Benjaminite. Then the tradition turns to the extremely brief, and yet potent mention of Shamgar.

Shamgar's description is the very least detailed presentation of any judge in the book. Thus, the introductory judges of the first round establish a precedent for the judges to follow through lengthy descriptions of two minor judges and then abruptly breaks completely with that precedent with an extremely brief description of a judge who very well may have been an Egyptian soldier (Shamgar).

His name does not seem to be Hebrew but perhaps Hurrian.[10] He is called "Son of Anath," which may mean that he served the Canaanite goddess Anath, who was Baal's consort and the goddess of war. The Egyptians adopted Anath into their pantheon of gods as the goddess of war and personal protectress of the Pharaoh. There is archaeological evidence

---

10. For the following discussion on Shamgar see Block, *Judges*, 173–75.

of a group of Egyptian soldiers called "the troop of Anath," among whom were soldiers of a certain designation, "Habiru." The "Habiru" designated people of many different ethnic origins, including Hurrians. It is possible that Shamgar was a member of a Habiru troop of mercenaries in Pharaoh's army named after the Canaanite goddess of war. The Egyptians did repel the Sea Peoples (Philistines) in northern Egypt. Perhaps they engaged them up the coast into northern Palestine where the Song of Deborah may have located Shamgar in Judg 5:6.

At any rate, it is interesting that Samson, the last of the Judges who is presented as a thoroughly Canaanized man, was raised up against the Philistines just as Shamgar, the last minor introductory judge of the first judges cycle—the non-Israelite judge—fought against the Philistines and saved Israel. If Shamgar was indeed from Egypt, then what a turn of events from the exodus! Israel was saved by an Egyptian soldier!

Shamgar's segment is a short but incredibly important note on the Canaanization of Israel and on the direction to which the rest of the book of Judges is heading. Shamgar also seems to represent a pattern followed by the later introductory judges instead of the pattern of the major judges introduced by Othniel and Ehud. This is a mark of literary competency well in line with oral traditional tendencies of repetition and echo, as Shamgar's inclusion represents the direction of the entire book of Judges. It marks the breaking of the quality and structure of Israel's judges and points forward to Samson, the final judge presented in this downward spiral of patterned idolatry and Canaanization.

Shamgar's inclusion just after these two judges demonstrates the final state of Israel and her judges—fully Canaanized and fully broken from the established pattern. The performance is going to end in total ruin. The overall pattern will continue toward the conclusions forecasted in these introductory judges through continued examples of repetition.

First Paired Major Judge—Deborah and Barak: 4:1—5:31

The first round of major judges appears as two sets of paired individuals, Barak and Deborah followed by Gideon and Abimelech. Judges chapters 4 and 5, like Exod 14–15, present a prose/narrative account of an event followed by a poetic/song expression of the same event. It is often assumed that the songs came first and the narratives later, filling out and explaining the poetic account. Some have held the opposite. Also possible is that both the prose and the poetic refer to the same traditional information embedded in the community and are simply multiform performances of that tradition. From our perspective, there may not be much benefit from figuring out which came first, but from seeing the two as complementary versions of the same event.

However, the first question for the performance of this episode from the book of Judges is: Who is the judge, Deborah or Barak? One may get the impression that Deborah is the fourth judge discussed in the book of Judges, and Barak is a side character offered only to move the strong female theme forward. After all, Judg 4:4 says that "she was judging Israel at that time." Judges 4:5 says that people came to Deborah for "the judgment" (לַמִּשְׁפָּט).

This certainly seems to make a strong case for Deborah being the judge of this story, since it was Deborah who "was judging Israel at that time." But 1 Sam 12:9–11 and Heb 11:32 both identify Barak as the judge. Block lists several reasons why the context may not indicate that Deborah is the judge: she is not "raised up" by YHWH; the Spirit is not said to be upon her; why does she call Barak?; why is she not the savior of Israel (yasa)?; why is Sisera sold into the hands of "a woman" and not into Deborah's?; why is Sisera given into Barak's hands?; etc.[11] To the above we would add that she is called a prophet, which would place her as the very first prophet to follow Moses (according to an Accordance Bible software search, Deut 34:10 is the last place the root for "prophet" is used before Judg 4:4). In the Gideon cycle, a prophet is used in the narrative of the calling of the judge. Perhaps the same is true here with Deborah and Barak.

It is an intriguing question. Regardless, Deborah is certainly the most virtuous character in the book of Judges, perhaps followed by Barak if there is truly no negative association to his refusal to go to battle without Deborah. It is very possible that we are to read Judg 4:1–6 within the overall cycle of the book of Judges as follows: (1) The people turn away from YHWH and do evil; (2) God hands them over into the hands of Canaanites; (3) the people cry for deliverance and go to Deborah for YHWH's answer; and (4) God raises up Barak as judge/deliverer through the prophetess Deborah. In the flow of the narrative this probably means that they came to her to hear God's reply to their cries. They came to her, and her response was to call Barak.

---

11. Block, *Judges*, 193–94.

Barak says that he will not go unless Deborah goes with him. This is not necessarily a cowardly act. Barak may be displaying true humility. Barak desired the presence of God, which is assured by the presence of YHWH's prophetess, Deborah. The sign Deborah gives that Barak is called by God is that God will deliver Sisera into the hands of a woman. The hearer may anticipate this woman to be Deborah, and perhaps that is what Barak would think as well. At any rate, Deborah leads Barak to lead the army against Sisera.

The LORD routes the enemy army so that Barak's military efforts are victorious. After being routed, Sisera retreats to the tent of Jael, where he is lulled to safety by a woman's loving touch. Then he gets hammered. Jael drives a tent peg through his head. Just look at God's enemies—destroyed in battle and killed in their sleep; the powerful and feared general fooled and overpowered by a housewife. Indeed, Barak was called by God, and the glory of victory was given to this tent-dwelling woman. The reversal of roles at the hands of Jael is highlighted in the Song of Deborah in Judg 5 as Sisera's mother, portraying the normal role of a woman in the face of a battle, is pictured gazing out of the window and waiting for Sisera's return—a stark difference from the general slayer Jael.

What a testimony to God's people in exile! When his people are faithful, even the wives of foreign people become instruments of salvation! The victory of the Deborah/Barak cycle intentionally connects to and activates elements of the overall performance of the book of Judges as well as the greater tradition.

For example, some have held that the mention of Ehud's death in Judg 4 may imply that the inclusion of Shamgar was a later addition, interrupting the flow between 3:30 and 4:1. However, the echoed mention of Ehud at the introduction of the Deborah/Barak cycle could be an intentional move to activate that cycle for rhetorical purposes. There is a chiastic repetition between Ehud's story and Deborah/Barak's. In Ehud's story, the leader is assassinated with sexual innuendos (A), followed by military victory (B). With Deborah/Barak, the military victory occurs first (B), followed by the leader's assassination with sexual innuendos (A), creating the classic chiastic shape—A, B, B, A. The repetitive connections between the two cycles are clear. Block elaborates on other comparisons of the assassination scenes:

> The stylistic and verbal links between vv. 17–22 and a part of the Ehud narrative in 3:16–26 are obvious: (1) the absence of the divine hand; (2) the focus on individual actions; (3) the use of

speech to get the victim into a vulnerable position; (4) the motif of treachery and deception; (5) the sequence of murder and discovery; (6) the use of the verb *tāca'*, "to thrust," at the critical moment (3:21; 4:21); (7) the sequence of entry and discovery.[12]

There are also connections to the first judge, Othniel. In 1:14 Achsah "pierced down" to the ground (צנח) off of her donkey, an odd verb for the motion, though perhaps it demonstrates Achsah's heightened passion. The same verb describes the tent peg as it "went down" into the ground in 4:21. This key word further connects these two judges who found land/glory by the works of women. Block discusses the social customs challenged by Jael, which certainly find connections to Achsah's initiative as well.[13]

Women will continue to play a vital role in Judges. Gideon's mom will act as the lead in the narrative of Gideon's call. Abimelech's relationship with his mom will make possible his claim to rule. Jephthah's daughter stands as a tragic example of the Canaanization of Israel's leaders and heroes. Samson's inability to control his lust for women will lead him to hand over his secret to Delilah. Finally, a Levite's concubine will be thrown to a lustful mob and raped to death, inciting civil war, and the broken social structure will be "cured" as virgin girls are kidnapped and given over to the men of Benjamin. The book of Judges portrays a world in which the image of God, male and female, is not functioning in Shalom among God's chosen people.

The victory poem, the Song of Deborah, is arranged after the narration of the event, and it echoes Israel's great epic-primordial battle-psalms (like Hab 3). The structure of the narrative followed by an epic victory song resembles the narration of the parting of the Reed Sea which was followed by Moses' victory song and Miriam's dancing and singing. Indeed, the pivot point of Barak's battle comes in Judg 4:15 when YHWH "routed" (the Hebrew is, המם) Sisera and his chariots. This is exactly what YHWH did in the pillar of fire and cloud to Pharaoh's chariots in Exod 14:24, "And in the morning watch YHWH in the pillar of fire and of cloud looked down on the Egyptian forces and threw the Egyptian forces into a panic (Hebrew is, המם)." The Egyptians fled before YHWH only to be crushed by the waters. The Song of Deborah says, "The torrent Kishon swept them away, the ancient torrent, the torrent Kishon" (5:21). This is a clear sign of activation of the great exodus event.

---

12. Block, *Judges*, 205.
13. Block, *Judges*, 208–10.

At this point in Judges, God delivers his people through battle. Enemy generals are defeated by tent-dwelling women! God's people are being obedient, and God is bringing the victory. This is depicted as an almost exodus-level victory, and the audience is invited into all of the emotions of the great salvation-event, anticipating a renewed example of their covenant identity. The audience wonders, "Perhaps things will not get so bad after all."

And yet the performance of the Judges tradition still began with a satirical/sarcastic introduction. The first judges included a non-Israelite judge who hid behind his wife after his heroic father-in-law tried to weasel them out of a decent parcel of land, directly followed by a trickster of Canaanite-ish assassin in Ehud. And as much as the story of Deborah and Barak may activate the exodus tradition, it also echoes these other judges—a man seems to hide behind a woman, and the assassination scene connects chiastically to Ehud (further implied by the introduction of "when Ehud died"). The story celebrates YHWH's victory through Jael, but why does Israel need a non-Israelite, tent-dwelling deception in the first place? Where is the absolute faithful obedience of Israel and the uncompromised victory of YHWH through his people? Additionally, the last judge mentioned before Deborah/Barak was Shamgar—a non-Israelite, possibly even an Egyptian; called the son of Anath, Baal's consort! Shamgar, who also saved Israel!

What a mixed bag of hope and cynicism.

In the end of chapter 4, the indisputable hero is named. Who is said to have subdued Jabin? God. God is the hero. This is the ongoing truth of Judges that is never shrouded in sarcasm.

Second Paired Major Judge—Gideon and Abimelech: 6:1—9:57

Gideon: 6:1—8:35

Just like Deborah and Barak, and unlike Jephthah and Samson, the second episode of the first round of major Judges comes in a pair. The first round of major judges is a pair of pairs.

While the introductory judges, intertwined with the story of Deborah and Barak, left us with a mixed bag of hope and glory and cynicism and suspicion of failure, the Gideon/Abimelech episode will not leave us guessing. The hope and glory of this second pair in the first round of major judges will quickly dissipate into full-fledged failure.

Gideon, in his own weakness, begins by submitting to God's strength, even to the extent of diminishing his army from thirty thousand to three hundred in obedience to YHWH. But then Gideon begins to lean on his strength, and he fails to pass down his original humility to his children. Instead, his legacy is marked by idolatry and a pursuit of power and vengeance.

In the Gideon/Abimelech cycle we see a metaphor of the nation as a whole. They began as a weak people—not because of their greatness did God choose them from the nations. But God chose them, and they put away other gods to serve YHWH, just as Gideon destroyed the Baals and Ashtaroth as he began his judgeship. But the people whored after their own glory and idols, and they became just as Canaanite as those they were instructed to displace from the land. Though the father started off well, he declined, and his offspring screwed up royally (pun intended). Likewise, Gideon will begin as a humble man submitting to God, but he will diverge from the covenant with YHWH. His legacy of aborted glory will continue into the lives of his children. Moving on from the story of Gideon, the story of Abimelech "looks like a leaf from a Canaanite history notebook"[14] as Gideon's children rule over portions of Israel like kings and are upended through pursuits of power and vengeance.

Should the story of Judges reflect the elements of hope seen in the Deborah/Barak episode, one would expect faithful and obedient Israelites inquiring of YHWH, hearing from YHWH through his priests and prophets, and enjoying the glory and joy of the victories wrought for them through YHWH's move. Instead, even as the people suffer due to their sin, God's people do not go to his prophet to inquire "the judgment" (as they did from Deborah, 4:4–5). This time God must send an unnamed prophet to rebuke Israel (6:7–10).

Block said this about the story of Gideon: "The heroic women of the [Song of Deborah] give way to the unheroic 'man of Israel' (7:14) who not only does all he can to evade the call of Yahweh but in the end abandons God."[15] Gideon's home of Ophrah was a place of clan idolatry (6:25–32). Gideon followed God and tore down the idols. But later he will lead Ophrah to become a place of national idolatry (8:27).[16] The judge who would refuse to rule Israel will act like a king, lead the nation

14. Block, *Judges*, 250.
15. Block, *Judges*, 250.
16. Block, *Judges*, 250.

to idolatry, and his son, Abimelech ("My Daddy is the King"), will lead the nation to civil war and chaos.

Gideon's cycle begins with the classic introduction of the established pattern of the judges—Israel did evil, YHWH gave them over to the hands of the Midianites (etc.), and they cried out to God. Though the text does not say, "God raised up a deliverer/judge," the call of Gideon is the most expansive call narrative in the book, followed closely by Samson's birth narrative. It begins with a prophetic word just as Barak's raising/calling included a prophetic word from Deborah. God replies to Israel's cries through a word from an unnamed prophet.

The text does not say who this prophet was or where he came from, but an important truth can be mined from his ministry. Even when "all Israel" does what is evil in the sight of the LORD, there always seems to be a remnant of faithful YHWH worshipers, a remnant of people and prophets.

The reference to the exodus from the Deborah/Barak cycle is made explicit with the prophetic word of judgment (6:8–10). The Deborah/Barak cycle demonstrated that Israel could have lived within the victorious covenantal relationship with YHWH, as demonstrated in Exodus. But Israel would not remain faithful. The prophetic voice here in the Gideon/Abimelech cycle states the issue emphatically. Still, God raises up Gideon in spite of Israel's pattern of not listening to YHWH.

Gideon questions God's faithfulness: "Where are all his wonders that our fathers told us about when they said, 'Did not the LORD bring us up out of Egypt?'" What irony! Not only are God's people following the downward spiral as outlined in the book of Judges, but they are even questioning God's faithfulness in light of the situations incited through their own unfaithfulness to the covenant—even in the face of the exodus-level deliverance in the Deborah cycle. Gideon asks, "Where are all of YHWH's wonders?" And yet we just heard about them in the story of Deborah and Barak!

The pattern of Gideon's call—(1) meeting with God or his messenger; (2) an introductory address of the person being called; (3) the divine commission; (4) the raising of objections by the person called; (5) divine words of reassurance; and (6) a sign authenticating the call experience— "intentionally presents Gideon as sort of a second Moses."[17] Indeed, in 6:16, after Gideon hesitates, the angel of YHWH says, "כִּי־אֶהְיֶה עִמָּךְ" (for

---

17. Block, *Judges*, 257.

I will be with you), which is a direct citation from Exod 3:12. The greater context calls to mind Exod 3:14: "I will be who I will be / I am who I am." Like Moses, Gideon will be transformed into a deliverer by the powerful presence of YHWH.[18] In spite of Israel's faithlessness, and in spite of their blindness or amnesia to his current work, God is once again moving to his people with exodus-like intentions and power.

The normal pattern of the judges is interrupted as Gideon is charged to attack the true enemy of Israel—the Baal altar and the Asherah pole. He does so! But he does so at night because he knows his people would condemn him if they caught him in the act. This is backwards to the covenant. The idol-worshipers should be put to death, but Israel is already so Canaanized that they would kill the one who keeps covenant and destroys idols.

Gideon's father saves his life with a rousing speech for Baal to take care of his own problems, and Gideon gets the nickname "Jerubbaal," which, though with some form issues, essentially means "Let Baal contend against him."

The Midianites, Amalekites, and the people of the East gather, and this weak and meek man, whose hometown wanted him dead just verses earlier, blows a horn and sends out messengers. And everyone just runs to him to help him fight!

What changed in the hearts and minds of his town and countrymen? The answer is found in verse 34: "Then the Spirit of YHWH came upon Gideon . . ." God moved in Gideon in such a way that those who had wanted him dead and those who lived in neighboring tribes came running to his call to arms. Block said, "As in the cases of Jephthah in 11:29, and especially Saul in 1 Sam 11:6–8, the same Spirit which possesses the divinely called deliverer compels the recipients of the summons to respond to his call."[19]

Even with all of the clear signs and calls of God on his life, Gideon still hesitates and asks for signs that God is with him. The signs of the fleece were not about seeking God's will. Gideon knew what God had promised (6:37b—"then I will know that you will save Israel by my hand, *as you said*"). Block explained, "Despite being clear about the will of God, being empowered by the Spirit of God, and being confirmed as a divinely chosen leader by the overwhelming response of his countrymen to his

---

18. Block, *Judges*, 261.
19. Block, *Judges*, 272.

own summons to battle, he uses every means available to try to get out of the mission to which he has been called."[20] God continues to move in grace and gives the tentative Gideon the reassurance he asks for.

God then commands Gideon to dwindle down his army so that it will not be said that Israel's own hand defeated the Midianites. God's move in Israel through Gideon is not about the glory of Israel or any Israelite. It is all about the glory of God.

And Gideon obeys! He sends 99 percent of his force home so that the army's meekness reflects his own. This is a good sign. Gideon seems to be leading Israel to trust in the power of YHWH and not in their own strength.

Then God gives Gideon a reassurance for which he did not ask. Near the enemy camp he hears about a dream and its interpretation. The dream was of a runaway dinner roll that crushed the tent of Midian. The interpretation was that the destructive pastry represented the very sword of Gideon! Empowered by the interpretation of the dream, Gideon goes back to his company of three hundred and takes command with an interesting plan. His forces surround the enemy camp, break their jars, blow their trumpets, and raise their torches. God confuses the enemy and gains the victory, sending a remnant running back to the desert.

Then Gideon does a curious thing. He calls for greater numbers of Israelites to finish the job. Is this a sign of Gideon backtracking on God's call to cut back his numbers? If the people were too many for God to get the glory earlier, why is it now the time to call out greater numbers? The text does not say explicitly whether this was an act of obedience or disobedience, but the hearer is left wondering. Gideon's activities from this time forward grow more and more questionable, leading the audience to believe that Gideon began to step out of his trust in YHWH once he tasted victory.

Ephraim comes to Gideon upset that Gideon failed to call them out earlier. Gideon does not stand strong in his decision to obey YHWH. He does not say, "I did what YHWH called me to do. YHWH commanded me to dwindle down my forces for his glory. This battle is not about our glory but the glory of YHWH. Look not to your own hands or your own reputation, but submit to YHWH for the victory belongs to him!"

Instead, Gideon appeals to their human pride, essentially saying, "You guys are better than us! You did better than we did!" He does confess

---

20. Block, *Judges*, 273.

that it was God who gave Oreb and Zeeb into their hands but only after he says, "What have I accomplished compared to you? Aren't the gleanings of Ephraim's grapes better than the full grape harvest of Abiezer?" (8:1). The battle that was supposed to be all about the victory of God has dissolved into a comparison of which Israelites have accomplished more.

After this scene, we encounter a very different Gideon. As opposed to a quivering, nighttime obeying, sign-seeking, divine dream encouragement-needing, humble follower of YHWH, we see a vengeful warlord ready to treat Israelites like Canaanites.

It is important to note:

1. Yahweh is not involved in this phase of the plot at all (except in Gideon's own glib comments).

2. The two captured Midianite leaders have strange names and are called "kings" (*mĕlākîm*) rather than "commanders" (*śārîm*).

3. The campaign takes Gideon and his men far afield to Karkor east of the Dead Sea.

4. Gideon runs into serious conflict with his Transjordanian countrymen.

5. Gideon is personally involved in the capture and execution of the enemy kings.

6. Personal blood vengeance replaces national deliverance as a motive for Gideon's action.

7. Gideon, the fearful young man, has become a brutal aggressor.[21]

Gideon sets out to hunt down these kings. In the process, he is turned away by two cities. To Ephraim Gideon said, "You're better than us." To his Transjordanian countrymen he says, "I'll teach you a lesson of subjugation."

Gideon leaves the promised land in pursuit of his own personal crusade. What a metaphor for exiled Israel and for us all. How often we abandon God's promises for our own pursuits—just like Adam and Eve when they wanted to pursue equality with God through their strength and had to leave the garden.

We discover later that Gideon wanted revenge for the killing of his brothers—the sons of his mother. He has gained great confidence in the

---

21. Block, *Judges*, 287.

victory that God gave him—the victory that was meant to liberate the land and give glory to God. Gideon has utilized his newfound confidence in himself, and his newfound militia, to go and get revenge outside of the promised land, perhaps as far as one hundred miles east of the Dead Sea, as the most likely place for Karkor may be Wadi Sirhan.[22]

Gideon captures the kings, beats the elders in one of the Israelite cities, and then destroys the defense tower of the other and kills the men. This would have left the town absolutely defenseless. It was essentially a death sentence to the women and children who were left behind. All he had promised to do was tear down the tower, but Gideon seems to have developed some sort of war-induced bloodlust.

Finally, he turns his attention to the kings he had taken. He makes it clear that they are going to die because they killed his brothers, the sons of his mother. He tries to get his young son to engage in his vengeful blood lust, but since he was only a boy and afraid, Gideon's son would not kill the kings.

Gideon's son reflects the young man Gideon used to be, demonstrating for the audience how much Israel's savior has changed—from leaning on YHWH's strength in his own fear and weakness, to exerting his own vengeance on his personal enemies and even on his fellow Israelites. He even tries to get his young son to follow in his footsteps.

The kings say, "Come, do it yourself. 'As is the man, so is his strength.'" Gideon accepts these words touting his strength. He now believes that he is a warrior worthy of slaying these kings. He has shifted from moving in God's strength in light of his own weakness, to walking in the weakness of his own strength.

He takes from these kings the ornaments of kings from their camels. After all, the slain kings had said that Gideon, just like his brothers who had died, had the appearance of a son of the king. Why should Gideon not take a king's bounty?

Gideon responds well when the people ask him to rule over them. Unlike his response to Ephraim and unlike his vengeful behavior, his answer seems humble. He says, "I will not rule over you, nor will my son rule over you, but YHWH will rule over you."

While Gideon's words seem faithful, his actions are directly opposed to his words, another move of biting satire. First of all, while he verbally denied kingship, he did not say, "Besides, it was not me who saved you but

---

22. Block, *Judges*, 291.

YHWH." Gideon demonstrated some slick political skill in his discussion with the Ephraimites, and he might be doing the same thing here. He smooths them over with what he knows they would like to hear. Second, he has already treated his Transjordan countrymen as an evil king would. Third, he asked for a portion of the spoil—something kings receive. This was a clear symbolic request of submission from the people, again, without mention of YHWH's victory. Fourth, he made a national icon and set it up in his hometown. An ephod is something worn by priests. Is Gideon claiming to be a royal priest? The high priest of Israel? Or did he put the ephod on an idol? At any rate, all of Israel whored after the idol, and it was a snare to Gideon and his household (the word "household" can have dynastic overtones). Basically, Gideon set up a national shrine in his hometown reminiscent of David bringing the ark of the covenant into the city he had conquered with his own personal militia. Fifth, he had a harem of wives and concubines. Sixth, he named his son Abimelech, which is likely to be interpreted as "My father is king." And seventh, his sons are assumed to be ruling over Shechem in chapter 9, which is why Abimelech has them all killed (except for Jotham, who escapes).

While Gideon publicly denies the title of king, he behaves as king in everything he does in his latter years. Furthermore, when one compares his rule to Deut 17, Gideon acts as a king outside of the covenant. He acquires excess gold and silver and many wives (Deut 17:17), and he does not write or follow the book of the law (Deut 17:18–20).[23]

Even though Gideon set up an idolatrous ephod in his hometown, something about his rule over Israel apparently kept the people from full out Baal worship (8:33)—unless this is another mark of sarcasm in the book. After his death, the people again prostituted themselves to the Baals.

ABIMELECH: 9:1–57

This is "the longest single pericope" in the central section of the book of Judges. In it, God will only be referred to as Elohim and Gideon as Jerubbaal. "These features reflect the author's unambiguous stance toward the nation and the characters: Israel has been totally Canaanized; Baal has contended for himself and prevailed."[24]

---

23. For further discussion on Gideon's "sham rejection of kingship," see Block, *Judges*, 296–301.
24. Block, *Judges*, 308.

Abimelech, half-Canaanite on his Shechemite mother's side, persuades the elders of Shechem to help him hire mercenaries to kill Jerubbaal's seventy sons, so he alone, and not the many sons of Jerubbaal, will rule over them. They agree, and only Jotham survives.

Jotham, which means "YHWH is perfect/honest," climbs up Mount Gerizim and delivers a fable about trees seeking a king. Jotham's name and speech is the one part of this section that seems to reflect some sort of awareness of a need for loyalty to YHWH, his standards, and his pattern of disciplining unacceptable behavior.

The fable goes something like this: the trees seek someone to act as king over them. The three trees who are first asked—the olive tree, fig tree, and grapevine—all argue that they are too busy doing productive things, so they should not stop and take on the worthless job of the king.

The trees then ask the bramble to reign over them. The bramble says to the trees, "If you are anointing me as king over you in good faith, then come! Take refuge in my shade."

The satirical ridicule of trees taking refuge in the shade of the bramble is unmistakable.

The bramble continues, "But if you are not acting in good faith, fire will come out of the bramble and consume the cedars of Lebanon."

Jotham then offers the interpretation. If Shechem has acted in truth and integrity in anointing Abimelech, then let him be their joy. But Jotham leaves no doubt. Shechem has not acted in truth and integrity in respect to Jotham's father, Jerubbaal, so the entire fable and interpretation lands as a curse: "Let fire come out of Abimelech and consume you and let fire come from you and consume him!" Jotham then goes into hiding.

Mount Gerizim was one of the two mountains utilized in a ceremony of Torah blessing. Moses commanded that the people, once they enter the promised land, set the blessings on Mount Gerizim and the curses on Mount Ebal (Deut 11:29–32). The ceremony was a reminder for the people to keep covenant with YHWH—to "be careful to do all the statutes and the rules that I am setting before you today" (Deut 11:32). Joshua 8:30–35 records the ceremony. Jotham's satirical blessing lands as a curse upon Shechem and Abimelech, and its declaration from Mount Gerizim, the mount of blessing, heightens its sarcastic bite. The audience knows that just as Shechem does not deserve the blessing from Mount Gerizim but the curses from Mount Ebal, the fable is calling forth fire upon Abimelech and the Shechemites. Equally, the fable reminds the exiles that they deserved the exile for their own relationship with their kings.

In the following narration, we see the curse come to fruition. The Shechemites begin to despise Abimelech's rule and set up places to rob those who would pass by, which would include those bringing deliveries to Abimelech.

Gaal calls upon the Shechemites to follow him. Perhaps Gaal was a Shechemite who had left at some point and had now returned. He claims to be a descendant of Hamor, the founder of Shechem. Zebul, the city ruler, sends word to Abimelech who responds with violence, destroying the forces of Gaal. Abimelech also turns violent against the townspeople when they try to resume their daily schedule of going out to the fields. He destroys the city and sows it with salt.

Some from the town fled to the tower in the temple of Shechem, and so Abimelech burns the tower, killing all the men, women, and children. "As the bramble in Jotham's fable had predicted (v. 15), fire had burst forth from the king and consumed the cedars of Lebanon."[25]

When Abimelech tries to go and repeat this atrocity in another town, he is struck in the head by a stone dropped from the tower by a woman. And so "the story of Abimelech the macho man is framed by two women: the first, who gave him life (8:31), and the second, who took it (9:53)."[26] Block points out the irony that the one "who had slaughtered his brothers 'upon one stone' has his skull crushed beneath one stone."[27]

Repetition again emerges in this first round of major judges. Like Sisera, a blow to the head by a woman destroys the villain. But this time the villain is a "king" in Israel. He is the son of Gideon. This entire round of major judges is a swirling display of how Israel has come full circle. Their "king" is half-Canaanite on their mother's side and half-anti-covenantal king on the side of his father, Gideon, the one who stole glory from YHWH and set up a national idol. And Abimelech, the son of the great judge and king in Israel, is killed by a blow to the head from a woman just like Sisera who oppressed Israel.

Yet "neither human pretension (8:22–32) nor human ferocity (9:1–55) could dislodge Yahweh from his throne. In the end Abimelech's egomaniacal ambition must yield to the kingship of God, and with this the story of Gideon is complete."[28] Again, God accomplishes his purposes in spite of evil human activity.

25. Block, *Judges*, 332.
26. Block, *Judges*, 334.
27. Block, *Judges*, 335.
28. Block, *Judges*, 334.

Round 2—Jephthah: 10:1—12:7

Minor Judges—Tola and Jair: 10:1-5

The first round of major judges was introduced by three minor judges—Othniel, Ehud, and Shamgar. The first round had two major judges, and both of them were paired up with another person that helped the cycle reflect and expand upon the minor judges: Barak, paired with Deborah; Gideon, paired with Abimelech.

The second round begins with two introductory judges, Tola and Jair. Notice the new pattern of these judges. These judges are not said to have been raised up by YHWH. The text simply says, "There arose . . ."

This sounds more like the short note on Shamgar—"And Shamgar also saved Israel."

"And Tola arose to save Israel." He judged, he died, and he was buried.

These new introductory judges do not even have the introductory note of Israel doing evil in the eyes of YHWH, crying out, etc. The narrative of the major judge of this second round of judges, Jephthah, will include aspects of the original pattern, but, like these introductory judges, nothing is said of God raising up Jephthah. It seems as though YHWH enters the picture later on in the story out of his own compassion, mercy, and grace in order to put his Spirit upon Jephthah and give the enemy into Jephthah's hand. In these introductory judges, and in the Jephthah cycle, nothing is said concerning the land or people having rest due to the ministry of these men.

Jair does not even save Israel. He just arose and judged. He was a Gileadite just like the following major judge, Jephthah. Jair had thirty sons who rode on thirty donkeys and had thirty cities in Gilead.

The introductory/minor judge in the book just following Jephthah, is Ibzan of Bethlehem. The text says of Ibzan, "He judged Israel. He had thirty sons and thirty daughters he gave in marriage outside his clan and thirty daughters he brought in from the outside for his sons."

Jephthah, the judge who only has one child, a daughter, is surrounded by a minor judge with thirty sons and a minor judge with thirty sons and daughters, plus thirty extra daughters he brought in from the outside for his sons. This is yet another example of intentional repetition used to highlight a portion of the story.

Jair is a man of great means. With so many sons he certainly had many wives. He is able to buy each son a brand-new donkey and manage to offer a city for each of them to govern. Jair is a man of means and persuasion in Gilead.

Jephthah is not like Jair. We will read that Jephthah is an outcast of Gilead who haggles his way into authority. He only has one kid, a daughter, and he even ends up sacrificing her. The point is clarified by the repetitious presentation of the minor judges—even what Jephthah had, he destroyed due to his (and all of Israel's) lack of covenant faithfulness to YHWH.

Major Judge—Jephthah: 10:6—12:7

The Jephthah cycle begins with "the most elaborate description of Israelite apostasy in the book."[29] The extensive identification of the foreign gods that Israel has served along with the blatant description of Israel's forsaking of YHWH and his service highlights the totality of their apostasy.

The narration identifies YHWH's anger as the emotion driving his discipline of Israel for the first time since chapter 3, and, instead of one foreign oppressor, two nations—the Philistines and the Ammonites (literally, "sons of Ammon")—are called forth.

The Philistines, sea peoples from the west, settled on the western shores. The Ammonites, as we can tell from the Jephthah cycle, operated in the Transjordan territories to the east. God has raised up two nations to box in Israel. Israel's apostasy is filled to the brim, and they are surrounded by the discipline of YHWH. The Philistine threat will not be addressed until the third round of major judges in the Samson cycle.

In Judg 10:6–17, YHWH never moves to save Israel. He is totally passive in the story until 11:29 when his Spirit falls upon Jephthah. The name of YHWH is evoked by Jephthah. He speaks before YHWH. But YHWH is never said to appoint or accept the dealings of these Gileadite men. It is only YHWH's mercy and grace that can account for his sudden movement upon Jephthah before Jephthah makes his horrible oath.

Along with the most elaborate description of Israelite apostasy, the Jephthah cycle also offers the most detailed account of Israel's response to the discipline of YHWH. Though they confess their apostasy, they do not seem to be ready to repent at first.

---

29. Block, *Judges*, 344.

YHWH replies with biting sarcasm, essentially saying, "How many times have I already saved you and you keep on going back to other gods? Let those gods save you if they are so worth your worship."

The book says that Israel repents and puts away the foreign gods and serves YHWH.

And how does YHWH respond? That is indeed the question.

Scholars differ on interpreting YHWH's response due to some ambiguity in the meaning of the Hebrew idiom וַתִּקְצַר נַפְשׁוֹ, "and his soul was short," and the word for the "misery" of Israel (בַּעֲמַל).

The idiom is fairly straightforward in how it is used elsewhere in the Old Testament in Num 21:4, Judg 16:16, Job 21:4, and Zech 11:8. The meaning of this phrase reflects impatience, vexation, or great frustration with the situation at hand. In Judg 16:16 Samson was so vexed by Delilah's nagging that he gave away the secret to his strength, even though she had clearly betrayed him three other times!

The word "עָמָל" can simply mean "hard work, effort," but more often it has the connotation of suffering—"pain, trouble."[30] Some scholars opt for the meaning of "hard work, effort" because YHWH does not seem to make any moves to help Israel (at least at first). Block represents this group when he says,

> Yahweh may be dismissing the Israelite actions as further evidence of their iniquitous condition. The words themselves are ambiguous, but there is rejection in Yahweh's voice. The Israelites' present efforts are intolerable, and the attempts to wrest deliverance from him are an affront. The repentance is external only; theirs is a conversion of convenience . . . These people are interested only in relief from their oppressions. Because their confession lacks sincerity, Yahweh will withdraw and be used by this parasitic people no longer.[31]

This interpretation understands YHWH to be frustrated with Israel's efforts because, as hard as the efforts may seem on the outside, they are false external performances of insincere repentance.

However, it seems that the vast majority of the uses of the word, "עָמָל," especially in the Torah and Prophets, reflect some kind of hardship, pain, or trouble (Gen 41:51; Num 23:21; Deut 26:7; Isa 10:1; 53:11; 59:4; Jer 20:18; Hab 1:3; 1:13 all seem to imply something more of

---

30. HALOT, 845.
31. Block, *Judges*, 349.

hardship rather than effort). It is a frequent word in Job 3–16, occurring eight times and always implying some kind of hardship or harm.

Perhaps the introduction to this cycle reflects exactly how the cycle unfolds. YHWH expresses his lack of willingness to help Israel this time, taunting them to call on the gods whom Israel has chosen over YHWH. Yet as Israel tries to repent and operate in her own strength, YHWH grows impatient with their suffering, gives his Spirit to Jephthah, and delivers the Ammonites into his hand.

The focus is not on the sincerity of the Israelite repentance but on the mercy and grace of God that breaks through his frustration with his rebellious people. Whether their repentance was sincere or not, he cannot easily sit by and watch his people suffer. He grows so impatient over their suffering that he'll even use someone as flawed as Jephthah to bring relief to his people.

The Ammonites gather against Gilead, and so the Gileadites ask who will launch the attack. This reflects Judg 1 in which the people ask YHWH who will go up for them against the Canaanites. However, the Gileadites do not inquire of YHWH but of themselves. Block said, "This was a purely secular moment; as a Canaanized people the Gileadites were left to their own wits and resources, and, as in the case of Abimelech, a bramble would not be long in sprouting. Through this entire episode Yahweh's silence is deafening."[32] The Gileadites call Jephthah to be their hero.

The calling of Jephthah parallels the people's crying out to YHWH:

1. The Ammonite oppression (10:7–9)
2. Israel appeals to Yahweh (10:10)
3. Yahweh retorts sarcastically (10:11–14)
4. Israel repeats the appeal (10:15–16a)
5. Yahweh refuses to be used (10:16b)

1. The Ammonite oppression (11:4)
2. Gilead appeals to Jephthah (11:5–6)
3. Jephthah retorts sarcastically (11:7)
4. Gilead repeats the appeal (11:8)
5. Jephthah seizes the moment opportunistically (11:9–11)[33]

---

32. Block, *Judges*, 351.
33. Block, *Judges*, 354.

The difference, clearly, is Jephthah's move to seize power over the Gileadites. The Gileadites' first offer to Jephthah varies from the initial offer to the other Gileadites, and it also varies from their second offer to Jephthah after his sarcastic retort. As an outsider, they did not want to give him full authority at first, but their need persuaded them. This is a mediation between humans vying for power. The Ammonite display of power against the Gileadites prompted the Gileadites to haggle with Jephthah.

YHWH remains silent. The people's pattern of covenant unfaithfulness is not a pattern YHWH plans on sanctioning. He maintains his intention stated at the beginning of this narrative. He refuses to operate among the people as he had in previous cycles of rebellion. The Gileadites only evoke the covenant name as some kind of authorizing principle to seal the deal upon which the men themselves had agreed.

The Gileadites call Jephthah to lead them against the Ammonites and be the head over all the people of Gilead. Just as Jephthah successfully negotiated his terms with the Gileadites, he tries to negotiate with the Ammonites. Jephthah acts as the representative leader (even king) of Gilead as he sends delegates with a message—"Why have you attacked our country?"

The Ammonite king claims that he is merely reclaiming the land that was rightfully theirs. This seems to be patently false. As Block explained, "According to the biblical record the Arnon [river] served as the border between Moab and the Amorites (not the Ammonites), and the Israelites had gained title to the land between this river and the Jabbok by defeating the Amorite king Sihon, who ruled Heshbon."[34]

Jephthah's speech contains some errors of its own, but the overall argument is as follows:

1. First of all, our people were not aggressors to the Transjordanian peoples. We asked to go through and they attacked us. We obtained this land by defeating the Amorites, not the Ammonites.

2. YHWH gave us this land through that process. What our God gives us is ours, just like what your god gives you is yours (a very Canaanite way of talking about gods).

3. We have had this land for three hundred years now (exaggeration?); why are you and your people just now claiming it as your own?[35]

---

34. Block, *Judges*, 359.
35. See Block, *Judges*, 359–63, for his discussion of Jephthah's arguments.

Some of Jephthah's claims seem to be orthodox. He places victories in YHWH's hands, and he commits the judgment of the present dispute to YHWH. But he also affirms the decisions and victories of Chemosh in his speech, and he later follows through with his vow by sacrificing his daughter for victory, something that the sons of Ammon did for their deities, Milkom and Molech.

At any rate, the Spirit of YHWH comes upon Jephthah, and just like the humble Gideon, Jephthah's rallying cry is heard. YHWH is impatient with their suffering, and so he intervenes in his grace.

Tragically, the outpouring of the Spirit of YHWH was not enough for Jephthah. He needed something else to seal the deal of his victory. He desired some way to manipulate or affirm YHWH to his will, just as a Canaanite would with his gods. Block said, "He was still negotiating—manipulating God and seeking to wrest concessions and favors from him like he had from the Gileadites and Ammonites."[36]

With the Gileadites, Jephthah got exactly what he wanted. With the Ammonites, he received a refusal. With YHWH, Jephthah only received silence.[37]

The vow was neither instigated nor acknowledged by YHWH.

What exactly did Jephthah have in mind with his vow? It is not customary for animals to come out and greet their conquering heroes. Jephthah seemingly knew that he was promising a human sacrifice.

Block observed, "In 10:10 the narrator testifies to the fact that at this time the Israelites worshiped Milkom, the Ammonite god, and Chemosh, the god of the Moabites, whose leaders are known to have sacrificed children (2 Kgs 3:27)."[38] Also, Jer 32:35 draws a connection to the sons of Ammon, who worshiped Molech through the sacrificing their children, and Israel who did the same thing in the valley of Hinnom.

It is no coincidence that the judge at this point in the downward spiral of apostasy, who fought against the sons of Ammon, tried to worship YHWH just like the Ammonites worshiped their gods. This performance stands as a testimony as to why Israel, who also sacrifices her children before the exile, deserved the discipline of YHWH.

Perhaps Jephthah expected someone else to come out of the door first, but that seems to be about as much credit as we can give him. It sure seems as though the phrase "whatever comes out of the house to meet

---

36. Block, *Judges*, 365.
37. Block, *Judges*, 365.
38. Block, *Judges*, 367.

me" "envisages the exuberant welcome by children of a father who has been away on a military campaign,"[39] and the only child Jephthah had was his daughter.

After YHWH gave victory to Jephthah, both he and his daughter believed the deed must be done. They believed that it was the only right thing to do. That's how bad things had gotten in Israel. Jephthah's daughter operated within her Canaanized role. She is depicted as humble and submissive. She is trampled by Israel's Canaanization.

Jephthah the judge stands in the text surrounded by Jair with thirty sons and Ibzan with thirty sons and daughters, while Jephthah has killed his only offspring, a daughter. Seeking to secure his immediate victory over the Ammonites, Jephthah sacrificed his future. With the death of his daughter, his family dies. "The conquering hero is reduced to nothing,"[40] and YHWH's people worship their God as if he is a Canaanite god receiving human sacrifices.

The placement of Jephthah's tale at this point in the book of Judges makes it clear that the author/tradition-bearer holds this action to be completely outside of covenant faithfulness to YHWH. The book of Judges condemns this behavior as a low point in almost the worst season of Israel's apostasy. YHWH's evaluation of the events in the narrative can be seen in his condemnation, rejection, and silence. Only a fleeting moment of merciful salvation brought any good out of this sad epic.

YHWH hands the enemies into Jephthah's hands in spite of the fact that YHWH himself did not raise up Jephthah. YHWH saves Israel from the Ammonites by using Jephthah, but Jephthah's story mentions no rest for the land. "Like the short notes on the secondary governors, this cycle ends simply with a notice of the length of his tenure (a short six years), his death, and his burial somewhere in Gilead."[41]

Jephthah's legacy included a form of civil war against the Ephraimites who suffered "almost as many losses as the Benjamites would later in 20:35, 46, when they were virtually wiped out as a tribe."[42] With Jephthah we get an Israel about as bad as it gets. He secures no rest or peace for the land, and the closing of his cycle resembles more of the minor judges of the second two rounds of judges than of the earlier major judges.

39. Block, *Judges*, 368.
40. Block, *Judges*, 375.
41. Block, *Judges*, 342.
42. Block, *Judges*, 384.

The consistency of the oral traditional use of repetition does not let up as we reach the Jephthah cycle.

As to Gideon:

> Both open with a confrontation between God and Israel (6:7–10; 10:6–16). Both men begin as nobodies and become tyrants in Israel. Both are empowered by the Spirit of God, an event that is immediately recognized by the rallying of the troops (6:34–35; 11:29). Both follow up the divine empowerment with expressions of doubt (6:36–40; 11:30–31). Both win a spectacular victory over the enemy (7:19–25; 11:32–33). Both engage in confrontations with jealous Ephraimites after the battle has been won (8:1–3; 12:1–6). Both brutalize their countrymen (8:4–17; 12:4–6).[43]

As to Abimelech:

> Both he and Abimelech are born of secondary (probably foreign) wives (8:31; 11:1) and surround themselves with brigands and good-for-nothings (9:4; 11:3). Both are opportunists who negotiate their way into leadership positions (9:1–6; 11:4–11). Both seal the agreement with their subjects in a formal ceremony at a sacred shrine (9:6; 11:11). Both turn out to be brutal rulers, slaughtering their own relatives (9:5; 11:34–40) and engaging their countrymen in battle (9:26–57; 12:1–6). Both end up as tragic figures without a future (9:50–57; 11:34–35).[44]

Round 3—Samson: 12:8—16:31

Samson is the judge at the bottom of the barrel of the performance's downward cycle of apostasy. In Samson we see the final stage of the diminishing pattern set forth in the opening judges—Othniel, Ehud, Deborah/Barak, and Gideon/Abimelech.

Whatever is to be said about Samson, he should be seen as the worst judge in the darkest days of Israel set forth in this book. As discussed above, he will echo other judges through key words and themes, and Samson will epitomize Israel herself as he chases after foreign women, flaunts his special position before YHWH, and fails to learn from his failures.

---

43. See Block, *Judges*, 342–43.
44. Block, *Judges*, 343.

In the end, we will see in Samson a vision of Israel from the time of the exile—an Israel abandoned by YHWH on one hand, yet an Israel that YHWH is still determined to faithfully and graciously move to and through. YHWH has a plan to build his people and bless all nations, and he accomplishes his plans in spite of his people's shortcomings.

Minor Judges—Ibzan, Elon, and Abdon: 12:8–15

These three introductory judges are the last set of introductory judges found in the book. Like the two introductory judges in round two, they do not follow the pattern set by the first two of the first three minor introductory judges, Othniel and Ehud, but they follow more closely the brief note on Shamgar. Or perhaps better said, Shamgar and these final introductory judges follow the pattern set by Tola and Jair. We should analyze these final judges within the interpretive framework given to us by the current performance of the Judges tradition—the downward spiral of apostasy.

As discussed in the Jephthah cycle, Ibzan's thirty sons and daughters contrast boldly with Jephthah's only daughter whom he sacrificed and burned as an offering to YHWH. While Ibzan's many offspring and his wide influence (marrying his daughters "outside" and bringing in wives for his sons "from outside") are certainly impressive and demonstrative of his prosperity, the interpretive framework of the book of Judges calls us to look beyond the appearance of prosperity and understand the depravity of this first of the last of the judges in the book.

Certainly, Ibzan did not have all of these children with one wife. A sixty-proof womb would be quite the exception. These thirty sons and thirty daughters remind us of Gideon's seventy sons from his many wives and at least one concubine. Ibzan's prosperity is a flaunting of Canaanite culture and values.

He even gives his daughters away as wives to those "outside" and brings in wives for his sons from "outside." Herbert Wolf is right to point out concerning the word "outside" that "in its only other occurrence in a similar context, 'outside' (ḥûṣah) refers to outside the immediate family (Deut 25:5)."[45] However, as Wolf goes on to say, "The fact that Ibzan's marriage policy is mentioned . . . may indicate a break with tradition."[46]

45. Wolf, "Judges," 459.
46. Wolf, "Judges," 459.

Ibzan is in the last grouping of judges, at the bottom of the barrel of the book of Judges. He had many wives, and he is not said to have saved Israel. We should probably expect the worst and not the best from him. It is highly likely that his "outside" marriage policy refers to marrying his kids to those outside of the nation and faith and covenant—a faith and covenant to which he was clearly unfaithful. Indeed, Ibzan's "outside" marriage policy clearly reflects Samson's lust for women outside of the covenant.

Ibzan only led Israel for seven years.

And what can we say of Elon? He ruled ten years, died, and was buried. There is nothing more to say of him. Israel's rulers are running out of steam.

Abdon had forty sons. Again, this plethora of children did not come from one woman. He also had thirty grandsons. Abdon had seventy male heirs just like Gideon. And they each had a donkey just like Jair's thirty sons.

The book of Judges is part of the larger prophetic perspective—the Former Prophets—which explains the catalyst of and offers an apologetic for YHWH's greatest disciplinary move against Israel, the exile. The period of the divided monarchy that led to the exile had many periods of prosperity. Some are described in the Bible, like the period of Uriah and Jeroboam II (2 Chr 26 and 2 Kgs 14:23–29 respectively). Some, like the Omride dynasty that ruled some fifty years in the ninth century, were largely glossed over in the biblical record. The prophets often railed against the flaunting of prosperity of the rich as a sign of covenant unfaithfulness (Amos 2:6–7; 5:11–12; Isa 3:14–15; 10:1–2; Mic 2:1–2; 3:9–11). Seasons of prosperity do not often project seasons of healthy faith for the people of God.

Indeed, as the signs of prosperity displayed by these judges largely reflect attitudes far from covenant faithfulness (many wives and outside marriages), and since the Israelites' approach to prosperity during the divided monarchy—the neglect of the poor, gluttony, and idol worship—was an aspect of Israelite life that called for the discipline of YHWH, we should probably see these presentations of prosperity as ironic expressions of covenant unfaithfulness.

Major Judge—Samson: 13:1—16:31

The deteriorating cycle of the judges finds its final crumbled form in Samson. The cycle is introduced with a very short description of Israel's apostasy and discipline: "Again the Israelites did evil in the eyes of the LORD, so the LORD delivered them into the hands of the Philistines for forty years" (13:1).

But Israel does not cry out about the oppression. Indeed, later in the story Judah will complain that Samson, the judge, is causing too much tension with the oppressors. They complain to Samson, "Don't you know that the Philistines rule over us?!" (15:11). The judge marries, prostitutes with, and flirts with women from the oppressors while the nation is content to be ruled by them. YHWH must seek to "create an occasion to disturb the relationship between oppressor and oppressed."[47]

The tradition presents Samson's call with great fanfare, utilizing an entire chapter to narrate the raising up of this judge whom Israel never requested. Samson never rallies the troops. He never leads an army against the foreign oppressor. He does not have the foreign oppressor handed over to him by YHWH. There is no victory. There is no peace in the land. There is no focus on tribal or national deliverance. Instead, we receive a series of episodes in Samson's private life. The Samson cycle divides into three parts:

> The Birth Narrative: 13:1–24
> The Saga of the Timnite Wife: 13:25—15:20
> The Saga of the Gazite Women: 16:1–31[48]

THE BIRTH NARRATIVE: 13:1–24

The birth narrative begins with the proclamation of Israel's apostasy and the LORD's deliverance of the nation into the hands of the Philistines for forty years. The tradition mentioned the Philistines in the introduction to the Jephthah cycle for the first time since the non-Israelite Shamgar was said to have saved Israel by killing six hundred Philistines with an ox-goad in 3:31. But the Philistine oppression alluded to in the Jephthah cycle was not addressed again until now. Israel never cries out to be

---

47. Block, *Judges*, 392.
48. Block, *Judges*, 393.

delivered from the Philistines in this cycle, but God graciously moves to a barren couple to give them a miracle-child for the salvation of his people.

The story of Samson is surrounded by themes of legacy. The minor judges surrounding him boast progeny of royal numbers. The major judge before him sacrificed his only offspring, and Samson is the miracle child of a barren couple. As Samson stands as a representative of Israel, the question hovers over the nation as it hovers over this last judge—what will the legacy left behind?

YHWH demonstrates his grace in the selection of a barren woman as the agent through whom God will raise up this unrequested judge. The potential of his gracious move is demonstrated in the guidelines for the holy lifestyle of the woman and child, in the wonderful and mysterious identity of the messenger, and in YHWH's explicit blessing of the child as Samson grows up.

At this point in the downward cycle through which the book has already brought us, we are at once surprised by this miraculous and hopeful birth narrative. But we are also uneasy. Could this really be the turnaround for which we've been hoping for Israel? The pessimistic and sarcastic tone of the book thus far leads the audience to receive this positive introduction with a dose of cynicism.

The birth narrative sets the scene for aspects of Samson's story, as well as for the following final section of the book of Judges. Zorah is located in both Judah's (Josh 15:33) and Dan's (19:41) territory. Judah will seek out Samson to deliver him to the Philistines, and the tribe of Dan will be central in Judg 17–18.

Samson's mother is the central character of the birth narrative. Block says:

> Throughout she is referred to simply as 'the woman,' or 'Manoah's wife.' The notice of her barrenness echoes Gen 11:30 both in its vocabulary and its redundancy, not only inviting a comparison with the earlier birth narrative, but especially highlighting what happens in this chapter as a work of God. God is at work on Israel's behalf miraculously raising up a deliverer for his people.[49]

The husband, Manoah, seems to be cast as a comical figure bound by ignorance and obtuseness, always trying to get a handle on the situation but always coming in second behind his unnamed wife. Just as Samson's mom predominates his birth narrative, women will predominate his

---

49. Block, *Judges*, 400.

activity in life and eventually his death. Samson will reflect his father's obtuseness.

The messenger comes first to Manoah's wife, and after Manoah asks for another visit, the messenger comes to Manoah's wife again. Finally, they go and see him together. Manoah asks for instructions, but the messenger essentially tells him to listen what to he had already told his wife.

Manoah desires to honor the messenger with a meal, but the messenger instead instructs Manoah to give an offering to YHWH. The messenger rises up in the flame with the offering prompting Manoah to fall down in fear and expectation of death. His wife comforts him with something like, "If YHWH were going to kill us, why would he accept our offering? Why would he give us this promise?" (13:23).

God does not promise that Samson would deliver Israel but that Samson would "begin the deliverance." He is to be treated as a Nazarite. The Nazarite law preserved in Num 6:1–8 prescribes a specific time of commitment which included abstaining from wine or any other intoxicating drink, from having one's hair cut, and from contact with a corpse. The mother is also told that she is not to eat any unclean food. Abstaining from unclean food should have been the normal behavior for Israelites, but their faithfulness to the covenant is not expected at this point in the narrative of the book.

The offering given before the messenger of YHWH closely parallels that of Gideon's sacrifice in Judg 6, and we are supposed to see the comparisons in order to feel the contradictions of the stories as well. Though Gideon failed to remain faithful, the beginning of his career was marked by a timid humility as he walked in submissive obedience. Samson on the other hand will only and always boastfully follow what is right in his own eyes and do what seems best for himself in the moment. Gideon's story concluded with a merciless quest for vengeance. Vengeance (and lust) will mark the entire story of Samson.

The identity of the messenger is a mystery. The messenger describes his name as "wonderful" (an adjective—פלא). In Isa 9:6 (BHS 9:5) we find another name connected to this root: "For to us a child is born, to us a son is given; and the government shall be upon his shoulder, and his name shall be called Wonderful Counselor, Mighty God, Everlasting Father, Prince of Peace." The word "wonderful" in Isaiah is actually in noun form. The child's name is "Wonderful," comma, "Counselor," not, "Wonderful Counselor."

The only other time the adjective is used is in Ps 139:6[50]—"Such knowledge is too wonderful for me; it is high; I cannot attain it." Interestingly, Ps 139:13–14 also discusses birth: "For you formed my inward parts; you knitted me together in my mother's womb. I praise you, for I am fearfully and wonderfully made. Wonderful are your works; my soul knows it very well." The creation of this person in Ps 139 is a fearful work of God—he or she is wonderful since YHWH's works are wonderful. The creation of a human is something so wonderful it is counted among the fearful things for which YHWH is to be praised.

The messenger's name is described as wonderful, as he brings this news of the opening of this woman's womb. While this does not directly identify the messenger, these details wrap his promise in hope and anticipation for who this specially formed person will be and what he will do. The name of the messenger ties his promise of Samson's birth to the greater tradition of birth, creation, and rescue.

What of the name, Samson? The name consists of a diminutive added to the word for "sun." Samson is "little sun." There was a solar cult that worshiped the god Shemesh, and Beth-Shemesh lay just a few miles from Zorah.[51] Perhaps Samson was named after Shemesh—Samson, "the little sun god." At any rate, if the name was not outrightly pagan, it was dangerously compromising. Even though YHWH caused her to conceive, the mom may have named her son after the Canaanite sun god.

Samson's compromising name, along with the necessity for the messenger to remind the woman to not eat unclean foods and the couple's seeming slowness to identify the messenger of YHWH, all point to a family well-situated in Israel at this juncture in the book of Judges. They are not covenantal Israelites. This portion of the tradition is presented as the darkest period of the judges—the final report of the judge cycle before the final summary of the religious and social ruin in chapters 17–21.

Block said, "No other deliverer in the Book of Judges matches his potential... Despite all these advantages and this special attention, Samson accomplishes less on behalf of his people than any of his predecessors... He never leads Israel out in battle; he never engages the Philistines in martial combat; he never experiences military victory. All his accomplishments are personal; all his victories, private."[52] Samson

---

50. Block, *Judges*, 413.
51. Block, *Judges*, 416–18.
52. Block, *Judges*, 420.

will lightheartedly violate his Nazirite status, he will fraternize with the enemy, and he will only always act on his own behalf.

The Saga of the Timnite Wife: 13:25—15:20

To fully understand this crazy string of events we must remember that Samson is the final judge in the downward spiral of the book of Judges and that Samson as a representative of Israel as a whole. The tradition of Judges finds its final form in the Deuteronomic performance of the Former Prophets. Block draws out the tension and the shock of the story, and YHWH's part in it, by listing the events of this saga in reverse:

1. En Hakkore received its name because Samson was revived by the waters of Lehi (15:19b).
2. Samson was revived by the waters of Lehi because God opened up the hollow place and water came out of it (15:19a).
3. God opened up the hollow place because Samson cried out (15:18b).
4. Samson cried out because he was thirsty (15:18a).
5. Samson was thirsty because he had exhausted himself slaying a thousand Philistines (15:14b–17).
6. Samson slew a thousand Philistines because they had come to capture him (15:14a).
7. The Philistines came to take custody of Samson because Judah had handed him over (15:13).
8. Judah handed him over to the Philistines because he sought refuge from them in their territory (158b–12).
9. Samson sought refuge in Judah because the Philistines were after him (15:8–9).
10. The Philistines were after Samson because he had ruthlessly slaughtered many of their men (15:7–8a).
11. Samson slaughtered many of the Philistines because they had burned his wife and his father-in-law (15:6).
12. The Philistines burned Samson's wife and father-in-law because Samson had burned their crops (15:3–5).

13. Samson burned the Philistines' crops because his father-in-law had given his wife to someone else (15:1–2).
14. Samson's father-in-law gave his wife to someone else because Samson had returned home to his own father's house (14:20).
15. Samson returned to his father's house because the Ashkelonites were after him (14:19b).
16. The Ashkelonites were after Samson because he had killed thirty of their men (14:19a).
17. Samson killed thirty men of Ashkelon because the Philistines had solved his riddle (14:18).
18. The Philistines solved Samson's riddle because they "plowed with his heifer" (14:15b–17,18b).
19. The Philistines "plowed with Samson's heifer" because she was his wife (14:10–15).
20. She was Samson's wife because he wanted her (14:1–3).
21. Samson wanted the Timnite woman because . . . Yahweh was seeking an occasion to confront the Philistines (14:4).[53]

Samson had a high calling directly from YHWH but took this high calling lightly. Instead of passionately pursuing purity and intimacy with YHWH, he went after foreign women. And yet God still used Samson, even his weaknesses and shortcomings, for YHWH's glory and the salvation of his people. This is, of course, a direct reflection of Israel.

Israel may hear these tales and think, "Why would God use Samson? How could Samson take his miraculous birth and high calling for granted? How could God use Samson's lust for 'the foreign' for YHWH's own glory?" And yet, Samson is a direct reflection of pre-exilic Israel.

Block said, "Through it all [Samson] seems totally oblivious to what God is trying to accomplish through him"[54]—even though it was spoken forth and promised by YHWH at his birth.

Israel, when God began a people through the miraculous opening of Sarah's womb, was set apart for a specific mission—to be a blessing to all nations. The nation had a miraculous birth with supernatural promises, and she lived as if she was totally oblivious to her identity and high

---

53. Block, *Judges*, 421–22.
54. Block, *Judges*, 423.

calling, except when she cried out for her own needs and desires. "With brilliant irony the narrator describes a free spirit, a rebel driven by selfish interests, doing whatever he pleases without any respect for his parents and with no respect for the claims of God on his life, but in the process he ends up doing the will of God"[55]—just like Israel.

Block said:

> One concludes that, left to himself, Samson would never have become involved in God's or even Israel's agenda; and, left to themselves, the Israelites would have been satisfied to continue to coexist with the Philistines. But Yahweh has other plans. He must preserve his people as a separate entity. Therefore, through his Spirit, God intervenes in Samson's life so that the agenda set for him in 13:5-7 may begin to be fulfilled. Accordingly, the narrator interprets Samson's trip to Timnah as an expression of divinely induced restlessness and the Timnite woman who catches his eye as an agent of Yahweh's grand design. This is verified in 14:4, in which the narrator writes that he [Yahweh] was seeking an opportunity to incite the Philistines and thereby disturb the comfortable status quo that existed between them and Israel.[56]

Similarly, God has been faithful to work through his people even when we are obstinate and unfaithful. He led Israel through her history toward the birth, life, death, resurrection, and ascension of Jesus. He has led his church these two thousand years to this moment, even through imperfect and often rebellious followers. How great is his faithfulness.

As this Timnite saga progresses, the performance repeatedly utilizes the verb "to see," which clarifies the fact that Samson is operating on appearance and for personal interest. This theme of seeing will continue through this Timnite section, and it becomes ironic at the end of Samson's life as he has his eyes plucked out. The word "to see" occurs fifteen times in chapters 1–12, nine times in the last five chapters, and seventeen times in these four chapters, 13–16. Interestingly, the word stops appearing after 14:11 when Samson is assigned a group of "companions." The word does not appear again until chapter 16 when he sees the prostitute in Gaza. Throughout Samson's activity of revenge, even at the very end, he is blind. During the rest of his career, he does what is right in his own eyes just like the rest of Israel in the following section of the book.

55. Block, *Judges*, 427.
56. Block, *Judges*, 424.

When Samson asks for a foreign wife, Samson's parents do not call Samson to loyalty to YHWH. They do not remind him that marrying outside is frowned upon by YHWH (Deut 7:1–5), nor do they say, "The LORD has called you to special Nazirite status within Israel. This is a step beyond compromising that call." They also do not say, "The LORD's agenda is for you to deliver us from the Philistine oppression, not to marry them" (13:5). All this remains unsaid. Samson's lust for women outside of the people of Israel is foreshadowed by Ibzan's outside marriage policy with his children. Samson and his parents seem to be totally insensitive to YHWH's purposes, character, and plans, despite everything that occurred in chapter 13. Samson may end up running around blind, but God sees his people and will work to establish his will for their lives.

The saga discussed above begins as Samson and his parents go to Timnah. Samson kills a lion with his bare hands, and later he returns to the carcass. Even though he is breaking basic Israelite purity laws by marrying an outsider, surely he won't break his specific Nazarite call by interacting with this corpse.

However, there was honey in the dead lion. How could he resist his eyes? He scoops honey out of the carcass and casually walks away while eating it. He even gives some of it to his parents, the honey's origin unbeknownst to them, making them impure. The holy deliverer is defiling his parents as they work toward this unholy wedding.

Bees do not normally develop a community of honey in a carcass. This is God's work, perhaps testing Samson or making Samson's lack of commitment clear. Also, bees do not normally "develop a community" in the Bible at all. They swarm. But the narrator chooses a word for "community" that almost always "refers to a company of people, usually the Israelites as a faith community, called to be agents of grace and light in the decadent world."[57] Samson denies his special status that was established for the deliverance of his own community and grabs some honey for himself.

The living lion was a test of his ability to receive the power of God. The dead lion was a test of his ability to abide in a faithful relationship with God and the people. Samson failed the second test.[58]

---

57. Block, *Judges*, 429.
58. Block, *Judges*, 429.

Samson then throws a party for his bride. This sort of party would have included drinking to excess. Did Samson remain true to his Nazirite vow in this area? Who knows.

Thirty men are assigned to him, whether as an honor or as a guard, and he asks them the riddle:

From-the-eater	out-came eat[s]
And-from-the-strong	out-came sweet[s][59]

Some commentators see the easy answer to the riddle to be "love" or some aspect of a sexual relationship.[60] If the easy answer is love, it is interesting that the answer to the riddle given back to Samson, "What is stronger than a lion, and what is sweeter than honey," may ironically point to Samson's own life. Love is sweeter than honey, and love will overpower Samson in the end, even when a lion was not strong enough to do so. "Despite Samson's great physical strength and the force of his Nazirite vow, he is completely helpless when confronted with the love of women."[61] The men force the answer to the riddle from Samson's wife and deliver the answer to an embittered Samson who accuses them of "plowing with his heifer."

Having lost the bet of the riddle, Samson goes to Ashkelon and kills thirty men and brings back their clothes. Angry, he goes to his father's house.

Samson returns to see his wife whom he had earlier referred to as his "heifer." This would have sounded as bad in that culture as it sounds to us. The word for heifer, *egla*, harkens back to Eglon from Judg 3. Indeed, when Samson returns with a goat to see his wife in chapter 15, he asks to go into her inner chambers just like Ehud had done with Eglon. Samson says, "I will go into my wife, the inner chamber." Ehud went into the inner chamber with Eglon and pierced him with the sword. Samson wanted to go into his heifer in her inner chambers. But her father had given her to another man.

Block said this concerning the ordeal of Samson's marriage:

> In the narrator's eyes, Samson represents the nation. This person—uniquely set apart, called, and gifted for divine service—not only fraternizes with the enemy, but he also seeks to live among them. But God is in control and the story ends exactly where he wanted it. Yahweh is provoking tension between Israel

---

59. Block, *Judges*, 432.
60. Niditch, *Judges*, 157.
61. Block, *Judges*, 435.

and the Philistines. Unaware of their roles in divine providence the characters are creating the very situation Yahweh had planned. At the end of [chapter 14] (1) the work against the Philistines has begun, (2) Samson is back in his father's house, and (3) the adventure in mixed marriage has collapsed. The woman has betrayed her husband, the husband is calling his wife disparaging names, and the father-in-law has given his daughter to another man. What was planned as an interracial marriage turns into war![62]

Will Samson thus turn into the great military leader? Will he live up to his holy calling? Nope. He pitches a fit that he cannot go into the inner chamber of his heifer, declaring, "This time I will be absolved of all guilt from the Philistines when I execute evil (*rāʿâ*) with them."[63]

Samson ties the tails of some foxes together with torches and sends them the fields of the Philistines, who in turn burn Samson's wife and father-in-law. Samson lashes out against them for further revenge, and then he runs and hides. This judge is anything but a leader of the people. He is only focused on himself.

Ironically, Samson's wife had nagged the answer to Samson's riddle away from him so that she would *not* be burned with her father.

The Philistines gather for revenge.

Judah intervenes.

Judah is the first tribe YHWH calls upon to rid the land of the Canaanites in Judges chapter 1. From their line comes the Davidic line. What will these super-Israelites do? God wanted to incite Israel against the Philistines so that Israel might be delivered. Perhaps Judah will rally behind Samson in all their glory!

They do rally. But they rally only to capture Samson on behalf of their oppressors in order to maintain the status quo under Philistine rule.

Where has the downward spiral of the book of Judges led? "The Judahites are willing not only to substitute the rule of the Philistines for the rule of Yahweh, but also to sacrifice the divinely appointed leader to preserve the status quo."[64]

The dialogue is comical. The Philistines say, "We want to do to him what he did to us." Samson says, "I only did to them what they did to

---

62. Block, *Judges*, 438.
63. Block, *Judges*, 440.
64. Block, *Judges*, 444.

me!" There is no sense of the will of God but only turn-for-turn personal vengeance.

Judah hands Samson over, and the new ropes with which they tied him melt off of him by an act of YHWH. The Spirit rushes upon him, and he reaches out and grabs part of a corpse—a fresh jawbone of a donkey. He proceeds to act in the power of the Spirit, utilizing a tool that is totally contrary to his Nazirite vow.

A fresh jawbone would seem to be less valuable as a weapon than a dried out and hardened jawbone, but God seems to work to give Samson victory even as Samson is actively breaking the special covenant YHWH had made with him.

Again, this sounds just like Israel. God is always working in the lives of humans who do not deserve his help. If God only helped those who deserved his help, then no one would ever be helped by God.

With the jawbone he strikes down a thousand men. This certainly recalls the story of Shamgar, who struck down six hundred Philistines with an ox-goad.

Samson claims all the credit for himself in his little poem, and he asks God, "Are you going to let your servant die of thirst now?"

The sense of Samson's petition is, "I just did all this for you, and you are just going to let me die?" Samson will not cry out for God's people who suffer under the rule of the Philistines, but he will call out for water for himself.

Samson's "fear" of falling into "uncircumcised hands" is laughable. He is willing to go to bed with uncircumcised people and defile himself with carcasses for a taste of honey, but in this moment, we are to believe that he is so very concerned about purity and ritual issues.

Samson sounds like Israel in the wilderness: "Did you save us just so we would die in the wilderness of thirst?" And God graciously responds to Samson just as he did for Israel in the wilderness—he brings water out of a rock, further identifying Samson as a representative of Israel.

Samson's narcissism expresses itself even in the name he gives to the place, something like "the spring of the caller" or "the spring of the namer." He seems to name the place after himself, "the namer," rather than after YHWH, "the provider." He does not call the place "YHWH satisfies" or "YHWH brings victory." He names it after himself, "the spring of the one who calls out."

This chapter ends resembling the formulaic conclusion of a cycle in Judges. Samson judged Israel for twenty years in the days of the

Philistines. With a summary statement like this, we would expect a new cycle to begin, but that is just another aborted hopeful expectation in Samson's story.

THE SAGA OF THE GAZITE WOMEN: 16:1–31

We begin again with Samson's eyes. He sees a prostitute in Gaza.

Why was Samson so far into Philistine territory, forty miles from his home? The only logical answer is that this man just does what he wants. He is Samson. Who is to stop him?

Samson sleeps with a prostitute and somehow escapes a trap set for him by picking up massive gates and carrying them forty miles, uphill to Hebron—the territory of Caleb deep in the heart of Israelite territory. This time the narrator is silent about the empowerment of the Spirit. At any rate, the Samson story has now connected itself to Othniel (through Hebron's connection to Caleb), Ehud (heifer), Shamgar (Philistines), and Gideon (birth narrative). Samson is now a national fugitive of the Philistines known in their southernmost great city and not just in Timnah.

Samson falls in love with another woman from Gaza—Delilah. Samson cannot stay away from unbelieving foreign women, and his inability to learn from his past will be his undoing, just as it will be for Israel.

This section of the Samson cycle is rich with the theme of testing. The first three tests are as follows:

> First, the Philistine lords test Delilah: is she a Philistine, or is she Samson's lover? Second, Delilah tests Samson: Does he love her, or is he just teasing her? Like the riddle in 14:14, for Samson this test becomes a trap. Third, Yahweh tests Samson: Will he remain true to his Nazirite vow (vv. 17, 20)? Verses 15–17 contain the keys to the development of this motif as all three tests come together and Samson admits that the game is more than a test of love . . .[65]

Judges 16:15–17 reads:

> And she said to him, "How can you say, 'I love you,' when your heart is not with me? You have mocked me these three times, and you have not told me where your great strength lies." And when she pressed him hard with her words day after day, and urged him, his soul was vexed to death. And he told her all his

---

65. Block, *Judges*, 452.

heart, and said to her, "A razor has never come upon my head, for I have been a Nazirite to God from my mother's womb. If my head is shaved, then my strength will leave me, and I shall become weak and be like any other man."

Samson knows what is at stake. He has always known about his special calling. He only takes it as seriously as he must in order to maintain his special status and power. But he is even willing to give that up for his love of this foreign woman.

There are other tests in this section:

> Fourth Yahweh tests Dagon: Can he stand up for himself and his people (vv. 23–30)? Fifth, Samson tests God: Will he intervene to defend his agent in the end (vv. 28–30)? Indeed, in this section every speech is a test. As for Samson, the principal character, although he is able to shed the ropes and the web that bound his hair, he fails everyone's tests, ultimately being trapped in his own words.[66]

Only YHWH passes all of the tests.

The Timnites used Samson's wife to get the answer to Samson's riddle, and the lords of Philistia use a woman do get the answer to the riddle of Samson.[67] They offer to pay her in silver over three times the weight of gold Gideon received from his victory over the Midianite kings. Everything in the story of Samson is over the top.

Much could be said of Delilah's four attempts to get Samson to tell her his secret. I will offer just two highlights. First, Samson is tied in fresh and undried sinews, so that he once more comes into contact with a corpse. Samson toys with his Nazirite vow when he lies and says that binding him with fresh sinews would render him weak. Second, the Hebrew terms used for the fastening of Samson's hair in the loom—"to fasten, tighten" and, "peg, pin"—link this account with the account in 4:21 of Jael and Sisera.[68] This connection ominously paints Delilah as looming over Samson with death in her hands.

How many times does Delilah have to do exactly what Samson promises will rob him of his strength before he sees her as a spy? How could one make sense of how he continues to offer himself up to her?

---

66. Block, *Judges*, 452.
67. Block, *Judges*, 454.
68. Block, *Judges*, 458n409.

After she betrays him three times, why would he give her the true secret to his strength? There is no rationale behind his lust for this foreign woman.

Just like Samson, Israel returned again and again to the Canaanite gods, toying with her special calling. The book of Judges has demonstrated the cycle of how, over and over, Israel's love for those gods delivered Israel to oppression. But she would not learn. She continued to throw her special calling away for a lust for foreign gods.

Block says, "Samson's problem with his vow is not so much that he willfully violates it; he simply does not take it seriously."[69] Samson claims in verse 17, "I have been a Nazirite to God from my mother's womb," but the audience has seen him act flippantly with this Nazirite status throughout his life.

Israel claims to be the covenant people of YHWH, and yet the audience has seen her act flippantly with their covenant status throughout the book of Judges. The original audiences of the book of Judges knew the consequences of the nation's Samson-like behavior intimately. Any modern-day follower of YHWH will also recognize the same pattern in his own life, just as Paul proclaimed in Rom 7:19–25.

Samson's use of the generic word for God instead of the covenantal name is telling. Samson handed over his special relationship with YHWH to a foreign woman. The tragedy of Samson's life was his lack of covenant faithfulness to YHWH and to the covenant people, not his arrest and torture.

Similarly, the exile of Israel was not the tragedy of the nation. The tragedy of the nation of Israel was when she gave herself over to other gods.

After Delilah had his hair cut, Samson arose to fight off the Philistine men, but he did not know that the LORD had left him.

What a horrible statement.

He did not know that the LORD had left him.

This calls to mind Zedekiah who would not listen to the counsel of Jeremiah. Second Kings 24:20 says, "For because of the anger of the LORD it came to the point in Jerusalem and Judah that he cast them out from his presence. And Zedekiah rebelled against the king of Babylon." Zedekiah did not know that the LORD had left him, and so he stood against Babylon. He also was captured, and his eyes were put out after he

---

69. Block, *Judges*, 459.

was forced to see his family and rulers murdered in front of him (2 Kgs 24:18–20; 25:6–7; Jer 39 and 52). Block said of Samson:

> Overnight this man is transformed from one whose life is governed by sight and whose actions are determined by what is right in his own eyes into a blind man with eyes gouged out. Overnight a life of coming and going as he pleases turns into a life of bondage and imprisonment. Overnight the person who had spent his life insulting and humiliating others becomes the object of their humiliation. Overnight a man with the highest conceivable calling, the divinely commissioned agent of deliverance for Israel, is cast down to the lowest position imaginable: grinding flour for others in prison.[70]

Samson was imprisoned in the foreign land of Gaza. "Like Samson, the nation will be seized, blinded, exiled, imprisoned, and humiliated with forced labor."[71] Samson is the picture of Israel:

> Samson is a *Wunderkind*, miraculously born by the will of God.
>
> Samson is called to a high life of separation and devotion to Yahweh.
>
> Samson has a rash, opportunistic, and immature personality.
>
> Samson is inexorably drawn to foreign women, like Israel was drawn to foreign gods (both "play the harlot").
>
> Samson experiences the bondage and oppression of the enemy.
>
> Samson cries out to Yahweh from his oppression.
>
> Samson is blinded (cf. 1 Sam 3:1–3).
>
> Samson is abandoned by Yahweh and does not know it.[72]

Block pointed out, "Yahweh obviously knows that Samson has been called. Manoah and his wife know, the narrator knows, and the reader knows,"[73] and we find out later that Samson was indeed aware of his calling. But "there is little evidence that he has any respect for his divine vocation. On the contrary, the narrator notes his repeated deliberate violation of the call."[74] He handles corpses (forbidden by the Nazorite vow),

---

70. Block, *Judges*, 462.
71. Block, *Judges*, 462.
72. Block, *Judges*, 392.
73. Block, *Judges*, 396.
74. Block, *Judges*, 396.

is bound by fresh sinews, grabs a fresh donkey jawbone, and even gives his secret away to the woman who has three times betrayed him.

Israel seems to be acutely aware of her position as the people of YHWH. They discuss the works of old—the exodus salvation and the giving of the Law are always remembered by the people (see Gideon). But they do not seem to take the covenant agreement seriously, and instead they lust after foreign gods over and over, though the results are always the same.

Samson is done. No longer will he see. Now all that is left of his strength is spent grinding grain for the enemy. But the narrator gives us a brilliantly penned stroke of hope. The narrator says, "But the hair on his head began to grow again after it had been shaved" (16:22). "'With a single stroke of the artist's brush the ominous skies give way to the promise of brilliant sunshine; all is not lost, for hair grows back.'"[75]

Samson is brought out before a crowd, and he asks God for one more favor.

He acknowledges the name of YHWH!

He cries for help!

Are his last thoughts for his nation? Is he saddened by his life spent on lust and vengeance?!

Nope. Block said, "He seems totally oblivious to the national emergency and unconcerned about the divine agenda he was raised up to fulfill . . . All he seeks is personal vengeance."[76]

Earlier he had called for help because he was thirsty and did not want to die with the uncircumcised Philistines. Now he cries out with his last words, "Let me die with the Philistines!"

Samson killed more Philistines in his death than he did in his life. "This is a tragic note. This man, with his unprecedentedly high calling and with his extraordinary divine gifts, has wasted his life. Indeed, he accomplishes more for God dead than alive."[77]

Unlike the prosperous Canaanized judges before him, he dies with no children, and the only donkey in his story is the corpse he used for vengeance. His story ends with satirical hope. His whole family comes to receive his body, and he is buried in the tomb of his father. He judged Israel twenty years.

What do we learn from the life of Samson?

75. Block, *Judges*, 463, citing Crenshaw, *Samson*, 501.

76. Block, *Judges*, 467–68.

77. Block, *Judges*, 469.

If anything good came from Samson's life, it was due to the grace and unending relational move of God and the powerful presence of his Spirit. God is faithful to his covenant, and he is faithful in moving salvation history forward.

If anything good came from Israel's life, it was due to the grace and unending relational move of God and the powerful presence of his Spirit. God is faithful to his covenant, and he is faithful in moving salvation history forward.

If anything good will come from our lives, it will be due to the grace and unending relational move of God and the powerful presence of the Spirit of Christ. "Yahweh is determined to build his people. Even if she becomes her own worst enemy and her human leaders fail her . . . in the end, by the grace of God she will triumph."[78]

The Chiastic Chaos of Canceling Covenant: Judg 17–21

This final section of the book of Judges is rough. At the same time, this section is the highlight of the magnificent literary work that is the book of Judges. This final section abandons the overarching, deteriorating pattern of the book of Judges. However, the performance flows from the previous section with the echo from 13:2, "Now there was a man . . ."

The book began with drips of scathing satire—"Who shall go first before us against the Canaanites? Judah will go! They are awesome! Remember how they conquered Hebron and Jerusalem and all of those Philistine strongholds!"

Except that they never did.

Actually, we remember that their kings were part of the reason Israel went into exile. They fell prey to their own glory just like the Canaanite king they did actually conquer—Adoni-Bezek.

In this final section of Judges, what might have been seen as a satirical drip transforms into a veritable flood of caustic critique of the pre-monarchial tribal confederation of Israel.

The book closes with two stories tightly knitted together through chiastic echoes. In 17:1—18:31 a Levite travels from Bethlehem (A) to Ephraim (B), with the echoing refrain given in the following order: "In those days there was no king in Israel and everyone did what was right in his own eyes" (A); "In those days there was no king in Israel" (B).

---

78. Block, *Judges*, 472.

In 19:1—21:25 we get these aspects of the story in reverse. A Levite travels from Ephraim (B) to Bethlehem (A) with the echoing refrain given in the following order: "In those days there was no king in Israel" (B); "In those days there was no king in Israel and everyone did what was right in his own eyes" (A)—giving the chiastic pattern ABBA.

A. Bethlehem	A. No king in Israel everyone does right in his own eyes
B. Ephraim	B. No king in Israel
B. Ephraim	B. No king in Israel
A. Bethlehem	A. No king in Israel everyone does right in his own eyes

Bethlehem is identified as "Bethlehem in Judah." Ephraim is a common name for the Northern Kingdom of Israel. This connection of religious ruin in the north and moral/ethical ruin in the south makes it clear that all of Israel, both the north and the south, "suffer from the same spiritual disease."[79]

These sections have other connections as well. For instance, "Both accounts conclude with a reference to Shiloh" (18:31; 21:19–24); "In both accounts military contingents consisting of six hundred men played a critical role."[80]

After reaching the lowest point in Israel's cycle of idolatry, marked by the troubling tales of Jephthah and Samson, and witnessing the complete breakdown of Israel's attempts to seek aid, as well as God's refusal to be manipulated for their salvation, the tradition presents a structured portrayal of utter societal chaos. What's particularly striking is the connection of this chaos to the descendants of Moses and Aaron, the leaders of the exodus.

The first section (17:1—18:31) depicts the culmination of Israel's idolatry. The tribe of Dan, instead of relying on YHWH to help them conquer the land from the Canaanites, resorts to stealing an idolatrous Levite from their countryman. Ironically, the countryman's name is "Who is like YHWH," which mocks his actions of establishing a false place of worship with an idol, an ephod, and an unfaithful priest. Dan further exacerbates the situation by attacking a peaceful area and settling there, disregarding the land allocation described in Josh 19, and erecting an idolatrous sanctuary. This represents the low point of Israel's spiritual decay.

---

79. Block, *Judges*, 485.
80. Block, *Judges*, 475.

The second section (19:1—21:25) presents Israel's moral ruin. They become just like Sodom—a community that deserved immediate destruction by fire from heaven. The people seem to understand the atrocity of Gibeah, and they even seek YHWH's instruction for the battle against Benjamin.

And here is found perhaps the clearest of satirical remarks of the entire book.

Israel finally assembles as one man to attack the social influence of Canaan and to rid the land of this evil. But when they are finally assembled to attack the great evil, the evil is Israel herself, even the beloved Benjamin.

Israel asks YHWH, "Who is to go up first to fight the people of Benjamin?" This is a clear echo of chapter 1, "Who is to go up first to fight the Canaanites?" Just as in chapter 1, Judah is called to go up first against the Canaanite evil. Benjamin is directly identified with the Canaanites.

One of the most surprising revelations in the book of Judges occurs when one of the spiritual leaders of this epoch is revealed by name. Judges 20:28 says, "Phinehas the son of Eleazar, son of Aaron, ministered before [the ark of the covenant of God] in those days." Phinehas's service situates this event well within one hundred years after Israel began her conquest of the land under Joshua.

Phinehas was alive and old enough to go into battle in Num 31, and he was old enough to spear through the bodies of a man and woman simultaneously in Num 25. Indeed, Phinehas activates a tradition of purifying Israel from idolatry through violence—purging Israel of the evil in her midst. Perhaps the tradition mentions Phinehas at this point only to activate ideas of violent purification, and no chronological conclusions are supposed to be made, but the earlier connection to Moses' descendant in the previous section argues otherwise.

If any chronological connection is to be made, then within this last section of the book that summarizes the depth of Israel's depravity we discover that she was at her worst within one generation after Joshua died.

Whatever may be the exact chronology of the historical events discussed in the book of Judges, the tradition's presentation at this point highlights the downward spiral of covenant unfaithfulness. And the tradition underscores that the worst of the community's unfaithfulness to YHWH—the very epitome of religious and social collapse—may have occurred within the first generation after Joshua.

The final performance of Judges has so structured the tradition that the hearer experiences a dreadfully deep pit of apostasy—three hundred years of declining judges—only to look up and discover that the worst of the filth actually bubbles up right near the surface, within the lifetime of Phinehas.

Only once after Joshua's leadership did Israel rally against the influence of the Canaanites, and the Canaanite-spirit was manifested within herself. Even then, despite rallying together in condemnation of the gang rape of a concubine, the tribes unanimously consented to the abduction and violation of six hundred virgins from among their own people. In those days there was no king in Israel, and everyone did what was right in their own eyes. Israel needed no king to lead her into the depths of her depravity.

Religious Ruin 17:1—18:31

The first half of this final section deals with the Danites, the tribe of Samson. Just as the Samson cycle focused more on the judge's private life than on national/tribal events, this final section will focus on glimpses of normal Israelite lives.

Starting with chapter 17 we are introduced to a thieving son named Micayah-Yahu, or "Micah" for short. His name means, "Who is like YHWH?" with the expected answer "no one!"

He steals eleven hundred shekels of silver from his mother, which "is equal to the amount each of the Philistine governors had given Delilah as a reward for delivering Samson into their hands (16:5)."[81] After hearing about his mother's curse spoken against the unknown thief, Micah returns the silver, and his mom blesses him by YHWH. Maybe this mom is a devoted YHWH worshiper! She named her son "Who is like YHWH," and she blesses him by the name! She even consecrates the money to YHWH! However, any suspected devotion to YHWH is short-lived.

She immediately gives two hundred shekels back to her son, instructing him to take his cut to make an idol. Two hundred shekels would not have made a very impressive idol. Micah's later words in chapter 18, "my gods which I have made," demonstrate that this was either an explicit Canaanite image, or at best, it was syncretistic. Not only is Micah's mother a false worshiper of YHWH, but she is a cheapskate of an idolater!

---

81. Block, *Judges*, 478.

Likely, the ephod and the other cultic devices were made as a rival or replacement of the high priest's ephod "and the Urim and Thummim which YHWH sanctioned for oracular purposes (Exod 28:30)."[82] Finally, Micah set up one of his own sons as a priest. Every action of Micah and his mother stands totally contrary to covenant faithfulness. Block expressed the satirical subtext of this opening:

> Looking back on vv. 1–5, the incongruities and ironies in the account produce a farcical tone in this paragraph. A woman, who, in her namelessness represents any female head of the household in Israel, openly confesses her devotion to Yahweh in blessing and dedications, but her actions run directly counter to that confession. Her son, who bears a thoroughly orthodox name, commits the ultimate crime, establishing a cult system in direct violation of Yahweh's incomparability, as expressed by the name, and Yahweh's explicit command not to worship any gods besides him nor to make any physical representations of deity. The tragedy is that the actors do not realize the incongruity of their actions.[83]

There was no king in Israel in those days, and everyone did what was right in their own eyes. Something like the form of Judges we have was performed well into the divided kingdom, at least after the exile of the northern kingdom.[84] Judges is the second book in the Former Prophets—a prophetic explanation of how the history of Israel led to exile. The book of Judges explicitly demonstrates that none of this evil can be attributed solely to any king or royal line. With or without a king the human condition leans toward apostasy. Micah and his mom represent all of Israel. "Everyone" was treating their devotion to YHWH in like fashion.

Verse 7 introduces a young Levite sojourning in Ephraim, seemingly aimlessly, having come from Bethlehem in Judah. This nameless Levite, just as Micah and his mother, represents the greater group—all Levites. Micah invites this young boy to be his "father and priest." He promises to pay the Levite and give him a place to stay. The Levite stays,

---

82. Block, *Judges*, 482.

83. Block, *Judges*, 482.

84. See Judg 18:30: "There the Danites set up for themselves the idol, and Jonathan son of Gershom, the son of Moses, and his sons were priests for the tribe of Dan until the time of the captivity of the land." The "time of the captivity of the land" probably refers to the time after 734–32 BC when the neo-Assyrians conquered the region and removed the Danite population (Block, *Judges*, 66). The form of this performance, then, is at least after this date.

and though he is promised to be a father to Micah, he becomes like one of Micah's sons.

Micah believes that with a bona fide Levite serving as his priest, YHWH will now favor him, as though the presence of the Levite acts as a lucky charm, making YHWH more amicable. The Levite sacrifices his call to holiness for security, status, and money. Block said:

> Instead of serving as an agent of life and peace, revering Yahweh and standing in awe of his name, offering truthful and righteous instruction, walking with Yahweh in peace and uprightness, turning Micah back from iniquity, preserving knowledge, and serving as a messenger of Yahweh of hosts, this Levite has himself apostatized. He has lent his support to the perversion of his countryman, failed to keep Yahweh's ways, and demonstrated partiality to this man with money (cf. Mal 2:1–9). The religious establishment in Israel has been thoroughly infected with the Canaanite disease.[85]

This performance of the tradition behind Judges chapter 18 intentionally echoes and activates a sort of type scene from Num 12:16—14:45 and Deut 1:19–46[86] in which landless Israelites dispatch scouts into the hill country who return with a report eliciting a response from the people. Of course, the narrative of the scouts in Judges varies from the other two examples.

In Judges, the search for land and the sending of scouts are not sanctioned by YHWH. Indeed, they seem to represent a blatant rejection of the commands of YHWH to take the land he allotted to the tribe. This parody of the larger tradition sits ironically in the period of time in which everyone was doing what was right in their own eyes. There is no human king on the throne, and YHWH's reign and statutes are disregarded.

The older traditions of spying out the lands stem from the initiative of YHWH as he moves according to his covenant with the nation, but in Judges a tribe tries to recreate the past as they see fit in their own eyes. In this case, the greater tradition is activated as a rhetorical foil standing behind the events being performed. YHWH initiates the scouting mission in Num 13, but the people rebel against YHWH's desire to go and take the land. Here, the people are leaving the land they were called to conquer and respond favorably to the scouts' reports to go and conquer land not allotted to them. The activated tradition highlights Israel's (and

---

85. Block, *Judges*, 490.
86. See chart in Block, *Judges*, 491–92.

all of humanity's) tendency to do what is right in their own eyes—often the very opposite of God's calling.

The Danites seemed to have had at least a temporary occupation in their original allotment. In Judg 1:34–36 the Danites were driven out of their allotment into the hill country by the Amorites. Their response at this later stage in the book of Judges is completely humanly derived— "Instead of confessing their sin of unbelief and appealing to Yahweh for aid, they do what is right in their own eyes."[87]

Another reconnaissance mission from the tradition becomes pertinent as we approach Judg 18:2. Certain elements in Judg 18:2 bear resemblance to details in Josh 2:1, where Joshua dispatches scouts to Jericho, specifically to the house of Rahab the prostitute.

In this case, the activation of the larger tradition implies that the house of Micah is identified with the house of the prostitute in Joshua. Block elaborated, "This interpretation certainly suits the overall tenor of the book, especially in view of the narrator's earlier application of the language of prostitution ("playing the harlot") to Israel's idolatrous practices (2:17; 8:27; 8:33)."[88]

The Danites recognize the voice of the Levite. Perhaps he performed some sort of priestly duty that could have been overheard and recognized. At any rate, the Danites ask the Levite a series of questions. Who brought you here? What are you doing in this place? Why are you here? Those are good questions for both parties. The answers from either party would reveal their apostasy. YHWH did not send any of them. Whatever they are doing at Micah's house, no one is walking in obedience to the covenant with YHWH. There is no good reason for any of them to be there.[89]

The Danites treat YHWH like a common deity, seeking a blessing for the endeavors they had already decided upon (like Balak's summoning of Balaam to curse Israel in Num 22).

The Levite gives the Danites what sounds like a promising answer: "The course on which you are going is before the LORD." However, to those hearing the current performance, it rings with an ominous tone. YHWH is indeed watching over these acts of apostasy and disobedience.[90]

---

87. Block, *Judges*, 495.
88. Block, *Judges*, 496.
89. See Block, *Judges*, 497, for a discussion on these questions.
90. Block, *Judges*, 498.

The Danite scouts leave and visit Laish and see a good and prosperous and peaceful land, far-removed from any oversight, ripe for plundering. They report back to the tribe encouraging an attack.

The Danite force of six hundred (a significant number also the second part of this final section of the book of Judges) travels toward the fight. The five scouts report to the rest of the force concerning the ephod and the other idolatrous items, so they stop at Micah's house. The gang decides to take the items, but they run into the Levite who asks, "What are you doing?" They invite him to come and be a father and a priest to them (like Micah had offered him before), saying, "Is it not better that you serve a tribe and a clan in Israel as priest rather than just one man's household?" And the priest is glad. He grabs the ephod, the other household gods, and the carved image and goes along with the people. The Levite had betrayed his station before God, and now he betrays his idolatrous adopted family.

Micah summons a group of soldiers to go after his priest and his gods, much as a judge might rally an army to fight off foreign oppression.[91] But Micah is not pursuing salvation from foreign oppressors or faithfulness to YHWH. He is chasing after fellow Israelites so that he might reclaim his idols and false priest.

The Danites threaten to kill Micah and his family if he persists, and Micah retreats. The thief from the beginning of this episode has become the victim of having his household robbed of his most valuable items. Indeed, one of the objects stolen from him was made from the very silver he had stolen.[92]

The performer repeatedly mentions the peacefulness of the people attacked by the Danites, evoking sympathy for the Canaanites. The Danites destroy the people and the town according to the *herem*, and they proceed to set up their cult center.

In a surprising turn, the Levite is finally named—Johnathan, son of Gershom, the son of Moses. The term for "son" could mean grandson or descendent, but it is noteworthy that only two generations removed from Moses are identified, and it is more than surprising that a descendent of Moses, especially one so close in time if the term is to be rendered "son" and not descendent, would break from the faith of the iconic leader of the Hebrew people.

---

91. Block, *Judges*, 508.
92. Block, *Judges*, 508–9.

Judges 2:10 says that after Joshua's generation, "there arose another generation after them who did not know the LORD or the work that he had done for Israel." This identification of the grandson of Moses, the generation after Joshua, would confirm this timeline. The note about Phinehas in the following section further suggests this short time span between the death of Joshua and Judg 17–21.

The apex of apostasy was not found centuries after Israel entered the promised land but in the very next generation after Joshua. About this episode Block said, "There is not an admirable character in the chapters. No one displays any devotion to Yahweh; no one demonstrates any concern for national well-being; no one behaves with any integrity. The Israelites have become as shameless in their religious expression and ethical conduct as they need to be to get their way."[93]

The apostasy of Dan continued in this way, at least as long as the house of God was in Shiloh.

Societal Ruin 19:1—21:25

Chapter 19 opens the "longest coherent account in the book."[94] The only named character is Phinehas. When Phinehas is named, "it catches the reader by surprise and has a shocking rhetorical effect. Phinehas the priest is the grandson of Aaron, which means that the events transpiring in this chapter occurred within one hundred years of the death of Moses and probably within decades after the death of Joshua."[95] The namelessness of the rest of the major characters allows them to stand in as representatives of Israel at large. "The Levite represents every Levite; the concubine, every woman; [etc.]."[96]

In the end, the Levite will dismember his concubine to call Israel together as one man so that Israel might "dismember herself."[97] Block argued, "This episode represents the climactic and supreme demonstration of the Canaanization of Israel."[98] She acts like Canaanites, and she rallies against herself just as she was supposed to have done against the

93. Block, *Judges*, 514.
94. Block, *Judges*, 517.
95. Block, *Judges*, 517.
96. Block, *Judges*, 517.
97. Block, *Judges*, 518.
98. Block, *Judges*, 519.

real Canaanites. As the tradition evoked pity for the Canaanites in Laish in the last episode, we cheer the holy war against the Israelite tribe of Benjamin in this episode.

The only time YHWH shows up as a director of any human action is in 20:18, 23, 27–28. All other decisions and moves are done without consulting or hearing from YHWH, and these decisions serve the satirical purpose of Judges as Israel is painted as one who continually becomes what YHWH called her to fight against.

After she defeats the Benjaminites for the gang rape of the Levite's concubine, they end up sanctioning the raping of six hundred Israelite virgins.

Block said, "In this final composition Israel discovers her greatest enemy, and the enemy is in her very own midst."[99] Indeed, Judges leaves Israel looking completely ignorant of the fact that she is circling the drain of her ongoing tendency to become what she is supposed to battle. Even as the eleven tribes battle against Benjamin for the raping of the one, they quickly become what they fought against in sanctioning the raping of hundreds. The comparisons of Gibeah to Sodom are so stark they need not be rehearsed. Israel has become an icon of godlessness.

In 19:1–9 a Levite travels from Ephraim to Bethlehem to retrieve his concubine who was either unfaithful to him or angry with him. Regardless, one might ask, "Why does this nameless Levite have need of a concubine, a second-hand wife?"

The father of the concubine is happy to see the Levite and pours out his hospitality on the priest for many days. The major role for the father's hospitality is to act as a foil to the lack of hospitality of the citizens of Gibeah, and to work toward the overall flow of the plot through the theme of the waning day. "In this chapter timing is everything, and it is the unfortunate timing of the Levite's departure from his father-in-law's house that precipitates the crisis that follows."[100]

The Levite's entourage leaves and comes to Jebus, that is Jerusalem. Judges 1:8 said that "the men of Judah fought against Jerusalem and captured it and struck it with the edge of the sword and set the city on fire." If they had really done so, the Levite and his concubine would have found an Israelite city for refuge. On the other hand, we will discover that

---

99. Block, *Judges*, 519.
100. Block, *Judges*, 527.

an Israelite town is not always safer than a Canaanite town when Israel herself has been Canaanized.

In Gibeah no one is found to take in the Levite and his company until an old man from the hill country of Ephraim brings them out of the town square and into his house, providing the expected and appropriate hospitality. Just as in Sodom in Gen 19, men come pounding on the door demanding the male visitor in order to rape him (in Genesis there were two strangers).

These men in Gibeah are called "men of the sons of Belial." This term is found sixteen other times in the OT for "murderers, rapists, false witnesses, corrupt priests, drunks, boors, ungrateful and selfish folk, rebels, those who lead others into idolatry and who do not know Yahweh."[101]

The host tries to talk the men out of their lust for the Levite, and he offers his own daughter and the Levite's concubine to the men to do to them whatever they please—literally, "do to them what is good in your eyes." This phrase connects the entire episode to the refrain that helps to hold Judg 17–18 and 19–21 together—In those days there was no king in Israel and everyone did what was right in their own eyes.

Lot also offered women in the place of men in Gen 19 (offering his two daughters), but in that story the supernatural strangers struck the worthless men blind. The host's honor and obligation to a male guest apparently supersedes his devotion to his own daughter, and in this case, the host expected the same commitment from the Levite concerning his concubine.

The text is not clear concerning who grabbed the concubine and threw her outside to the mob. Since the Levite is the main character of the overall episode, and since he does not seem to demonstrate any care for the woman the next day, he may likely be the culprit. Indeed, the next morning he gets up to leave "to continue on his way," but, "Behold! Surprise! There was his concubine!" Fallen at the doorway with her hands on the threshold. He was on his way to leave, presumably without her, and he found her on his way out.

This poor woman. "They knew her" and "they abused her" all night until morning. And at dawn "they discarded her."

She drug herself to the door and stretched out her hands to the threshold for safety, unable to knock or cry out for help.

---

101. Block, *Judges*, 535.

That morning the Levite said to her, "Get up, let's go. But no one answered. Then the man put her on his donkey and set out for home." He is not even called her husband at this point in the narrative. He is but her master.

This last account offers a final poignant example of the ongoing theme of the broken relationship between men and women in this season of Israel. Block explained:

> The narrator here describes a social system in which men rule over women in the worst sense of the phrase and sacrifice them for their own interests rather than providing responsible leadership and sacrificing themselves for the best interests of women. This is cancerous patriarchy expressed according to Canaanite standards. The Levite had preferred Gibeah over Jebus to avoid the dangers of Canaanism, only to discover that Canaan had invaded his own world.[102]

Division between the sexes is one of the first and most clear marks of the impact of sin on the world. Adam tried to pass his guilt over to Eve, and Eve was told, "He will rule over you, and your desire will be for him." Just as sin desired Cain, women will desire to usurp power over men even as men lord power over women. Sin has brought division between the foundation of the image of God—male and female. In the time of the Judges, this aspect of sin's effect on the world is fully manifested.

The following scene is difficult, and it calls to mind 1 Sam 11:7—"Then he took a team of oxen and he cut them up and he sent throughout the territory of Israel by the hand of messengers, saying, 'Anyone who does not go out after Saul and after Samuel, thus it shall be done to his oxen.' Then the dread of the Lord fell on the people, and they went out as one man."

The Levite carves up his concubine—the one whom he threw to a mob to be raped to death. There is no recorded threat similar to the one described in 1 Sam 11:7, though perhaps the ritual of dismembering an animal or person and sending the body parts to various recipients was representative of some sort of custom of marshalling soldiers. A Mari document, dating to the eighteenth century BCE, discusses the dismemberment and disbursement of a prisoner in order to strike enough fear into the people in order to get them to gather for a campaign.[103]

---

102. Block, *Judges*, 543.
103. Block, *Judges*, 546.

The atrocious act of the Levite worked. Chapter 20 finds "all of Israel from Dan to Beersheba and from the land of Gilead" gathered "as one man and assembled before YHWH in Mizpah." Block observed:

> Viewed within the context of the book as a whole, it is truly remarkable that this nameless Levite from an obscure place in Ephraim was able to accomplish what none of the divinely called and empowered deliverers had been able to do. Not even Deborah and Barak had been able to galvanize support and mobilize the military resources of the nation to this extent.[104]

Israel is finally gathered together as they should have been, and they are gathered to rid the land of Canaanite atrocity. But the atrocity is from within.

The Levite describes what happened in Gibeah to the congregation, expressing no concern for his concubine and transforming the events into a "self-centered apologia."[105] The Levite describes the series of events something like this: the men of Gibeah (the Levite does not discuss why they were at Gibeah in the first place) wanted to kill him (not rape him?), and somehow they got a hold of his concubine instead and raped her. And she died.

As a member of the priestly line, he makes no reference to YHWH or to the covenant. After this interesting account, the Levite leaves the story and never returns.

This Levite, not directed or raised up by YHWH and not full of the Spirit, did what the other judges could not do—galvanize the entire nation to concerted military action.[106] Or perhaps the performance makes it evident that YHWH was behind the call of the people and not this nameless, compassionless Levite.

The tribes make selections by lot, which could indicate a less personal approach to YHWH than what we read in Judg 1:1–2. They ask for the men of Gibeah to be handed over, and the Benjamites declare "their solidarity with the rapists rather than 'the assembly of God,' thus setting the stage for a direct military confrontation."[107]

---

104. Block, *Judges*, 550.
105. Block, *Judges*, 554.
106. Block, *Judges*, 554.
107. Block, *Judges*, 556.

The Benjamites gather a rather large army of their own, including seven hundred men "constrained in the right hand" just like Ehud the Benjamite.

The activation of Ehud in this narrative prompts us to temporarily halt our recounting of the civil war events and delve into the recurring themes we've encountered thus far in the book of Judges.

Now that the time frame of Judges has been totally dismantled with the mention of Moses' grandson (and the upcoming mention of Phinehas), what are we supposed to think about Ehud, the left-handed Benjamite from the beginning of the performance? We are guided by the activation of his narrative in this sad saga, as well as through his connection to these covenant-less and heartless Benjamites, to realize more than ever that his tactics were probably more Canaanite than covenant.

We are also left with a chronological conundrum. When did the Ehud cycle actually occur along Israel's time line? Was it before these Levitical accounts of Judg 17–21? Could this account have occurred after the eighty years of rest made possible when Ehud led a band of Israelites, including Ephraimites, into battle against Moab? How old would Jonathan and Phinehas be at this point after the eighty years of rest provided by Ehud's leadership? And yet Jonathan was described as a "young man" in Judg 17:7. On the other hand, would any tribe follow a left-handed Benjamite into battle after the episode described in Judg 19–21?

Oral traditional cultures vary in their use of chronology compared to our Occidental, post-Gutenberg culture. This reality argues against forming any strict chronological theory from the "data" offered in the performance of Judges. However, it seems possible that this episode of civil war occurred before Ehud's achievement of eighty years of rest (Jonathan being a young man in the previous account and Phinehas still living and ruling in the current account), in which case the immediacy of the total destruction and Canaanization of Israel is shocking. Also shocking is that a Benjamite could rally troops from Ephraim after this debacle. Of course, if the nation would rally behind Benjamin to kidnap six hundred virgins for the men, perhaps they would also rally against Moab with Ehud from Benjamin.

Therefore, this final account of the despicable apostasy of Israel projects the audience to the beginning of the performance. Through internal activation and repetition, we realize that the moment we stepped into this performance, we were not tip-toeing into shallow waters of rebellion, but we were already wading into the abyss of depravity.

As to these seven hundred "left-handed" men in Judg 20:16, it is remarkable that their left-handedness is never mentioned again. Since their "left-handedness" leaves no identifiable impact on the battles, it seems as though this special band of warriors were only mentioned to remind us of Ehud and activate elements of the performance for rhetorical effect. Are we to see Ehud as one of these seven hundred?

Even if the mention of the troop's "left-handedness" was not given to help us figure out the performance's chronology, it evokes a certain line of thinking: From the very beginning, all of our judges have been unworthy, like left-handed gang-rapist-defenders, and our people have been falling fiercely from covenant faithfulness like brimstone raining from the sky upon Sodom.

With Othniel we were provided with a king of double evil coming from the north from between the two rivers, language clearly chosen to evoke the double evil of the exile—Assyria and Babylon, the Mesopotamian empires. The cycle of judges began by informing us that this narrative addresses the root cause of the exile. As it draws to a close, we are carried back to the beginning, to Ehud, just after the attack of the double-wickedness from between the two rivers, and there we are confronted with a hero of Israel connected to the worst Israelites imaginable—the Israelites who reflect the depravity of Sodom.

In Judg 17–18 we meet six hundred Danites who might as well be Philistines. In Judg 19–21 we meet six hundred remaining rapist-defending Benjamites who hold out until Israel helps them rape six hundred women. The repetition of "six hundred men" in this final account of the book of Judges echoes for the audience the six hundred Philistines killed by Shamgar. The last of the first introductory judges projected this final event, and his earlier note also now connects representatives of Israel to their Philistine enemies.

The book of Judges stands as a product of an oral traditional culture. It is brilliantly arranged through repetition. The performance contains elements of repetition within the book itself (such as these activated elements of Ehud and Shamgar) that direct the audience to interpret the meaning of the events. The performance contains elements that activate the greater traditions such as law and king and covenant (such as the phrase "there was no king in those days" and the prose/poem structure of the Barak/Deborah cycle) that help interpret the flow of the narrative, and the performance contains elements of repetition that connect to the situation of the community contemporary with its current form—exile and beyond (such as the satirical conquest summary in chapter 1 and the story of Adonai-Bezek). All of these elements work together to activate the greater traditional identity of the people with rhetorical force for the current life-situation of the community.

As we continue our recounting of the civil war, we see that the first battle begins after Israel inquires of Elohim, "Who will go up first against Benjamin?" Just as in chapter 1, Judah will go up first.

The text does not say at this point that they inquired of *YHWH* but that they inquired of *Elohim*. The shift is likely significant. While Israel wants God's direction and aid, they are not coming to him as the personal, relational, covenantal God as Israel had at other times when they called upon the name of YHWH.

YHWH is not supporting this entire episode as he had originally intended to do with Israel's holy war against the Canaanites. In this instance, the holy war is waged against the Canaanized tribe of Benjamin, and YHWH is not perceived by the people as the intimate, personal God of Israel, as he was in the days of Moses and Joshua.

Two times Israel suffers defeat before the Benjamites. After these two defeats, Israel may finally have "come to realize that their covenant relationship with Yahweh is in doubt,"[108] for they fast and present burnt offerings and peace offerings to YHWH.

The house of YHWH was at Shiloh, but we read in 20:27 that the ark of the covenant of God was in Bethel in those days. It seems that Israel brought the ark with them to battle as some sort of good luck charm. After all, carrying the ark had significance when Joshua crossed over the Jordan (Josh 3) and in the circling of Jericho (Josh 6). Of course, the presence of the ark did not save Israel in 1 Sam 4 when the ark was brought with similar intentions—Israel was defeated and the ark captured by the Philistines. At any rate, there seems to be hope for covenant renewal along with lingering signs of continued Canaanization.

As discussed at length already, Phinehas's presence is a chronological atomic bomb. Genealogies can be telescoped (generations can be skipped in order to highlight the relevant members of the line). Perhaps this was really Phinehas II, the predecessor to Eli from 1 Sam, but that does not explain the parallel presence of Moses' grandson in the previous saga.

Exact chronology may not be the primary point anyway. The presence of Moses' and Aaron's "grandsons" in this final chiastic section of

---

108. Block, *Judges*, 560.

Judges works to contrast this generation of apostasy with previous generations of faith, even while they also remind us of the ongoing struggle for God's people to walk in faithfulness.

By taking all of the difficult content from the downward spiral presented by Judg 3:7—16:31 and situating it within the memory of the grandsons of the great leaders of the exodus, the depth and power and tragedy and immediacy of Israel's appalling apostasy is compressed into a density that crushes the audience with shock. The audience is triggered and jolted into a desire for covenant faithfulness.

YHWH moves in tragic grace, promising to deliver Israel's brothers into their hands.

The final battle involves a plan to ambush Gibeah. The plan works, and the Benjamites are defeated. Only six hundred men escape to the rock of Rimmon, where they stay four months.

Israel returns to Benjamin and enforces the *herem*. All life was slaughtered—human and animal alike. The tribe of Benjamin was basically wiped off of the map. Block said this:

> This is one of the most effective examples of ironic narrative in the Old Testament. A nation increasingly Canaanized appears before Yahweh as the covenant community of God (vv. 1–3). Where divinely called and empowered judges had failed to mobilize the nation into concerted action, a nameless Levite of questionable character and with questionable methods is able to rally all the troops 'as one man.' The tribe that embodies right-handedness (Benjamin, 'son of the right hand') not only demonstrates its left-handedness metaphorically by being completely out of step with orthodox theological and ethical standards, but also, ironically, is able to field an entire contingent of first class left-handed warriors. A little army of twenty-six thousand, seven hundred of whom are 'handicapped with respect to the right hand,' is able to put to rout an army more than fifteen times its size, not once, but twice. In the process they slaughter forty thousand Israelite soldiers, without a single stated casualty of their own. Perhaps most ironic of all, this chapter portrays the nation of Israel engaged in a holy war against their own kinsmen with all the passion they should have displayed in their war against the Canaanites. Israel has discovered who her greatest foe is: she is her own worst enemy."[109]

---

109. Block, *Judges*, 569.

The irony continues into the following chapter. Israel seemed to have little qualms throughout the previous sections of the book marrying Canaanite or Philistine women (think of Abimelech, Jephthah, Ibzan, and Samson), but here the Israelites had made an oath not to give their daughters in marriage to the Benjamites. They refuse to let their daughters consort with the Canaanized tribe. And finally, they actually keep their oaths! (At least, perhaps, by some interpretation of the letter of the law.)

The people weep until evening at the possible loss of the tribe of Benjamin. This signals back to Judg 2 when Israel gathered at Bochim:

> 1 Now the angel of the LORD went up from Gilgal to Bochim. And he said, "I brought you up from Egypt and brought you into the land that I swore to give to your fathers. I said, 'I will never break my covenant with you, 2 and you shall make no covenant with the inhabitants of this land; you shall break down their altars.' But you have not obeyed my voice. What is this you have done? 3 So now I say, I will not drive them out before you, but they shall become thorns in your sides, and their gods shall be a snare to you."
>
> 4 As soon as the angel of the LORD spoke these words to all the people of Israel, the people lifted up their voices and wept. 5 And they called the name of that place Bochim. And they sacrificed there to the LORD.

Here in chapter 21, they don't weep at their lack of covenant loyalty but at the potential loss of the tribe of Benjamin. "There still appears to be no concern for their spiritual well-being."[110]

The people cry out, "YHWH, why has this happened to Israel." At this point in the narrative the question is comical. Nothing "happened" to Israel. Are they really that clueless? Are they really placing some of the blame on YHWH? Block said, "Whatever the Israelites' motive, the silence of God is deafening."[111] They try to make offerings again, but God is not manipulated by ritual works. He remains silent.

He has spoken in his covenant—his Torah has been given. Let them listen to that.

But they do not.

They set out and make plans of their own. They seem confident that they must not break their oath to refrain from giving their daughters to Benjamin in marriage, but neither can they fathom allowing Benjamin to

---

110. Block, *Judges*, 570.
111. Block, *Judges*, 571.

become naught. They remember that they had earlier agreed that whoever did not show up to battle against Benjamin should die. They were content to ignore Jabesh Gilead's absence until their own oath to keep their daughters away from the Benjaminites put them in this situation. Now, they use their first oath to justify the merciless methods of keeping their second.

This reflects the oath of Jephthah. Israel has trapped herself in an oath that God never asked them to make, and it is no coincidence that this oath affects those in Gilead from where Jephthah judged. Just like Jephthah, Israel sticks to her oath and kills her kindred—men, women, and children—and they give the virgins over to Benjamin for the raping. They sacrifice their daughters just like Jephthah sacrificed his only daughter.

They take the young virgins to Shiloh. The performance calls it "Shiloh in Canaan." The place where the tabernacle rests is referred to as a city *in Canaan*. "Since this is the most sacred Israelite shrine, [the narrator] invites the reader to generalize the characterization to the entire land and to evaluate all the activities that transpire at Shiloh in this chapter as essentially Canaanite in character and intent."[112]

The kidnapped girls who were brought to Shiloh in Canaan were too few. Israel decides that the best course of action is to allow the Benjamites to kidnap young girls from a festival at Shiloh. Perhaps these young girls were professional dancers at the cultic site? This would reflect some kind of Canaanite ritual. Given the timeframe, it's likely that some sort of grape festival was celebrated, undoubtedly accompanied by plenty of wine. Since the festival is not named, it is likely a Canaanized celebration full of drunkenness and revelry—the covenant people of YHWH decide to add kidnapping and rape to the festivities.

Block observed, "The verb that describes the authorized action of the Benjamites, *ḥāṭap*, appears in only one other place in the Old Testament. In Ps 10:9 the verb appears twice, comparing the forceful seizure of an innocent person by a wicked and violent man to that of a lion pouncing on its prey to devour it."[113] Block also pointed out, "In the midst of joyful celebration these young women are suddenly to be abducted and dragged away from home. It does not seem to matter to the elders that these same Benjamites have only recently defended their fellow tribesmen after they had gang-raped a young woman."[114] Indeed, it

112. Block, *Judges*, 576.
113. Block, *Judges*, 581.
114. Block, *Judges*, 581.

is not impossible, though perhaps statistically unlikely, that among these abductors of young women abide some of the men who participated in the gang rape in Gibeah.

If nothing is done against the blatant breaking of Torah guidelines of rape, how is this better than breaking an oath? Is it okay to break Torah blatantly for a fragile technical loophole around an oath that was never required or sanctioned by YHWH? Block called this a "comedy of legality."[115] It was certainly no comedy for the victims—just a picture of the abominable wickedness of which legalism is capable.

After all the surviving rapist-protectors received their virgin prize, they went back to rebuild their towns. "This report must be interpreted in light of Deut 13:13–19, which describes how cities and regions that have been subjected to the law of holy war are to be dealt with: they are to remain in ruin in perpetuity, and they must never be rebuilt (v. 16) as a warning of the grave consequences of abandoning the standards of covenant commitment to life."[116] Instead, the atrocity of Benjamin was only initially treated as the horrific affair that it was—the holy war ban was set upon the tribe, and Israel gathered just as it should have against the Canaanites. Afterwards, steps were taken to repeat the same sin that started the entire episode, and they rebuilt the cities that were supposed to stand in ruin and judgment.

Israel promised to fight against the Canaanites and secure the promised land. Instead, they became the Canaanites.

Israel promised to fight against the tribe of Benjamin due to the tribe's support of the rapists of Gibeah. Instead, they destroy another Israelite town, murdering everyone except for four hundred virgins, and they give those four hundred virgins over to the remaining Benjamite men to "take as wives"—rape. Since there were not enough virgins kidnapped from that town, they give the rest of the Benjamites permission to kidnap young girls at a festival and rape them as wives.

What Benjamin did in Gibeah, the nation later sanctions on behalf of Benjamin.

They promised to fight against the Benjamites, but they became the Benjamites.

At this point, even when Israel assembles in unity against Canaan, only chaos ensues, and Israel becomes the very thing they are supposed

---

115. Block, *Judges*, 581.
116. Block, *Judges*, 582.

to battle. There is no king in Israel, and everyone does what is right in their own eyes.

Block said, "If the reader will read on to the beginning of the next book of the Hebrew canon (1 Sam), however, he or she will discover that while the darkness continues, the grace of Yahweh will begin to penetrate that darkness. He will remove those who embody Canaanite values (Eli and his sons, Saul) and replace them with agents of light and grace (Samuel, David)."[117] However, it will not take long for David to participate in the sin of Benjamin, using his power and influence to take Bathsheba into his bed and murder her husband, Uriah. Perhaps never recovering from the shame of that act, David will also turn a blind eye to the incestuous rape of his own daughter, Tamar. Solomon will multiply the polygamous sin of his father and, like Samson, allow his lust for many foreign women drag him away from covenant faithfulness to YHWH and sacrifice his God-given wisdom. The nation will then split and experience an almost perpetual cycle of unfaithful kings.

The heights of Samuel's faithfulness, David's heart, and Solomon's wisdom seem to only highlight the depths of how far Israel falls from covenant faithfulness as she follows the example of her kings. Judges stands as a testimony that Israel's covenant failures cannot be blamed on any royal lineage. She experienced absolute religious and social depravity even when there was no king and everyone did what was right in their own eyes.

Judges was performed within the oral traditional culture of ancient, exilic/post-exilic Israel. In order to interpret the book's purpose and meaning, we must engage its content with an understanding of how oral traditional cultures communicate. We should look for elements of internal repetition—repetition of structure (the judges cycle), names (Ehud), words (pierced down, heifer), phrases (there was no king in those days), scenes (Eglon's upper room and the room of Samson's wife), and themes (progeny, marriage outside of Israel, the rally of Israel against Canaan). We should also look for repetition within the circumambient traditional material of the oral traditional community. In other words, we should expect *activation* through the repetition of structures (Judges chapters 4 and 5 repeat and activate the structure of Exodus chapters 14 and 15); repetition of names (Moses and Aaron); words (המם in Judg 4); phrases (Judg 5:21, the

---

117. Block, *Judges*, 585.

waters . . . swept them away); scenes (Gideon's and Moses' call); and themes (covenant faithfulness and the curses of apostasy from Deuteronomy).

These elements of repetition connect the audience to the rhetorical purposes of the performance so that the community can activate their communal identity within their current life-situation. The oral traditional material stands as a *Sprache des Volksleben* that performances can harness to help the community agree upon, and come together in, their current *Sitz im Volksleben*. The book of Judges leaves no question for the exilic/post-exilic community: the nation had been worthy of the covenantal curses practically from the moment they stepped into the promised land.

7

The Synoptic Tradition

THE TRADITIONS OF JESUS preserved in the New Testament emerged in a significantly different oral traditional environment than those of the Old Testament. By the time Jesus came on the scene, the Jewish people were already largely a people of the book, with extensive discussion of the written Torah and the traditions of the elders. When Paul collaborated with Tertius and Phoebe and others to pen and send the letter to the church in Rome, there was, in fact, an original letter, an original text. Though, as I will demonstrate below in chapter nine, even in this "original text" elements of orality dominate through Paul's use of repetition and activation, and it is necessary to understand the rhetorical purposes of his use of repetition to exegete the letter. I will focus specifically on Rom 9–11.

But first, chapter seven and chapter eight will look at the Synoptic Gospels and the Gospel of John respectively. Even if it is assumed that the evangelists penned an "original text" of their respective gospels, it is clear, as will be discussed below, that their "original" gospel presentations stood together as unique performances of the Jesus tradition—representing the fluidity and stability of the tradition.

So, while the "orality" of the New Testament differs from that in Old Testament, the principles of exegesis remain consistent. Indeed, as we move into the New Testament, we are immediately aware of the activation of the Old Testament tradition in the New and the need to identify the activated elements of the greater tradition for a full understanding of the rhetorical purposes of the given performance. Here in chapter seven I will discuss the repeating structure of Mark, the echo of the passion predictions in the Synoptic Tradition, followed by a look at the parallel Sabbath healings and didactic content of Luke 13:10—14:35.

Repetition in the Gospel of Mark[1]

The following demonstrates an echo of themes of *authority*, *response*, and *mission* on the part of Mark throughout his Gospel. Just as Judges utilized repetitions to structure its performance for rhetorical purposes, Mark organizes his narrative of Jesus ministry through intentional repetition of themes to instruct the believing community of their identity as followers of the crucified Messiah.

David E. Garland offers a threefold division of the book of Mark (1:14—8:21; 8:22—10:52; and 11:1—16:8).[2] He also identifies a threefold division in the first major section (1:14—3:6; 3:7—6:6a; and 6:6b—8:21). Each subsection of the first major section of Mark begins with (1) a summary statement followed by (2) a calling, commissioning, or sending out of the disciples and ends with (3) opposition, unbelief, or lack of understanding in reference to Jesus.[3]

Within Garland's threefold division of this first major section, the first subsection, 1:14—3:6, is clearly concerned with Jesus' kingdom *authority*. Jesus demonstrates authoritative teaching (1:22, 27), authoritative power over demons (1:27, 34, 39), over disease (1:31, 34, 42; 2:12), over sin (2:10), and over the Law (2:18–22, 28). In 3:1–6, the concern is over what is lawful to do on the Sabbath. Does Jesus have the authority under the law to heal on the Sabbath?

The second subsection, 3:7—6:6a, is concerned with the *response* to Jesus and the kingdom. Responses of Jesus' immediate family and scribes follow directly after the appointing of the twelve, and Jesus speaks on the need to pay attention in order to respond correctly in the parables of the soils, lamp, and seeds. In 4:35—5:43, Mark weaves stories together concerning fear and faith, climaxing with Jesus' words to the ruler of the synagogue concerning his response, "μὴ φοβοῦ, μόνον πίστευε (no fear,

---

1. For an overview of other perspectives on Mark from an oral traditional approach, see Botha, "Gospel of Mark."

2. With a thirteen-verse introduction, Garland, *Theology of Mark's Gospel*, 99–101.

3. Garland, *Theology of Mark's Gospel*, 100.

only faith!)." The subsection closes in 6:1–6a with Nazareth's response to Jesus—offense at him due to their lack of faith.

The third subsection, 6:6b—8:21, focuses on Jesus' *mission*. Jesus sends out the apostles on a successful ministry—"and they were casting out many demons and anointing with oil many who were sick and were healing them" (6:13). Their return is prefaced by the death of John the Baptist (6:14–29) as an instruction that kingdom mission, no matter how "successful," is dangerous, offensive, and sacrificial. This may also have *activated* in the mind of the original hearing community the impending death of Jesus. Jesus teaches his disciples to feed the crowds (6:30–44), but their hearts are hardened concerning the lesson (6:45–52). Nonetheless, Jesus is still on mission (6:53–56).

Then the focus shifts to a gentile-themed mission as clean and unclean are redefined (7:1–23), and Jesus ministers to a gentile woman (7:24–30) and a man in gentile territory (7:31–37). Finally, Jesus once again leads his disciples to trust in his provision and feeds the crowds (8:1–10). This section ends with the Pharisees demanding a sign and the disciples still not understanding Jesus' ministry (8:11–21). Like the blind man in the next scene, the disciples need their eyes opened to Jesus' mission as well as to their own. Therefore, the three subsections of the first major division in Mark can be broken down thematically to Jesus' *authority*, *response* to Jesus, and Jesus' *mission*.

The last of the three major divisions of the book of Mark begins in 11:1–33 as Jesus enters Jerusalem like a king, deauthorizes the temple, and then tells the chief priests, scribes, and elders, "Neither will I tell you by what *authority* I do these things" (11:33). This first section of the third division of Mark concerns Jesus' *authority*. Following this section concerning Jesus' authority are passages clearly dealing with *response* to Jesus—the parable ending with the rejected cornerstone (12:1–12), and tests of Jesus that end with a man being "not far from the kingdom of God" (12:13–34). And, of course, this section contains the lengthy discussion in Mark 13 that concludes, "And what I say to you I say to all: Stay awake." After chapter 13 the narrative turns directly to Jesus' *mission* of the cross. To see in the third major division of Mark what is seen in the first is not difficult—three subsections focusing on *authority* (11:1–33), *response* (12:1—13:37), and *mission* (14:1—16:8).

This is just what lies behind the central section (8:22—10:52) as well. This central section focuses on the clarification of the identity of the Messiah and of his disciples. The section begins with the healing of a man who only sees partially at first (8:22–26), resembling the disciples in the next scene—they see Jesus as the Messiah, but their vision of the Messiah is blurred.

Framed by the three passion predictions, Mark will present Jesus' lessons concerning the true identity of the Messiah/Son of Man and his disciples. The section will conclude with the healing of the named blind man, Bartimaeus, who *sees* Jesus as the Son of David.

Each time Jesus predicts his passion, the disciples falter, which leads Jesus to give instructions on true discipleship. This is the repeating pattern of this second major division—(1) passion prediction, (2) error of the disciples, and (3) instruction on discipleship. Within this passion prediction framework, the themes of *authority*, *response*, and *mission* arise again.

Like the other two main divisions of Mark, this division will begin by establishing Jesus' *authority*—the glory of the kingdom is seen in his transfiguration (8:38—9:13); Jesus commands demons that others cannot (9:14–29). Then Jesus emphasizes a *response* to him: "Whoever receives one such child in my name receives me, and whoever receives me does not receive me but him who sent me" (9:37). The discussion of a strange exorcist also focuses on one's attitude toward Christ: "For whoever gives you a cup of water to drink in the name, because you are of Christ—truly I say to you that he will by no means lose his reward" (9:41). The discussion on divorce, "Whoever would divorce his wife and marry another commits adultery against her..." (10:11–12), is reminiscent of Jesus' warnings about temptations and causing others to sin instead of being salt and peace (9:42–50). The section repeats the need to receive the kingdom like a child (10:13–16) and then presents the story of the rich young man's poor *response* to Jesus (10:17–31).

The third subsection, marked off by the third passion prediction, speaks of Jesus' baptism and cup (his *mission*) and the disciples' future of sharing in it (10:38–40). Jesus instructs them on how they should serve each other and concludes with the definitive statement of his own mission, which is to act as a guide for their mission: "For even the Son of Man came not to be served but to serve, and to give his life as a ransom in place for many" (10:45). The picture of the Messiah has been clearly painted. Jesus can open the eyes of the one who calls him "Son of David" and march *authoritatively* into Jerusalem to call people toward a *response* as he finishes his *mission*.

The first major division in Mark (1:14—8:21) establishes Jesus' authority as teacher, miracle worker, and one who is over and above the religious leaders of the day. The second major division in Mark (8:22—10:52) focuses on Jesus' instructions to the disciples and their response to his true messianic identity. The third major division (11:1—16:8) lands Jesus in Jerusalem and walks him toward his mission on the cross. Therefore, the three major divisions of Mark also proceed in the thematic order of *authority, response, mission.*

Whether intentionally or simply by his conformity to oral communication constructs, Mark has presented three major divisions that echo in succession Jesus' *authority, response* to Jesus, and Jesus' *mission*. These three major divisions are each divided into three subsections that follow the same thematic procession—*authority, response, mission.*

This thematic framework of Mark can aid in interpreting every passage in the Gospel by identifying in which major section and subsection the passage is found. Expecting oral echoes in the text can uncage the Bible from its print and help the interpreter discover nuance that oral traditional cultures may have received naturally.

Next, we will see something similar to the echo/ring composition discussed above in reference to the woe oracles in Hab 2—the echo of the passion predictions of Jesus in the Synoptic Gospels. This echo is interesting in that the echo/ring material reverberates across the multiform performances of the life and teachings of Jesus. Each Gospel intentionally performs the echo/ring material of the predictions toward the greater purposes of their unique performances of the Christ tradition.

The Passion Predictions in the Synoptic Gospels

Matthew, Mark, and Luke present Jesus predicting his passion at least three times. As will be seen below, each Gospel utilizes the three instances of shared passion prediction material as structural markers pointing toward Jesus' teachings on the true nature of his messiahship and on the true nature of being his disciple. Each Gospel retains similar material but adjusts the predictions to fit within its purposes—a clear example of the fluidity and stability found within oral literature. The following discussion should highlight how theories of orality and textuality can interact with modern exegetical methods—both toward critical issues, such as general literary structure, Mark/Matthew priority, and the historicity of the Gospel presentations, as well as toward exegetical conclusions of the various sections containing the passion predictions.

Mark

Mark's portrayal of the predictions of Christ's suffering aligns with the overall structure and themes of his Gospel discussed above. He is the only one of the three who constantly uses the following pattern: use of the title Son of Man (the one with *authority*), is rejected/delivered/condemned (*response*), will die and rise (*mission*). As will be discussed below, Matthew leaves out "Son of Man" in his first prediction. Matthew is also missing "and be rejected" in his first prediction. Luke does not mention the death or resurrection in his second prediction. Luke also does not share, "and they will condemn him to death," in his third prediction as do Matthew and Mark.

This data is not strong enough to catalyze an argument for the themes of *authority*, *response*, and *mission* within Mark, but it is supporting data for their intentional presence in the Gospel in that Mark's predictions contain the proper material for these themes at every point when Matthew and/or Luke do not. Mark's reportage of Peter's rebuke, which is not in Luke, adds to the discussion of Jesus' authority. Mark says, καὶ παρρησίᾳ τὸν λόγον ἐλάλει ("and he spoke the word plainly") indicating that the truth was out in the open to be seen, and, like the unnamed blind man, the disciples simply needed proper sight.

Mark's third-day formula, μετὰ τρεῖς ἡμέρας, may intentionally add emphasis on the crucifixion, and this seems to be in line with the thrust of a proper response to Jesus' mission—deny self, take up the cross, be ready to die in service like John the Baptist. Perhaps this is why Mark shares with Luke the additional content concerning the events of the passion in the third passion prediction. Mark's use of μετὰ τρεῖς ἡμέρας may also reflect a form of the predictions also preserved in Matt 27:63.

Matthew

Matthew is a complicated work to outline. Donald A. Hagner says, "Although much study has been devoted to the structure of Matthew in recent years, there has been little consensus as to the best analysis."[4] R. T. France agrees, "Any proposed outline of the gospel is thus imposed by the interpreter, not dictated by the author, and is therefore open to discussion

---

4. Hagner, "Matthew 1–13," 1.

as to whether it truly represents the intended shape of the narrative."⁵ Two major proposals for the structure of Matthew depend either on the five sections of Jesus' teaching or on the two times Matthew uses the phrase, ἀπὸ τότε ἤρξατο ὁ Ἰησοῦς ("from that time on"—Matt 4:17 and 16:21).⁶ Hagner says, "The narrative of the death of Jesus, however, is the goal and climax of the story, and any structural analysis must include it as a major element. Accordingly, the fivefold discourse structure should be recognized as a subsidiary structure rather than a primary one."⁷ France points out that the second option would align largely with Mark and Luke, which divide cleanly into material before the journey to Jerusalem and the material of and after the journey to Jerusalem.⁸ France says:

> From 4:17 onward Jesus's ministry in Matthew, as in Mark, is set entirely in and around Galilee until Jesus announces his intention to travel south to Jerusalem in 16:21. Like Mark, Matthew offers a substantial body of material, particularly concerned with the reorientation and training of the disciples, on the journey between Galilee and Jerusalem.⁹

Hagner agrees concerning the "reorientation and training of the disciples" saying, "The turn the Gospel now takes will necessitate the radical redefining of categories for the disciples."¹⁰

This clear shift in focus in Matthew aligns structurally with the first passion prediction in Matthew, so it is already clear that Matthew utilizes this first passion prediction as a major marker in his material. And the shift in focus is specifically toward the content of the passion predictions—true messiahship is the way of the cross. Hagner says that Matt 16:21 marks the beginning of "the second main part of the Gospel... placing Jesus on the road to Jerusalem and the cross,"¹¹ and, "from now on the focus is upon what is to befall Jesus in Jerusalem."¹² This focus on the cross and "reorientation of the disciples" all coalesces as "the shadow of the cross thus falls across this whole southward journey, [and] Jesus

---

5. France, *Gospel of Matthew*, 2.
6. France, *Gospel of Matthew*, 2–3; Hagner, "Matthew 14–28," l–liii.
7. Hagner, "Matthew 14–28," li.
8. France, *Gospel of Matthew*, 3–4.
9. France, *Gospel of Matthew*, 4.
10. Hagner, "Matthew 14–28," 477.
11. Hagner, "Matthew 14–28," 477.
12. Hagner, "Matthew 14–28," 477.

tries to get his disciples to understand the paradoxical and unwelcome nature of his mission . . . trying to instill into them the new and radically different values of the kingdom of heaven."[13]

While France and Hagner's commentaries argue strongly for a shift in Matthew at the first prediction, what about the structural importance of the second two predictions? The echo/ring principle greatly reflects the reappearance of predictions of Jesus' passion, and, since Jesus grew up in a culture that was largely oral, he may have intentionally structured his teaching along these cultural constructs. If interpreters would expect principles of repetition and echo of content, they may find the presence of such features to act as clues for interpretation. David McClister claims to have found such interpretive clues among the second two predictions in the Matthew's Gospel as he argues for a chiastic structure of Matt 17:22—20:19:

17:22–23: Jesus foretells his death
A. 17:24–27: Giving freely; money; sacrifice Challenge "Parable"
  B. 18:1–7: Little children are the essence of the kingdom of heaven
    C. 18:8–9: Sacrifice of the body for the sake of the kingdom
      D. 18:10–14: Do not despise what God values Parable (Lost sheep)
        E. 18:15–17: What to do when a brother sins
          F. 18:18–20: Agreement between heaven and earth
        E'. 18:21–35: What to do when a brother sins Parable (Unforgiving servant)
      D'. 19:1–9: Do not separate what God has joined
    C'. 19:10–12: Sacrifice of the body for the kingdom of heaven
  B'. 19:13–15: Little children are the essence of the kingdom of heaven
A'. 19:16—20:16: Giving freely; money; sacrifice Challenge Parable
20:17–19 Jesus foretells his death[14]

McClister says, "Matthew's chiastic arrangement in 17:22—20:19 is his own creation, but it does not appear that he created it from scratch. Instead, it builds on a framework common to the synoptic gospels. To this framework Matthew added materials to produce the chiastic structure. Therefore, all or parts of sections A, E, F, E', C, and A' are peculiar to Matthew."[15] McClister acknowledges what France argued above—that

---

13. France, *Gospel of Matthew*, 628.
14. McClister, "Where Two or Three," 550.
15. McClister, "Where Two or Three," 551.

the Synoptic Gospels seem to have a common framework. Additionally, McClister's work identifies the second two passion predictions as major markers in the structure of Matthew.

McClister argues that this chiastic structure demonstrates that Matthew centers this section on Jesus' words about the agreement in heaven and on earth when Jesus' disciples are unified. The entire chiastic section discusses how disciples should relate with each other, climaxing in the idea that whatever they bind on earth will be bound in heaven, whatever they loose on earth will be loosed in heaven, and if two agree on earth about anything they ask, it will be done for them by the Father.

With this argument in mind, the passion predictions in Matthew have the following effect. The first prediction acknowledges the disciple's new understanding of Jesus as "Messiah," but also begins the journey of redefining for them what the "Messiah/Son of Man" is supposed to do—namely, suffer as a ransom for many (20:28). This also redefines who they are to be as the disciples of such a Messiah (16:24–27). Jesus then reveals his glory on the Mount of Transfiguration and in rebuking the demon that the disciples could not. Matthew demonstrates here that the Son of Man is not walking to the cross in weakness but in humble power and sacrificial love. Having established the Messiah's topsy-turvy mission of glory and humiliation and the reflective call for the disciples to lose their life to save it, Matthew then utilizes the second and third prediction in a long section centering on disciples' intended communal perspective.

This section seems to make the same point as John's presentation of Christ's prayer in John 17—the disciples are to humbly engage each other as one, with Christ at the center, bringing heaven and earth together. Christ is in them as they are drawn into his relationship with the Father. Matthew closes this section utilizing one last correction of the disciples by Jesus as an opportunity to completely clarify the reason for the Son of Man's suffering—"a ransom for many." Jesus then opens the eyes of the blind ones who call him "Son of David." Has Jesus thus succeeded in opening the eyes of those disciples who call him Messiah? This is the thrust of this section in Matthew predominated by the structural placement and content of the three passion predictions.

Therefore, it may be possible to attempt some explanation of Matthew's decisions in his presentation of the passion predictions. Since Matthew centers his *passion prediction section* on the communal identity of the disciples, and specifically on the heavenly authority they have together in Christ to bind and loose in the heavenly places, he recorded

Jesus' words to Peter about binding and loosing in 16:17–19. Although Matthew may simply have a tendency to add direct speech,[16] perhaps he did so in the case of this first passion prediction to soften the specific authority he seemed to have given Peter. Peter's specific rebuke is recorded, as is Jesus' word to Peter that Peter was a σκάνδαλον to him. Matthew is also missing Mark's comment that Jesus looked "at his disciples" (Mark 8:33) when he rebuked Peter, which targets Peter more specifically in Matthew. This focused rebuke of Peter lessens the individual focus of Jesus' earlier words toward Peter so that Matthew can make those earlier words applicable to the entire discipleship community at the center of his chiastic structure at Matt 18:18–20.

There is little to say about Matthew's second prediction—it is so short. Perhaps he chose to say the disciples "gathered" to evoke a more *communal* tone. Matthew's conclusion—"they were greatly distressed"— may be just short enough to acknowledge a response on the part of the disciples before quickly moving into the chiastic structure Matthew had in mind.

As with the second prediction there is little to distinguish Matthew's version of the third from the others that apply specifically to his use of the prediction. Matthew's decision to specify the "privacy" of Jesus' words with the disciples and the cross as Jesus' mode of death are not extreme features toward his theme. However, if these last two predictions function largely as refrains of this ring-composition for this central content of Jesus' identity as Messiah and the reflective identity of his disciples, there is not much specificity required for Matthew's rhetorical purposes beyond what the predictions already specifically point to—the suffering, death, and resurrection of the Messiah.

Luke

In regard to Luke, a thorough overview of the entire Gospel outline will not be attempted, but it will be shown that despite Luke's variance from Mark and Matthew in his usage of the three predictions, he still employs them as a central shaping tool for his Gospel.

Luke is the outlier of the Synoptics in many respects. For instance, Luke is the first part of a two-part work, Luke-Acts. Luke is the only Gospel that states his pursuit and use of sources (Luke 1:1–4). And regarding

---

16. Bultmann, *History*, 312.

the passion predictions, Luke's use differs significantly from Matthew and Mark. Whereas Matthew and Mark have clear breaks in their structure right at the first prediction, Luke's major division is assumed to be at 9:51, when Jesus sets his face toward Jerusalem. Luke's first two predictions are very close together, with a tremendous gap between the second and third (first 9:22; second 9:43b–45; third 18:31–34). Luke lacks Peter's rebukes in the first prediction, lacks a *third-day formula* in the second, adds content about fulfilled Scripture in the third, and lacks James's and John's positioning request after the third.

In other words, Luke does not use the passion predictions as central thematic refrains *the same way* that Matthew and Mark do. However, it will be shown below that he still uses them as a sort of bookend, introducing and then leading to the conclusion of his discipleship material, and this discipleship material is also seen as a journey to Jerusalem, as in Matthew and Mark, which requires Jesus' reorientation of the disciples' views on messiahship.

Luke's Gospel is said to pivot on 9:51.[17] At this point Jesus sets his face toward Jerusalem, and Luke's Gospel ceases to align with Mark's. By this point Luke has already shared the first two passion predictions, and the third will not appear until 18:31. Did Luke completely disregard the shared centrality of the passion predictions in the tradition represented by Matthew and Mark? No.

The "pivot" in 9:51 is not quite as sharp as it first seems, with Jesus' clearly narrated focus and Luke's engagement of new source material. There are links between 9:48–50 and 52–56, 9:1–6 and 10:1–12, and an argument can be made for a unified section 8:1—11:13.[18] So, while the pivot at 9:51 is clear, it is by no means abrupt. Indeed, there is an ongoing progression beginning with 9:18 as Joel B. Green discusses in light of the disciples' new knowledge of Jesus as Messiah:

> This does not mean that Peter and the others understand fully the nature of Jesus and his mission, only that they have moved beyond their former incomprehension, and certainly beyond the helpful but inadequate perspectives of the crowds. Following this appraisal of his status, Jesus goes on to nuance it further with reference to suffering and vindication, and to draw out the immediate implications of his status for the character

---

17. Marshall, *Gospel of Luke*, 400–401; Garland, *Luke*, 408–10; Liefeld, "Luke," 931–32; Green, *Gospel of Luke*, 394–99.

18. Marshall, *Gospel of Luke*, 400.

presumed of those who would follow in his footsteps. In this way, (1) the miraculous deeds of Jesus that have characterized his Galilean ministry are fully integrated into his message of social transformation and transposition, (2) a fresh narrative need is established that focuses on the divine necessity of Jesus's execution and resurrection, and (3) a foundation is laid for the presentation of the nature of discipleship that will increasingly occupy center stage during the meandering journey of Jesus and his band of followers to Jerusalem in the Gospel's central section (9:51—19:27). Luke has thus begun to draw together the narrative threads of his portrayal of Jesus's ministry in Galilee at the same time that he establishes narrative needs that will occupy the narrator and propel the subsequent narrative forward.[19]

So, while 9:51 may be the clearest pivot point toward the journey to Jerusalem, it was the prediction material that set the foot spinning.

Green continues, "In retrospect, the degree to which this logion and the further explanations of discipleship in [9:24-26] serve as introduction to the travel narrative, and, thus, to Luke's understanding of discipleship, will become even more transparent. This is because the content of Jesus' 'recruiting speech' is repeated during the journey (see 12:8-9; 14:27; 17:33)."[20] Matthew's presentation of the content of these "repetitions" of Jesus' "recruiting speech" are all together in the same passage in Matt 10:32-39, indicating that Luke was intentional in spreading this material out through his travel section. Luke also adds unique prediction material (12:49-50, 13:31-33, and 17:25) within this central section that he has already bookended with the traditional predictions. So, while Luke may utilize the three predictions differently, he still sees them as a central definitive device in revealing the nature of Jesus' messiahship and the nature of discipleship, and he comes back to predictions of the passion like a refrain throughout his unique material.

Like Matthew and Mark, Luke utilizes the passion predictions to highlight the disciples' failures as opportunity for Jesus to teach them about discipleship,[21] but the most evident theological emphasis for Luke

19. Green, *Gospel of Luke*, 368.

20. Green, *Gospel of Luke*, 374.

21. See Luke 9:46-48. Also, it could be noted that Luke highlights the need for servant ministry through the disciples' ministry of exorcism. Jesus demonstrates the topsy-turvy kingdom by displaying his glory after predicting his passion, then Luke ties the second passion prediction directly to the amazement that Jesus was able to cast out a demon that the disciples were not. Their argument about who is greater is followed by John's jealousy that another besides them is casting out demons. The disciples are

in the predictions is what Marshall calls the "suffering secret."[22] He says, "Luke brings out more clearly than Mk. the thought of a divine purpose being fulfilled in the veiling of the prediction from the disciples (cf. 18:34). The predictions are understood only later after the resurrection when the risen Lord shows from the Scriptures the necessity of his path through suffering to glory."[23] Luke is drawing the narrative toward Luke 24:13–35 and 24:44–49 where the resurrected Lord, through a divine touch like what was required by Mark's unnamed half-seeing blind man, clarified for the disciples what the Scriptures said about his suffering and glory.

Therefore, Luke's unique usage of the three traditional passion predictions can be explained. Luke keeps the first passion prediction in the context of Peter's confession but removes the content of the rebukes. This removal directly connects messiahship to suffering and suffering messiahship to sacrificial discipleship. Within these connections, Luke can quickly draw out the "suffering secret" motif. Luke still draws out the weaknesses of the disciples through other means (see footnote 21 above). In 9:44 Luke leaves out the resurrection to highlight the humility that the disciples are lacking in their desire for authority over demons and people, and in 9:45 he uses the prediction to highlight the disciples' inability to understand the suffering Messiah. In the third prediction Luke adds the idea that the Son of Man's suffering is written about in the prophets and must be fulfilled. The disciples will not comprehend this until Jesus opens their minds to understand the Scriptures; hence in 18:34 they remain clueless, as the saying is hidden from them. Luke's *third-day formula* in the third passion prediction intentionally follows *what is written by the prophet* Hosea in Hos 6:2.

---

clamoring for power while Jesus is demonstrating humble service. Then James and John want to destroy the Samaritan village because they were belittled by the village's rejection. This is followed by a section on the cost of following Jesus. When the seventy-two return they glory in the fact that the demons were subject to them. Jesus reminds them that this power is not the point. And Luke goes on highlighting true kingdom ministry in the Good Samaritan and Mary . . . etc. All of this argues further against the idea that the pivot point of 9:51 detracts from the centrality of the traditional passion predictions to the Messiah/discipleship section of Luke.

22. Marshall, *Gospel of Luke*, 393.

23. Marshall, *Gospel of Luke*, 392–93.

Conclusion on the Synoptic use of the Passion Predictions

Rudolf Bultmann said that scenes like the passion predictions are the editorial work of Mark "or his predecessor," and "in such statements about situations we must not look for ancient tradition."[24] He takes issue with the organized, supernatural, unhistorical feel of the material. Albert Schweitzer also took issue with the organization of Mark since so much of it seemed historically implausible, and he said, "Either the Marcan text as it stands is historical, and therefore to be retained, or it is not, and then it should be given up. What is really unhistorical is any softening down of the wording, and the meaning which it naturally bears."[25] Bultmann and Schweitzer expected the Gospels to be works of rationalistic modernity in the post-Gutenberg age. But oral cultures work within different constructs.

The New Testament "was both born out of, and in turn gave birth to, oral performance"[26] within an oral culture very different from the culture that scholars like Bultmann and Schweitzer presupposed. As discussed earlier, oral performances are "almost always composed of a longer narrative plot line together with various smaller units that compose the bulk of the story in any given performance."[27] There is essentially a mental manuscript that is not focused on preserving a word for word repetition but instead is provided by the "narrative schematic itself." This mental manuscript is sort of a narrative frame that the performer can hang smaller units of material upon. Any given delivery of this mental manuscript can be edited "in terms of the placement, order, and length of the smaller units of tradition that fill out the narrative in any given performance."[28] These edits occur depending on any given "purpose, context, and time constraints of the performance in light of the situation of the community."[29] What is actually found among oral cultures is a sort of catholic narrative imbedded into the community's psyche, which certain tradition-bearers, or tradents, will perform utilizing different smaller units that can be reworded, resized, or rearranged to carry the agreed upon narrative to the proper place for the setting at hand. This describes

24. Bultmann, *History*, 331–32.
25. Schweitzer, *Quest*, 333–34.
26. Eddy and Boyd, *Jesus Legend*, 356.
27. Eddy and Boyd, *Jesus Legend*, 253.
28. Eddy and Boyd, *Jesus Legend*, 253.
29. Eddy and Boyd, *Jesus Legend*, 253.

exactly what is found in the Synoptic tradition—the same metanarrative, told in three different ways, utilizing many of the same smaller narrative units, told in different orders and lengths for different emphasis.

Regardless of what form critics like Bultmann assumed, oral cultures do discern between the historical and purely mythological data, and the historical genre within oral cultures most often tends to be "concerned about accurately transmitting recollections of their historical past."[30] Eddy and Boyd present many examples of oral scholars offering the cumulative claim that oral tradition-bearers are just as concerned with the faithful presentation of the actual historical events, based on evidence, as modern literate historians.[31] The communities themselves also distinguish between fact and fiction, and "it is not uncommon to find in orally dominant societies a clear conceptual and/or terminological differentiation between narratives considered to be factual and those considered to be fictional."[32] The major difference between the two approaches is the Western desire for perfect chronology and exactitude of detail on every level for the sole purpose of preserving the material, compared to the oral culture's desire to preserve the true nature of the history and then present that true history in whichever way best leads the community to draw together within the identity that the presentation reflects.

Jesus was an oral tradition-bearer teaching an oral community, the members of which had been indoctrinated within a general oral culture in the context of their specific oral traditions. His ministry was preserved within an oral tradition of its own (even if some of the tradition was recorded to writing early on, it was still done so within an oral/aural context). This tradition found its way to a more canonical written form. Studies regarding the "Synoptic Problem" should immediately begin to consider how Matthew, Mark, and Luke essentially represent the same long narrative plot constructed thematically by smaller units of narration and teaching. They utilize much of the same information with a fluidity of placement, order, and length of the shared content, which is stereotypical within an oral narrative performance culture. At any rate, any theory or hypothesis set forth by form and source criticism, or any other field of biblical study, that does not consider the memory retention and performance nature of oral cultures does not do justice to what is now known of tradition transmission within oral cultures.

30. Eddy and Boyd, *Jesus Legend*, 260.
31. Eddy and Boyd, *Jesus Legend*, 260–61.
32. Eddy and Boyd, *Jesus Legend*, 261.

That the Synoptic Gospels vary in detail and chronology has nothing to do with their historicity or chronology of "authorship," and it has everything to do with what the tradent-Evangelists wanted to communicate about the true historical events and teachings in the life of Jesus of Nazareth. In this regard, given that the three passion predictions play such a consistent and primary role within the Synoptic Tradition, it is very probable that something like these predictions were spoken by Christ himself as pedagogical devices preparing his disciples for his passion and laying the groundwork for a deeper understanding of their discipleship after his resurrection.

Indeed, this discussion may be just what Eddy was suggesting when he said:

> Now, to be clear, there is no way to prove at a very specific and concrete level whether the early oral Jesus tradition was reliable or not, since there is no way to dependably reconstruct this tradition. However, what we can do is: (1) gain an understanding of the various dynamics, genres, and models associated with oral transmission cross-culturally, (2) in light of these findings, analyze the data and dynamics of the written Jesus tradition found in the Gospels (and beyond), and finally (3) based on these prior considerations, draw plausible conclusions as to the likely nature of the early oral Jesus tradition—including its historical reliability. That we are, at best, left with generalities and probabilities should not bother us, since probabilities are what any field of historiography trades in, given the inherent limitations of historical method itself.[33]

Jesus' questions resound throughout the synoptic tradition, "Who do people say that I am? Who do you say that I am?" That the synoptic tradition is so centered on these questions and the passion predictions and didactic journey materials that follow them, and since more faith than ever can be placed on the historicity of the preserved tradition, these passion predictions and the content they frame are certainly the answer to the question, "Who did he say he was?"

---

33. Eddy, "Historicity," 146.

Luke 13:10—14:34

Acknowledging intentional repetition can help structure and interpret entire books of the Bible, and it can also help interpret smaller sections. For instance, an echo is apparent in Luke 13:10—14:35:

Chapter 13	**Parallel from Chapter 14**
13:10–17	14:1–6
Sabbath healing Religious ruler Is it lawful? How people treat animals Healing is "release"	Sabbath healing Religious ruler Is it lawful? How people treat animals Healing is "release"!
13:18–19	14:7–11
The kingdom is like a mustard seed that is very small but has surprising results.	Stop trying to make yourself "big." Make yourself "small." The self-exalted will be humbled. The humble will be exalted.
13:20–21	14:12–14
The kingdom is like hidden leaven that affects all the dough.	Stop seeking outward rewards. Spread fellowship without presumption into the entire community.
13:22–30	14:15–24
Many will miss out on the kingdom feast because they did not identify with Jesus. Some who are first will be last, and some who are last will be first. It is surprising who gets to attend the feast.	The first become the last because they refused to identify with the host. The outcasts take their place at the table.
13:31–33	14:24–33
Jesus does not love his life enough to try to save it by running from Herod. Indeed, he is going to *finish* by going to Jerusalem to die on the cross.	If one does not leave all behind, take up her cross, and follow Jesus, she is not able to be Jesus' disciple. One must be sure to examine her expenditures to make sure her house of discipleship will be/is *finished*.
13:34–35	14:34–35
Jerusalem was a city on a hill. It should have accepted Christ and represented him to the world. Instead, it is forsaken.	Salt that has lost its saltiness is good for nothing and thrown out.

Parallel Sabbath Healings as a Clue for Parallel Teachings

The clearest parallel found in this passage is the Sabbath healings.[34] There are four Sabbath healings in Luke, presented in two pairs—Luke 6:1–11 and the two discussed here. This also argues that the two Sabbath healings in this passage be read together. Both healings occur on the Sabbath in the presence of a religious ruler, leading to a controversy over healing on the Sabbath. Jesus responds to the controversies in both instances by arguing from least to greatest that if those hearing him treat their animals well on the Sabbath, then certainly humans should be treated at least as well. Both healings utilize the Greek term ἀπολύω, meaning "to release."[35] Interestingly, many commentators note the clear parallel aspects of these two healing stories, so close in proximity in Luke, but do not go on to investigate any other parallels in the material that follows them.[36] However, since repetition is a common way oral traditional cultures tell narratives and carry a point along through the story, noticing these echoes in the Sabbath healings from an oral traditional hermeneutic encourages one to explore their purpose. Indeed, these parallel Sabbath healings act to establish a ring composition in which common didactic content is introduced by these reoccurring Sabbath scenes. Before noting the parallels between each section and concluding on the overall purpose of these two parallel sections, I will first note some of the modern exegetical insights that argue for the parallel nature of the passages.

One of the first things noted by modern interpreters is how Luke 13:10–17 breaks from the normal miracle story pattern "and, in fact, from all normal form-critical categories."[37] Bultmann likened this shift to an example of failed skill on Luke's part,[38] but Green countered that Luke does not portray "clumsy constructions" in this passage but instead a "careful and deliberate attempt to frame the dialogue with the miracle story, so that the two are seen in intimate relationship."[39]

---

34. Most of the following parallels are noted in some form in most commentaries: Green, *Gospel of Luke*, 543–44; Culpepper, "Luke," 272–73; Garland, *Luke*, 563; Marshall, *Gospel of Luke*, 578; Bock, *Luke*, 392.

35. Green, *Gospel of Luke*, 542.

36. See the list above on note 34. Of these, only Culpepper makes an attempt to connect parallel sections between the following teachings, but Culpepper's sections are much more general.

37. Green, "Jesus and a Daughter," 644.

38. Green, "Jesus and a Daughter," 644.

39. Green, "Jesus and a Daughter," 648.

Relevant to this discussion is that this passage is located within the "travel section" of Luke, which is "overwhelmingly didactic in content."[40] Garland noted that this story is linked to the following teachings on the kingdom of God by οὖν or "therefore," which is "rarely used in Luke at the beginning of a unit."[41] All of this points to the conclusion that this first Sabbath healing story is not focused on the healing but is tying the miracle up within the dialogue and projecting it all into the teaching which follows. This Sabbath healing episode is a teaching construct launching into a section of instruction. The oral culture of the day would have picked up on this construction, and, upon hearing a parallel story later, would surely have been prepared for echoes of teaching to follow an echo of a narration so intimately bathed in instruction.

13:10–17 and 14:7–11

Immediately after the healing story in 13:10–17, Jesus gives two analogies for the kingdom of God. The first analogy, in 13:18–20, is that the kingdom of God is like a mustard seed. It is very easy to over-exegete passages like this.[42] Though it is true that the oral cultures would have picked up on commonly held symbols and metaphors that could have activated deeper meanings from their oral register, unless the use of those metaphors can be clearly demonstrated, it is probably wiser to take the most apparent meaning. The most obvious and simple meaning behind this analogy is that a mustard seed is really small and grows into something comparatively huge. This is what the kingdom of God is like.

Directly after the healing story in 14:1–6, Jesus tells a parable to the people at the dinner party with him instructing them to not select the most important seats at a meal, but instead to take lowly seats. They may be asked to rise from the lowly seats to the important seats. Jesus finishes this teaching by saying, "For everyone who exalts himself will be humbled, and he who humbles himself will be exalted."[43] In other words,

---

40. Green "Jesus and a Daughter," 645.

41. Garland, *Luke*, 543.

42. Much can be said about the nature of a mustard seed. One could wonder why the mustard "tree" was used as an example instead of the mighty cedar tree. Some have even tried to discuss the meaning behind the birds landing in its branches, Green, *Gospel of Luke*, 526–27. The analogy of the yeast is also often over-exegeted in arguing whether the yeast is good or evil in this context—Culpepper, "Luke," 276.

43. Luke 14:11.

"Be the seed! Do not try to make yourself big. Let yourself be small. Because the small will grow big, and those who puff themselves up will pop into nothing. Be the seed! Walk in the kingdom in the everyday events of real life."

13:20–21 and 14:12–14

The second analogy Jesus gives, in 13:20–21, is that the kingdom is like a little leaven that a woman hid in three measures of flour until it was all leavened. The most obvious meaning behind this analogy is that leaven is incredibly infectious, and when it is hidden, though it cannot be seen, it will be incredibly effective in transforming even the largest measures of dough.[44]

Directly after Jesus' teaching about the exaltation of the humble after the second Sabbath healing, he gives instruction on who the dinner guests and host should invite to their feasts. They should not invite the most obvious people such as friends, family, or rich neighbors who give the most obvious rewards; they should invite the least likely, such as the poor, crippled, lame, and blind who are totally unable to repay at all. This "hidden" service will be rewarded in the resurrection.

It is important to imagine what this sort of activity would do to a community. If the wealthy and elite humbled themselves to the point of hidden service to the lowly, this would transform the entire community into something entirely different—like a little leaven hidden in a lot of dough. Jesus says, "In the everyday sort of events in your life, be the transformative agents of the kingdom."

13:22–30 and 14:15–24

Then in Luke 13:22–23, someone asks Jesus, "Lord, will those who are saved be few?" Jesus teaches that many will miss out on the eschatological feast. The door is narrow, so those who desire to enter must strive to do so. The door will be shut on many who thought they had absolute access because of the connection they assumed they had with Jesus, but he will say to them, "Depart from me, all you workers of evil" (13:27). Though the door is narrow, Jesus declares that people will come from the

---

44. Three measures of flour could feed about 160 people—Marshall, *Gospel of Luke*, 561.

four corners of the earth and sit at the table. For "some who are last will be first, and some are first who will be last" (13:30). Just as this passage began by someone else's word, the parallel in 14:15–24 begins with one of the table guests, picking up on Jesus' reference to resurrection in 14:14, declaring, "Blessed is the one who will eat bread in the kingdom of God!" To this outburst of self-righteousness,[45] Jesus responds with a story of a master devastatingly humiliated as all of his dinner guests, who had already responded to an invitation to a meal, rejected the summons when the meal was all prepared.[46]

The master responds by inviting the lowly of the city, and even those blatantly cast outside the city walls, into his feast. Then, Jesus speaks directly to those feasting at the table with him: "For I tell you, none of those men who were invited shall taste my banquet."[47] The parallels between these two "table parables" are apparent. Many who think they are in will find themselves out, and many who are last will be first and dine at the master's table. What is gained from the second parable is the outright rejection of the master by those who were first invited. Certain guests are surprisingly rejected in the first instance, while the second demonstrates that they should not have been surprised to find the door shut in their faces since they were the ones who rejected the master of the feast.

13:31–33 and 14:25–33

In 13:31–33 the Pharisees warn Jesus that Herod is seeking to kill him. Jesus is adamant that he is not seeking to save his life but will complete his journey to Jerusalem and "finish his course." In 9:18, beginning with Peter's confession, Luke picked up on the echoes of the shared tradition of true messiahship and true discipleship represented in Mark (Mark 8:22—10:52 discussed above). But Luke diverted from Mark's material at 9:51, only completing the first two rounds of passion prediction and teaching on discipleship. At this point in Luke's performance the audience

---

45. The man most certainly did not declare this beatitude because he considered himself to be outside of the kingdom.

46. Green says this would be nothing less than something like premeditated social sabotage. All the guests say they will come to the party, but once the animals are slaughtered and prepared and the table is set, every single one of them comes up with a pithy excuse to not attend (Green, *Gospel of Luke*, 559–63).

47. Green's suggestion for the plural "you" in this passage to signify the master somehow speaking to those who skipped his feast is unconvincing. Green, *Gospel of Luke*, 562.

is experiencing material unique to Luke. Luke will begin to pick back up with the familiar themes as presented in Mark, utilizing a refrain of Bartimaeus's cry (perhaps as activating the greater gospel tradition), "have mercy on me," in Luke 16:24 and 17:13, to prepare the hearers for Luke 18:15, where he will enter back into the flow of the collective memory represented by Mark's performance. After the healing of Bartimaeus,[48] Luke, as a good creative oral performer, expounds upon Mark's developed theme with the story of Zacchaeus and the parable of the ten minas.

So here, at the point of Herod's threats in 13:1–33, the oral traditional community is already wrapped up in themes of messiahship, cross, and discipleship. When Jesus says, "I will finish my course," the audience knows what he is talking about. He is going to lay down everything—his very life.

The parallel passage occurs in 14:25–33 as Jesus teaches that one is simply incapable of being his disciple unless he or she renounces absolutely everything for him. Jesus gives analogies of someone building a tower or preparing for war. If they do not complete the endeavor at hand, they will be humiliated and likely destroyed. The point is *not* "Make sure you have enough to finish," but the context requires the point to be, "You do not have enough. You are incapable. Therefore, renounce all you have and follow Jesus."[49] Just as Jesus did not seek to save himself from Herod but instead renounced himself to "finish" in Jerusalem, the only way to "finish"[50] in discipleship is to renounce self and follow Christ.

13:34–35 and 14:34–35

Finally, in 13:34–35, Jesus mourns Jerusalem. Jerusalem was supposed to be the capital of the people of God. The temple stood in its midst reminding the people of their special relationship to God. Jerusalem was a city on a hill, and that city was supposed to be a beacon of God's promise to humanity through Abraham: "And through you all the families of the

---

48. The "blind man" is not named in Luke.

49. A tower is built for defense. If a tower remains unfinished, then the weakness of the property is evident. What should stand as a defense would instead stand as an invitation for attack. A king would be humiliated to go out to battle only to be defeated or surrender. Green, *Gospel of Luke*, 566–67.

50. There is a slight linguistic connection here between the two passages—see Luke 13:32, τελειόω, and Luke 14:29, ἐκτελέω; and a little weaker at 14:28, ἀπαρτισμός.

earth will be blessed."⁵¹ Instead, Jerusalem was rejecting her Messiah and seeking other gods of wealth and esteem.⁵²

Jesus was in turmoil. What should have been a great city of God's people had become a forsaken picture of idolatry. Jeremiah 5:7 captures Christ's heart: "Why should I forgive you? Your children have forsaken me and sworn by gods that are not gods. I supplied all their needs, yet they committed adultery and thronged to the houses of prostitutes" (NIV). Jerusalem, the capital of the people of God, is now an old picture giving way to the new picture of the disciples who would follow Christ, the new people of God meant to represent him to the world.

Just as Jerusalem was to be a beacon representing God, the disciples are supposed to be salty, revealing the world's true flavor and preserving its freshness.⁵³ Those who seek to follow Jesus are not called to try to build up fortifications to conquer their enemy. They are called to realize that they are unable to defeat the incoming army and surrender everything to Christ. The one who will not do this will lose himself and become nothing, like "unsalty salt."

One interesting clue to this passage is the word used for "lost its taste," μωραίνω, coupled with the phrase in 14:35, "He who has ears to hear, let him hear." The word μωραίνω literally means to be sluggish in mind or foolish, and "its main reference is to the intellectual life."⁵⁴ It is uncommon in the LXX, and when it is used it does not merely refer to ignorance, but to a lack of knowledge of God.⁵⁵ In Jer 5:21–22 the LXX uses this rare word in the direct context of the phrase "who have ears but hear not," identifying the "foolishness," or "tastelessness," of Israel with apostasy from God.⁵⁶ When one considers that Jeremiah prophesied the destruction of Jerusalem and the temple, and was almost killed for it, the comparison of these two texts is more firm. Jeremiah also discussed the "forsaken house" in Jer 12:7–8: "I will forsake my house, abandon my inheritance; I will give the one I love into the hands of her enemies. 8 My inheritance has become to me like a lion in the forest. She roars at me;

---

51. Gen 12:3.

52. As Jesus' teachings toward the Pharisees in this section imply.

53. For these two uses of salt in the ancient world see, France, *Gospel of Matthew*, 174.

54. There are some uses of the word to mean "insipid," as to foods. Kittel, *Theological Dictionary Volume IV*, 832.

55. Kittel, *Theological Dictionary Volume IV*, 833–37.

56. Kittel, *Theological Dictionary Volume IV*, 833–34.

therefore I hate her" (NIV). Jerusalem's house has become nothing, like unsalty salt. He who has ears to hear, let him hear.

Conclusion on Luke 13:10—14:35

Throughout the Gospel of Luke, the lowly are lifted up.[57] In this section of Luke 13:10—14:35, two parallel miracle stories demonstrate this theme. These miracle stories occur in a synagogue and at a feast, and on Sabbath. Sabbath and synagogue are symbols of Jewish exclusivity.[58] The feast at the Pharisee's house is a symbol of social/religious elitism. In the midst of each of these contexts the helpless and lowly were exalted to healing and release, signifying entrance into the kingdom. These stories are intimately tied, in structure, form, and theme, to teachings of the kingdom.

The humble are exalted, so be the seed. The hidden is rewarded; so be the leaven hidden in the dough. The first may be the last and the last the first, and nothing shy of absolute devotion will count for discipleship. A true disciple will represent God to the world and, as the disciple draws people from the four corners of the globe to worship Christ, they will all share a place at the eschatological table. The original hearer would have naturally absorbed this message from the performer of the text, and his or her natural communicational construct would have, upon accepting the teaching, allowed it to reconstitute him or her into a new or fresh expression of an ongoing tradition of communal identity.

These connections may be discovered through a simple literary approach to the text without regard to oral tradition. However, as argued above, the oral performance nature of the text can provide further warrant for such literary approaches. An approach to biblical literature as a product of oral tradition, as opposed to a written literary approach, calls for the investigation of literary devices common to oral cultures. Proper interpretation of material stemming from oral cultures requires the consideration of aspects of oral traditional culture such as activation, communal memory, structural repetition, and performance.

---

57. Green, "Jesus and a Daughter," 651–52; Torgerson, "Healing of the Bent Woman," 186.

58. Green, "Jesus and a Daughter," 649.

8

The Divine Proposal in John

THE INVITATION TO FOLLOW Jesus is simple, strange, and sometimes scary. In one way or another the invitation always sounds something like this: "Give up on everything you think you should have or want to have out of life. Give all of that away, follow Jesus, and discover a whole new meaning to life."

Jesus said things like, "Take up your cross, die daily, and follow me. If anyone doesn't hate his mother and brother and father and sister he cannot be my disciple. If anyone tries to save their life they will lose it, but if anyone loses their life for my sake, and the gospel, they will save it."

That kind of proposal could lead anyone to get cold feet!

But at least Jesus practiced what he preached. He gave his life away so that he could draw all humans to himself through his death and resurrection. Just as that lifestyle is not easy for any of us, it was not easy for him. Through blood, sweat, and tears he prayed the night before his arrest: "Father, if there is any other way, let this cup pass from me." Jesus identified with our sin, sorrows, and struggles.

The Synoptic Gospels begin Jesus' ministry with his baptism, connecting Jesus' water baptism with his crucifixion and resurrection so that Jesus' ministry begins and ends with a sort of baptism. This repetitive structure emphasizes the transformative theme behind Jesus' ministry—the theme of his identification with our sin and death. Jesus did not need to be baptized for repentance of sin, and Jesus had no sin of his own for which to die. However, he was immersed into both baptisms in order to identify with our sin, take our sin upon himself, bury it in the grave, and offer us his new life.

Perhaps Mark is most explicit in this endeavor as he intentionally draws out parallel aspects of both baptisms. For example, Mark is intentional in his use of the word σχίζω, "to tear." Mark only uses this verb twice, and in reference to the consequences of Jesus' two baptisms.

In reference to his first baptism, when Jesus came up out of the water, Mark says that the heavens were *torn*, a voice came out of heaven, and the spirit descended like a dove. The Father said, "You are my beloved Son; in you I am well pleased."

The second time Mark uses the word is found after Jesus died on the cross, and the curtain in the temple was *torn* from the top to the bottom. The voice of the Centurian echoed the voice of the Father from Jesus' water baptism, "Surely this man was the Son of God."[1]

Jesus' work of being baptized into the sin and death of humanity—his identification with human sin and suffering—tore the veil that separated God and humanity, the division between the heavens and earth. Now, in a new way, humanity can abide in the holy presence of the loving God. Just as Jesus identified with our sin and death, now the believer identifies with the death of Christ so that we can also identify with his resurrection. "The wages of sin is death, but the gift of God is eternal life in Christ Jesus our Lord" (Rom 6:23). He died the death we earned to offer us eternal life. We die to self, identifying with his identification with our sin through his death, and we leave everything behind in the grave and follow him in his resurrected life. The veil between heaven and earth is torn, and so as we abide in his resurrection, we abide in the kingdom of heaven here on earth.

The Gospel of John emphasizes God's invitation to intimate relationship differently than the Synoptics. In John, Jesus' ministry begins not with his baptism but with Jesus' sign of turning water into wine at a wedding. Just as the Synoptic Gospels connect Jesus' baptism at the beginning of his ministry to his baptism of the cross, John connects the

---

1. Mark 1:9–11; 15:33–39. Space does not allow for the investigation of what Old Testament themes might be activated in these scenes, but Rikk E. Watts is certainly correct to connect the "rending" of the heavens to Isa 64:1 and the surrounding context: Watts, "Mark," 120–22. Although it is interesting that Watts does not discuss Mark's second use of the term in Mark 15:38. The connection to the "second exodus" theme activated by Isa 64:1 is also supported by Rodriguez's discussion of Mark's use of *ekballō* in the scene immediately following Jesus' water baptism, *Oral Tradition*, 87–93.

inaugural wedding event of Jesus' ministry to the cross and resurrection, presenting the work of the cross not as a different kind of baptism but as a different kind of proposal and marriage and the inauguration of a new kind of spiritual family.

Through repetition and activation, John creates parallel scenes between the beginning of Jesus' ministry and his death and resurrection. This creative storytelling highlights the love of God and presents the cross, death, and resurrection of Jesus as the explicit demonstration of that love—a sort of divine proposal and marriage consummation with humanity, producing new spiritual children. Jesus is not only establishing the kingdom of God on earth; he is also establishing the family of God on earth.

John chapters 2–4 echo the themes of love and marriage and rebirth as they highlight the purpose of Jesus' ministry, and elements of the crucifixion and resurrection in chapters 19–20 intentionally parallel chapters 2–4 as a divine move of proposal and marriage and consummation. The Gospel of John is the last of the four gospels to be written, and it clearly varies from the performance tradition represented by the Synoptic Gospels. It is not unlikely that John may have intentionally written portions of his gospel to activate and interact with the synoptic tradition. Just as the Synoptic Gospels' focus on baptism invites humanity to die to themselves through baptism, John invites humanity to give their lives away to their eternal groom and live as the loving family of God.

Below I will demonstrate that John 2–4 focuses on the themes of Jesus as the bridegroom and the creation of a new spiritual family, and then I will outline the connections between John 2–4 and 19–20. First, I will give a brief summary of John 1 (focusing on 1:1–18) to establish some context of the gospel.

Summary of John 1

John 1:1–18 establishes the Christology toward which the Gospel of John will point its audience. Utilizing the activation of Gen 1:1 in his opening line, "in the beginning," John invites the audience to replay the creation scene with Jesus in view. Jesus is the Word of God at creation.

John pens the most succinct christological/trinitarian statement in all of Scripture in the first verse of his Gospel[2]—"the Word was with God,

---

2. See Wallace, *Greek Grammar*, 266–69. My translation is dependent upon

and what God was so was the Word." John's specific phrasing in this verse identifies the Word as God himself, and yet also as a distinct entity—not two deities, not a created being, but an entity equally identified as the one true God while still retaining a separate identity from the God who spoke the Word. Both God the speaker and God the spoken abide with the Spirit who hovers over the waters as one God in the reactivated creation scene. Nothing was created except what was created through the Word of God, spoken by God, in the presence and powerful outworking of the Spirit.

Within the creation framework, the Word is the source of all created life, and he is the light of humanity. John the Baptist came to bear witness of this light, though he himself was not the light. Though the very light of the world and source of human life came to his own, with John the Baptist as his witness, his own did not receive him. But all who did receive him were authorized by the very Word of God to become children of God through a birth process completely outside of human activity and control.

The very Word of God became flesh and operated as a tabernacle[3] amongst humanity—the meeting place between God and humanity.[4] The connection of Jesus and his body to the tabernacle and/or the Jewish temple will become incredibly important in the discussion below.

In his exploration of Jesus' identity as the "tabernacled presence of the glory of God," John unmistakably evokes a significant allusion to the concept of "seeing God's glory." In Exod 33:18 Moses says, "Please, show me your glory." God replies, "I will make all my goodness pass before you and will proclaim before you my name 'The LORD.' And I will be gracious to whom I will be gracious, and will show mercy on whom I will show mercy" (ESV).[5] God tells Moses that he cannot see the face of God in all his glory and live, so he passes by and allows Moses to see his back. Exodus 34:6 says, "The LORD passed before him and proclaimed,

---

Wallace's discussion on the passage.

3. The reference to the tabernacle is also an example of activation, and understanding John's use of the terminology in this passage is necessary to fully understand what John is saying about the incarnation.

4. This is further activated in Nathaniel's conversation with Jesus in 1:43–51. The consistent allusions to Jacob, along with Jesus' reference to "Jacob's ladder," all identify Jesus as the *Beth-El*. He is the house of God, the tabernacle, the very meeting place of God and humanity.

5. Unless otherwise indicated, such as here, Scripture passages in this chapter will be my own translations.

'The LORD, the LORD, a God merciful and gracious, slow to anger, and abounding in steadfast love and faithfulness'" (ESV). The Hebrew phrase וְרַב־חֶסֶד וֶאֱמֶת, "abounding in steadfast love and faithfulness," is a clear parallel of "full of grace and truth" from John 1:14.[6]

Jesus is the full manifestation of the glory of God that Moses longed to see. He is the unveiled and abiding shekinah glory that was hidden in a cloud in the tabernacle and temple. He is all of this manifested in human flesh. "And we saw his glory," John says, "glory as the one and only from the Father, *full of grace and truth*." John says, "For the law was given through Moses; grace and truth were through Jesus Christ." The glory of God—his very goodness that has been manifested as grace-and-truth—was always manifested through Jesus Christ.

In the beginning of creation and through Moses' giving of the law, the glory of God's goodness, grace, and truth was always present in the person of Jesus Christ, the eternal Word. Essentially, through the use of activation, John is saying, "We received the Torah from Moses, and the grace and truth that we find in Torah, found its being in Jesus Christ. And now, that very grace and truth—the glory of the Father—has become flesh. This human person, Jesus of Nazareth, was the very meeting place of God and man, the Word of creation, and the very manifestation of God's glory in human flesh. Every truth we know about God in the Old Testament was manifested perfectly physically in Jesus." That is why John finishes his prologue with "No one has ever seen God. The one and only God—the one upon the bosom of the Father—he exemplified him."

After the prologue, John the Baptist identifies Jesus as the lamb of God who takes away the sin of humanity, and Jesus calls the first disciples.[7] Then the evangelist begins to describe the ministry of Jesus.

The Cana Inclusio: John 2–4

The Wedding Sign—John 2:1–12

According to John, the ministry of Jesus began at a wedding on the third day (τῇ ἡμέρᾳ τῇ τρίτῃ). "On the third day" is a very common construction in the LXX. Some uses of this phrase contain possible connections to

---

6. This discussion, and immediately following, could be added to Rodriguez's discussion on John's prologue in *Oral Tradition*, 94–100.

7. See footnote 4 above for a brief mention of one aspect of activation present in the calling of the first disciples.

the Christian tradition. In Gen 22 it was on the third day that Abraham took Isaac up the mountain to sacrifice him, and God provided a ram in the place of Abraham's only and beloved son. It was on the third day that God descended upon Sinai in Exod 19. Other uses of this construction often reflect only a generic reference to a third day. One instance even reflects a more negative day—the day of Simon and Levi's revenge for their sister Dina in Gen 34.

However, I argued above that the intentionality of the authors of the Synoptic Gospels to frame their passion predictions around their overall purposes argued strongly for Luke's use of the phrase τῇ ἡμέρᾳ τῇ τρίτῃ, to be seen as an intentional reference to Hosea since Luke was arguing for Jesus' fulfilment of the Law, *the Prophets*, and the Psalms (Luke 24:44). Indeed, 1 Cor 15:4 is explicit in connecting the phrase to the Old Testament: "and that he was buried, and that he was raised τῇ ἡμέρᾳ τῇ τρίτῃ *according to the Scriptures*." There is no other Scripture as explicitly linked to the resurrection of Jesus on the third day than Hos 6:2, though honorable mention can certainly be made for Gen 22.

Additionally, it is no coincidence that this wedding sign is introduced by a citation from the wedded prophet Hosea. The prophet's marriage was used as a symbol of God's relationship with Israel. Hosea's people had run after other lovers and were suffering the consequences, but God, rich in love and mercy, could not continue to hand them over to their enemies (Hos 2:14–23; 6:1–3; 11:8–9; 14:4–7). Hosea, whose name means "salvation,"[8] ransomed his adulterous bride out of slavery, and John begins the story of Jesus' ministry with a citation from this prophet in connection with the wedding in Cana.

Hosea 6:2 LXX reads, "He will heal us after two days, on the third day we will be raised and live before him." John's citation from Hosea, clearly connected to the resurrection within the early church's traditions, would have certainly connected the salvation of Jesus through the cross and resurrection to the matrimonial message of Hosea. John is not being subtle, and by the time the narrative returns to Cana in chapter 4, the ministry of Jesus will have been immersed in themes of marriage, rebirth (as children of God), and salvation.

At the wedding, the hosts run out of wine. This would have been a huge source of social shame for the hosts, perhaps especially for the bridegroom who was the provider of the wine (John 2:9–10), and it

---

8. Note that Joshua's name is also referenced as Hoshea in Num 13:8 and 16. It is not a stretch to connect the name Hosea indirectly to the name of Jesus.

seems that Jesus' mother had some role to play in the feast, or at least some relationship with the hosts. She informs Jesus of the problem, apparently expecting him to do something about it. Jesus' reply seems rude at first glance. He answers with a Semitic idiom that apparently means something like "What do you have to do with me?" or "Why does our relationship argue for what you are doing to me or asking of me?"

The idiom in Hebrew reads מַה־לִּי וָלָךְ, while the Greek reads Τί ἐμοὶ καὶ σοί. Literally it translates to, "What to you and to me?" Demons say it to Jesus in Mark 11:24; 5:7; Matt 8:29; Luke 4:34; and 8:28, meaning something like, "Why do you bother us?" or "What do you have to do with me?"

The phrase was not necessarily used derogatorily. In 2 Chr 35 Josiah goes out to confront Necho of Egypt to battle him. Necho says, "*What to you and to me, king of Judah? I have not come against you today . . .*" In other words, "Our relationship does not argue for the role you are expecting me to play here. I'm not here to fight you!"

The general idea of this idiom is to say, "How does our relationship include me in this issue in the way you are expecting?" The phrase seems to be an intentional declaration that the speaker does not agree with the assumption of the other party as it relates to their relationship and how the speaker should engage the issue at hand.

Jesus essentially says, "Ma'am, does our relationship dictate that I get involved in the way you are assuming I should? My hour has not yet come." Mary's response is confusing. She simply commands the servants to do whatever he asks of them.

Deciphering the interaction between Jesus and Mary presents a challenge. Adeline Fehribach pointed out that Mary was essentially placing Jesus in the position of the bridegroom when she asked him to be responsible for the provision of the wine.[9] I believe that Jesus' question was posed ironically or instructively, meant to point those present to a deeper truth—a technique reminiscent of his encounter with the Canaanite woman in Matt 15:21–28. As Jesus dealt with the Canaanite woman publicly according to the disciples' own prejudices, the woman's faith instructed the disciples on the truths of Jesus' inclusive mission. Jesus managed his conversations in front of his disciples with didactic intent.

---

9. Fehribach, *Women*, 29.

Here at the wedding in John, Jesus' words essentially translate to "What could I possibly have to do with this situation? Am I the bridegroom? My wedding hour is not here." Yet he then acted exactly how his mother desired, and it puzzled his disciples. Jesus' questioning of the connection of the event to his hour led John to contemplate the significance of the sign within Jesus' greater ministry—especially the connection to Jesus' "hour." Later, John and the other disciples would understand its connection.

John leaves no doubt that the "hour" Jesus ultimately has in mind is his death and resurrection:

> John 7:30—Then they sought to take him, but no man laid hands on him, because his hour had not yet come.
>
> John 8:20—No one seized him, because his hour had not yet come.
>
> John 12:23—Jesus replied to them, "The hour has come for the Son of Man to be glorified."
>
> John 12:27—What should I say? "Father, save me from this hour?" But that is why I came to this hour.
>
> John 13:31—Jesus knew that his hour had come to depart from this world to the Father.

The word "hour" will play an important role in chapter 4. It is at the sixth hour that Jesus meets with the woman at the well (4:6). Jesus tells the woman at the well that the *hour* has come in which the Father will not be worshiped at Mount Gerizim or in Jerusalem (4:21) but in spirit and in truth (4:23). The word is used three times in 4:52–53 to highlight the timing of Jesus' healing of an official's son. As John develops chapters 2–4 into a unit focusing on the themes of marriage and new spiritual union, he also highlights connections of this section to Jesus' hour—his crucifixion and resurrection.

In the flow of the narrative, however, the disciples do not yet know that Jesus' hour is his death and resurrection. The word is always defined contextually. In John 16:21, "her hour" refers to the time of a pregnant woman's labor.[10] Within the context of the conversation, Jesus' response to his mother makes perfect sense. At the wedding, Jesus' hour would have most naturally referred to the time of Jesus' own wedding. It is as if

---

10. Fehribach, *Women*, 31.

Jesus said, "This is not my wedding (my hour). I am not the bridegroom. Why would I provide the wine?" It is only later that Jesus' disciples, and then the audience of John's Gospel, learn that his hour and his wedding refer to his crucifixion and resurrection.

The fullness of Jesus' question is later revealed: "How does providing wine for this wedding—acting as the bridegroom—connect to the hour of my crucifixion and resurrection?" Christ's question caused John to meditate on the connection, and so he includes Jesus' words to his mother for us to hear and ponder as well. John wants the audience to meditate on the connection between this first sign at the third-day wedding in Cana and Jesus' hour of the cross.

Fehribach explains what later reflection by John must have activated for him, and therefore, what he intended to activate for his audience:

> A first-century reader, familiar with the Hebrew Bibe, would have known that wedding feasts in the Hebrew Bible often illustrated the relationship between Israel and its God (Exod 34:10–16; Deut 5:2–10; Isa 54:4–8; Jer 2:2; 11:15; Ezek 16:8–13; Hos 1:2–9; 2:4–25) and that quality wine in abundance sometimes functioned in the Hebrew Bible as a symbol of messianic blessings (Isa 25:6; Jer 49:11–12; Joel 4:18; Cant 1:2; 2:4). Such a reader would have realized that Jesus's action of providing quality wine in abundance from the purification jars illustrated that he, in fact, accepted the role of the bridegroom, but that he was no ordinary bridegroom. As Sandra Schneiders and others have noted, the sign Jesus performed illustrated that he was accepting the role of the messianic bridegroom, and that as such he was assuming the role of Yahweh, the bridegroom of Israel.[11]

When Jesus seemed to deny his mother's request, Mary, understanding her son's character and personality, may have discerned a hidden meaning in his words. Thus, when Jesus expressed reluctance, Mary perceived a cue and confidently instructed the servants to follow Jesus' guidance. Or perhaps Mary had spiritual insight into just how the event would connect to the hour of Jesus' messianic mission. Maybe Mary was just a pushy mother. Either way, this episode may illustrate Mary's profound insight into her son's purposes.

---

11. Fehribach, *Women*, 29–30. Fehribach cites Sandra Schneider, *Revelatory Text: Interpreting the New Testament as Sacred Scripture* (San Francisco: Harper, 1991) 187, and others.

Perhaps most importantly, Mary acts as a structural/interpretive marker. She only appears in the Gospel of John here at the wedding of Cana and at the foot of the cross in John 19, connecting the scenes by her presence.

At any rate, Jesus acts and turns the water into wine—manifesting his glory (2:11; see also 1:14 and 17:5; 22; and 24). Jesus called for the purification jars to be filled with water, and he turned the water into wine. The purification vessels of the law were filled full by Christ. Christ is the fulfilment of the Law, and he invites us into his presence through the wedding celebration of his crucifixion and resurrection. This first sign demonstrated his glory and called his disciples to believe in him—just as his death and resurrection near the end of his earthly ministry would demonstrate his glory and invite them into a different kind of faith in him. Fehribach said, "It is through fulfilling his role as messianic bridegroom that Jesus gives people the power to become children of God and thus fulfills the promise made to Abraham."[12]

After this initial sign, Jesus goes and spends time with his mother and brothers. At the cross, only Jesus' mother will be present. His brothers do not seem to believe in him until after his resurrection. The absence of Jesus' biological brothers will play a significant role at his crucifixion.

Prediction of the Passover Sign—John 2:13–22

The very next scene takes place during Passover and in the temple. Jesus drives out the animals from the temple and pours out the moneychangers' coins, overturning their tables. Jesus says, "Stop making my Father's house a house of trade."

It is not explicitly stated in Torah nor implied in the narrative that the practice of selling sacrificial animals was inherently "wrong." Nor does the narrative imply that the traders or moneychangers engaged in extortion of the people. Perhaps insights to Jesus' actions can be drawn from the greater tradition activated from Jesus' words.

Zechariah 14:20–21 says:

> On that day HOLY TO THE LORD will be inscribed on the bells of the horses, and the cooking pots in the LORD's house will be like the sacred bowls in front of the altar. Every pot in Jerusalem and Judah will be holy to the LORD Almighty, and

---

12. Fehribach, *Women*, 32.

all who come to sacrifice will take some of the pots and cook in them. And on that day there will no longer be a Canaanite in the house of the LORD Almighty (NIV).

The words, "Holy to the LORD," were the words that were to be written on the turban of the high priest (Exod 28:36–38). On "that day" prophesied by Zechariah, horses will be as holy and set apart as the high priest himself—horses as holy as high priests. The most common cookware will be as holy as the basins before the altar.

The final phrase in Zech 14:21 calls for investigation: "On that day there will no longer be a Canaanite in the house of the LORD Almighty." Why would Zechariah make a point to declare the absence of Canaanites in the house of the LORD?

Had not God promised to bring gentiles into Zion as worshipers of YHWH on the day of the LORD? Earlier at Zech 14:16, *all* remaining nations are to come to Jerusalem to worship! Why is Zechariah celebrating the lack of Canaanites in the house of the LORD?

Were Canaanites in the temple so often that the promise "No longer will there be a Canaanite in the house of YHWH" would really register as such an awesome thing?

The discussion around the word "Canaanite" in Zechariah is fairly complex—it involves theories on how the original consonants of the text were pronounced and grouped, and the discussion extends into the translation of the LXX and beyond. But essentially, the word Canaanite could refer to Phoenicians who lived on the coast of Palestine, who were known for their extensive trading.[13] Because of this connection, sometimes the word "Canaanite" could actually mean "trader." This translation is applicable to quite a few passages of the OT such as Hos 12:8; Zeph 1:11; Prov 31:24; Job 41:6; and twice in Zechariah—here at 14:21, and also at 11:7.

If we are to understand "Canaanite" as "trader" in Zech 14:21 (or if John did), then it would mean, "In that day, there will no longer be any 'trader' in the house of YHWH." If there is no longer any need for the trading of sacrificial animals, then perhaps there is no longer any need for sacrifices. High priests and temple vessels are not needed as they used to be—after all, horses and Tupperware are just as holy. Jesus said, "Take these things away. Stop making my Father's house a house of trade."

---

13. BDB, 488; HALOT, 485.

The Divine Proposal in John

Jesus did not use the word "Canaanite" for "trade," but John is known for his allusions to the Old Testament without necessarily using exact vocabulary.[14]

F. F. Bruce pointed out that earlier in Zech 14 the prophet speaks of all the remnants of all the nations going up to worship in Jerusalem. The only place where gentiles could worship at the temple in Jesus' day was the outer courts. If this was the section of the temple that had become a marketplace, then the ability for gentiles to worship YHWH would have been hindered. Bruce says, "Jesus's action reinforced his spoken protest."[15]

If John was intentionally activating Zechariah (and the later clear reference to Zech 12:10 at John 19:37 increases the probable connection here at 2:16) Jesus was enacting a sign that essentially said, "Do you remember the day that Zechariah prophesied about? Today is the day. Today is the day for all nations to be able to worship in Jerusalem freely. Today is the day that horses can become as holy as high priests. Today is the day when Tupperware can be as holy as temple vessels. Today you shall stop making my Father's house a house of traders."

To Jesus' outlandish claims to the significance of his actions, the religious leaders' response could be paraphrased, "What sign do you show to prove that today is that day?"

But before John records the Jews' response to Jesus, he highlights that Jesus' disciples remembered what was written in Ps 69:9: "Zeal for your house will consume me." The passage cited continues, "and the reproaches of those who reproach you have fallen on me." Indeed, Ps 69 discusses a righteous sufferer who bears the reproaches of those who reproach God. Psalm 69 will be activated again at John 19:28–29, as Jesus is given sour wine for his thirst (69:21). This final reference in John 19:28–29 to Ps 69 in John (there is another reference at 15:25) is also the only time something like wine appears in John's Gospel besides the wedding at Cana.

Therefore, the current scene is now soaked in activation of the greater tradition. Jesus began his ministry *on the third day* at a wedding feast. He filled up the vessels of purification and brought new wine to the celebration. John the Baptist declared that Jesus was the Lamb of

---

14. See Hays, *Echoes of Scripture*, 284–88. Especially relevant are Hays words, "John's manner of alluding does not depend upon the citation of chains of words and phrases; instead it relies upon evoking *images* and *figures* from Israel's Scripture." Hays, *Echoes of Scripture*, 284.

15. Bruce, *Gospel*, 75.

God who takes away the sin of the world. The Lamb finds himself in the temple during Passover enacting Ps 69 and proclaiming Zech 14:20–21. The religious leaders demand a sign to confirm his claims. Jesus' response is "Destroy this temple, and in three days I will raise it up."

The audience already knows that Jesus has become the tabernacle of glory—his body is the temple. John explicitly clarifies the metaphor. The Lamb will be slain. The temple will be destroyed, but it will be rebuilt. The Lamb will live again. In three days, he will raise it up. For the audience, Hosea echoes again, "On the third day, we will be raised with him!"

They asked him, "What *sign* will you show us?" The first sign was the sign of the wine at the wedding—the Messianic bridegroom has made himself known. The sign that Jesus points to now is the last sign of the book of John, the sign of his death and resurrection. As John tells of Jesus' first and final signs back-to-back as an introduction to Jesus' ministry, he connects them to each other. They are meant to be interpreted together.

Later in this chapter I will demonstrate that John intentionally connects the scenes of Jesus' crucifixion and resurrection to these scenes (and the following scenes discussed in the Cana Inclusio). But at this point it must be stated that even if John did not double down on these connections later in his Gospel, the traditional audience, already immersed in the Jesus tradition, would have immediately made these matrimonial connections to the cross of Jesus. John has already succeeded in portraying the work of Jesus on the cross as God's proposal to humanity, fulfilling the Law, Prophets, and Psalms and inviting humanity into a new exodus-like salvation through the Passover Lamb.

Darkness, Light, and New Birth—John 2:23—3:21

There's a play on words in John 2:23–25. The word "entrusting" in verse 24—"Jesus himself was not entrusting himself to them"—is the same Greek word for "believe." So, humans were believing in him, but he was not believing in them enough to entrust himself to them.

Later in the Gospel, after feeding the five thousand with miraculously multiplied bread, Jesus tells the crowds, "Truly, truly, I say to you, you seek me not because you saw signs, but because you ate the bread and were filled" (John 6:26). The crowds then ask, "What sign do you do, that we may see and believe you?"

They had just seen the amazing sign of multiplied food! Jesus had been teaching and performing signs for a long time at this point. They believed in Jesus—at least, they believed they could get another free meal from him. But they were not ready to follow him. It is easy to get swept up and believe in something special that might benefit oneself, but faithfulness—relational commitment—is not so easy. Unfortunately, it is easy to mistake the first sort of belief for the second sort of faithfulness.

I think this is what John is getting at in these verses. The crowds may "believe in Jesus" because they see signs, but what are they actually pursuing with that "faith"? Were they ready to become children of God, as John mentioned in John 1:12–13—"To all who did receive him, who believed in his name, he gave the right to become children of God, who were born not of blood nor of the will of the flesh nor of the will of man, but of God"? Were they ready to step into a covenant relationship with Jesus, something like a marriage? Or were they more excited about the show of signs and how they might attain temporal blessings from this miracle worker?

We are soon to meet a certain human who believed in Jesus' name upon seeing the signs. Nicodemus meets Jesus at night and says, "Rabbi, we know that you are a teacher come from God, for no one can do these signs that you do unless God is with him." And Jesus responds, "Truly, truly, I say to you, unless one is born again, he cannot see the kingdom of God." Believing in the signs is not enough. One needs to be born again into a new and intimate committed relationship with Jesus—like a marriage.

It is easy to get swept away by something that seems special—a church that feels different or is experiencing significant growth, or a minister who seems to understand our current life situation. It is easy to be excited by a potential spouse who conjures enthusiasm about the future. It is easy to get swept up and carried away by something that feels special and to believe in the specialness of that something.

However, it is not easy to walk in relational, familial commitment. Every church, no matter how special it seems, is still full of people with their own hurts, hang-ups, and habits. Ministers may not always live up to our idealized expectations. Every romantic relationship will eventually face the daily realities of sacrificial love and relational development. Walking in relational commitment, for better or for worse, is not always easy. But it is always worth the joy that can only be found in faithful relationship.

Jesus knew that some kinds of belief come easily. "I believe those signs are amazing! I believe I want some more bread!" But relational commitment, the kind that says, "I'm ready to stick with you through better or worse; I'm ready for the sour wine of the cross," requires a willingness to let go of the old life and experience a rebirth into a new kind of life. With Christ, that means being born of God through the cross and resurrection of Christ. This type of rebirth requires letting go of the old. Jesus understood what is in humanity and what was required for saving faith.

Many of us have had the experience of someone getting swept up by something that seemed special. A friend or a spouse or a congregant seemed to believe in us and in what we seemed to share together, but then the daily relational commitment did not last. When the "special" faded, so did the "faith."

I have experienced this. It hurts. Jesus understands it too. We can rest in the assurance that his commitment to us will never falter and he can feel our pain when others abandon us. At the same time, we can also learn to be more discerning about to whom we entrust ourselves when they are simply excited by "the special." We can be intentional about how we open our hearts to relational commitment to Christ and others.

Also, we can grow in our understanding that following Christ is a relational commitment. It is like a marriage. It is like a new birth. Nicodemus was poised to receive that message from Christ when he came to meet with Jesus under cover of darkness.

John 2:25 says, "He himself knew what was in *humanity*."

John 3:1 says, "But there was a *human* from the Pharisees named Nicodemus."

John sets the stage for Nicodemus suggesting that he might not be exactly like the other humans who were seeking signs. At any rate, this conversation is deep, with many allusions back to the prologue (John 1:1–18).

On the outset, it is interesting that a Pharisee—a ruler of the Jews, which probably means he was on the ruling council called the Sanhedrin—would be such an exception. We have already seen the Pharisees acting as "interrogators" of John the Baptist, and their role will only get worse as the Gospel continues. However, we now see one of the first people outside the twelve disciples who seems to believe in Jesus and genuinely wants to understand and receive him, and he's a ruler among the Pharisees.

There is no demographic that Jesus cannot reach.

The Divine Proposal in John

Nicodemus, a member of the Sanhedrin, calls Jesus "Rabbi" and voices certainty that Jesus has come from God. This is no small admission from someone of Nicodemus's station. But Jesus knows that there is more to what Nicodemus must come to understand about Jesus' identity and mission. Jesus says, "Unless one is born anew, he cannot see the kingdom of God."

Jesus' statement contains wordplay, in that the word translated "anew" can mean both "again" or "from above."[16] Nicodemus responds, "How is it possible for a man to be born when he is old? Is he able to enter a second time into his mother's womb and be born?"

For a Pharisee like Nicodemus, to see the kingdom of God meant to experience the fulfillment of God's promises to the Jewish people as found in Scripture (the Old Testament).[17] Nicodemus's response could indicate at least two possibilities: (1) Nicodemus actually thought Jesus meant that one must be born *again*, and so he asked Jesus about getting back into his mother's womb to be born again; (2) Nicodemus understood what Jesus was saying, but Nicodemus just could not understand that what Jesus said could apply to a Pharisee such as himself.

If we look at the second possibility, then Nicodemus is responding to Jesus' rabbinical riddled speech with rabbinical riddles of his own. Nicodemus thinks, "I am a Pharisee! A member of the Sanhedrin. I'm about as close to being born from God as I can be. I'm already born from above! If anyone were to see the kingdom of God, it would be someone like me! The rabbi's words are as incredulous as if he is saying that he wants me to get in my mom's womb and be born again!"

If John intentionally distinguished Nicodemus from others who believe for the wrong reasons, perhaps we are to understand Nicodemus as confessing, "It's really hard to be born from above again at an old age—to let go of what I've been holding onto about God for so long. It would be just as easy to get in my mom's womb and be born again."

Either way, Jesus responds and addresses the deeper issue: "... unless one is born of water and of spirit, he is not able to enter the kingdom of God."

Being born of water and Spirit calls to mind Ezek 36:25–27: "I will sprinkle clean water on you, and you will be clean; I will cleanse you from all your impurities and from all your idols. I will give you a new heart and

---

16. Louw and Nida, *Greek-English*, 636.
17. Köstenberger, "John," 434.

put a new spirit in you; I will remove from you your heart of stone and give you a heart of flesh. And I will put my Spirit in you and move you to follow my decrees and be careful to keep my laws" (NIV). It is interesting that John the Baptist baptized with water but promised the coming of one who would baptize with the Holy Spirit.

This passage in Ezek 36 is directly followed by the prophecy of the valley of dry bones, where Ezekiel is called to prophesy that these dry bones be resurrected into new life—raised from the grave and filled with the Spirit of YHWH.

Jesus isn't just calling Nicodemus, and by extension anyone who comes to Jesus with genuine faith, to reset his mind. Jesus is calling for a complete resurrection—a new birth that involves a completely transformed life, infused with the very breath/Spirit of God.[18]

Jesus references Ezek 36–37 when speaking to Nicodemus to emphasize that believing in Jesus and becoming a follower is like being a pile of dry bones that are miraculously brought back to life. It is not something one can accomplish through genealogy, adherence to the Law, or works of the flesh. The new family that the bridegroom is creating is a work of God himself.

As John said in 1:12–13, "But as many as received him, to them he gave the authority to become children of God—to those who believe in his name, who were not born of blood, or the will of the flesh, or the will of man, but from God." We are completely incapable of saving ourselves. Our one act is the act of surrender. We surrender to the work of God on the cross, and he baptizes us with the Holy Spirit, kills the old self and raises up—"rebirths"—something new in us. Belief in the name of the Word is the open door to the authority to be reborn as the children of God.

The Synoptics saw this renewal as a sort of baptism—death and resurrection. John does not disagree, but he also presents this birth from above as a new life of love with the bridegroom—a rebirth into the heavenly family on earth. But even this divine proposal is not an invitation to fleshly works. To accept the divine proposal is to surrender to the work of the Spirit.

When someone is born of the Spirit, his way of thinking and moving and abiding in this life changes. It is no longer controlled by the ways of this world, and the world does not understand it—just like Nicodemus

---

18. In both Hebrew and Greek, the word for "spirit" also means "wind" or "breath." The context determines the appropriate meaning. In passages like this one and in Ezekiel, a play on words is often intended—God's "spirit-breath-wind."

The Divine Proposal in John

could not understand everything about the movement of the wind. F. F. Bruce said, "The hidden work of the Spirit in the human heart cannot be controlled or seen, but its effects are unmistakably evident."[19]

The final thing we hear from Nicodemus is the question, "How is it possible for these things to be?"

With what tone should that question be performed? With incredulity? With awe and reverence and anticipatory delight? We do not know the tone of Nicodemus's question. But we will see Nicodemus again at Jesus' burial. He won't speak. But his actions will help John define the cross and burial as the very consummation of God's love for all of humanity. Through the repetition of Nicodemus's presence in the narrative, John connects this conversation of rebirth to the cross and divine proposal of Jesus the bridegroom.

Bruce points out that, in light of the wisdom nature of the phrase, "Who has ascended to heaven and come down?" from Prov 30:4 and other comparable writings of the time, the point of Jesus' response to Nicodemus is that divine wisdom is only found in heaven.[20] The "earthly things," then, is very simply the fact that a spiritual rebirth is necessary to discern the things of God—to see the kingdom of heaven. If divine wisdom is only found in heaven, then we need divine assistance to discern heavenly things! Jesus is essentially saying, "If you cannot grasp the simple, earthy fact that spiritual awakening is required to attain a heavenly kingdom, how can you understand anything heavenly at all?" Indeed, Jesus' question stands for us all. If we don't believe the "earthy" reality that we need divine help to know God, how can we understand anything "heavenly" at all?

Then in 3:13 Jesus identifies himself as the Son of Man from Dan 7:13–14. He is the one who has both ascended and descended. Jesus is the only one, at least the only human, who's been in heaven and descended from heaven. He's the one with the divine wisdom. Not even people like Enoch and Elijah have ascended and descended like the Son of Man has.

And this Son of Man must now be lifted up just as Moses lifted up the serpent in the wilderness. The word translated "lifted up," in 3:14 is the word ὑψόω. The use of this word conveys both a lifting up (exaltation) and a laying down (abasement),[21] and its dual concept can be seen all through the teachings of Christ.

19. Bruce, *Gospel*, 85.
20. Bruce, *Gospel*, 87.
21. Kittel, *Abridged*, 1242.

For example, Jesus, to be lifted up (exaltation), had to die on the cross (abasement). To be resurrected (exaltation), Jesus had to die (abasement). If one would humble his/herself (abasement), God will lift them up (exaltation). One must die to self to be raised in relationship with Christ. Lose your life to save it. ὑψόω is everywhere in the Gospel of Jesus Christ.

And so in Num 21, Israel rebelled against God, and God allowed fiery serpents to torment the people. After they cried out for help, God instructed Moses to make a bronze serpent. Moses would *lift up* this abased creature so that any who looked upon it in faith would be healed.

This is what will happen to the Son of Man. Jesus will be lifted up in shame on a cross, but that shame will be his glory. He will die and rise again, so that any who look to him in faith will be saved.

Earthly and heavenly things.

These are the earthy things that Jesus was bearing witness to for Nicodemus. These are the earthy things that John was bearing witness to in his Gospel.

The earthly things of Jesus' life—his works, his teachings, and his death on the cross and resurrection—these are the things that allow for all the heavenly things—grace-through-faith salvation and the gift of the Holy Spirit that moves how he wills.

This is the way in which God loves the world. This is what it means that God gave his only unique Son so that any who would believe in him would have eternal life.

It is clear that God did not send his Son into the world to judge or condemn the world but in order that the world might be saved through him. As in Num 21, the bronze serpent did not judge the people. They were already judged. The bronze serpent was lifted up for the people to look to in faith in God for salvation. Therefore, whoever does not believe in the Son is judged already, but whoever believes has eternal life.

The sifting, or judgment, of humanity is twofold: (1) the light has come into the world; (2) humanity loves the darkness more than the light because their deeds were evil. Humans do not naturally seek to die to self, own our complicity in the darkness of the world, and drag our dark deeds into the light through confession and repentance. It is more natural for us to act like Adam and Eve in the garden—hiding from God, covering our shame from each other, and blaming each other for our position in life. We choose the darkness over the light. Choice is a defining element in the love/hate relationship. We love the darkness. We choose the darkness because our deeds are evil. And we are ashamed. So we hide in the darkness all the more. It is a vicious cycle of self-dehumanization.

Jesus invites Nicodemus, and us all, to step into the light and be reborn, not of the works of the flesh, but of God. Then it will be clearly seen that our works of truth have been carried out in God. The cure for this life—the means to being born from above—is not good works. The cure is exposure to the light of Christ.

Thus, through a conversation between Jesus and Nicodemus under the cover of darkness, John has illuminated the nature, purpose, and process of Jesus' mission. Jesus will be lifted up in shame and glory (process), as a means of salvation for all who would believe (purpose), rebirthing us into a new spiritual family (nature). John will now shift the focus back to the great witness of Jesus, John the Baptist, to reframe everything he has clarified about the saving work of Jesus back within the theme of marriage with Jesus as the bridegroom.

Celebrate the Bridegroom—John 3:22–36

John the Baptizer's entire ministry has pointed to the exaltation of Jesus who is now actively making disciples. The baptizer's ministry is reaching its fulfillment. At this critical juncture of the baptizer's ministry, his own disciples demonstrate a lack of understanding of his ministry as witness. John the Baptist's disciples learn of Jesus' effective ministry of baptism, and they seem jealous. John clarifies for his disciples the preeminence of Jesus by identifying Jesus as the bridegroom.

The baptizer calls Jesus the bridegroom from above. John is adamant that Jesus, the bridegroom, is the entire point of all of his ministry. He exists to bear witness to and prepare the way for the bridegroom. John is not working toward personal earthly esteem, but he is operating from a heavenly commission to enjoy the voice and exaltation of the bridegroom.

Every church and ministry does well to heed John's words. We do not minister to grow our ministry or brand. We are not moving toward earthly rewards, but we are operating from a heavenly commission to enjoy the voice of the groom. Anytime we hear that the groom's voice has been heard and honored, we rejoice.

As the groom's friend, John celebrates the groom's voice. John rejoices in the successful ministry of Jesus. Jesus must increase and John must decrease. John is the messenger who went before the Messiah. It is not the messenger or the ambassador who will save God's people, but the Lord himself because of his love. Jesus is the bridegroom and Son of God who carries the full measure of the Spirit, and those who believe in him have eternal life.

It would be beneficial to investigate what might have been activated for John the Evangelist as it pertains to God's divine proposal as he performed his gospel up to this point. Hosea 2:16–20 reads:

> "In that day," declares the Lord, "you will call me 'my husband'; you will no longer call me ['my Baal.'] I will remove the names of the Baals from her lips; no longer will their names be invoked. In that day I will make a covenant for them with the beasts of the field, the birds in the sky and the creatures that move along the ground. Bow and sword and battle I will abolish from the land, so that all may lie down in safety.
> I will betroth you to me forever; I will betroth you in righteousness and justice, in love and compassion. I will betroth you in faithfulness, and you will acknowledge the Lord (NIV).

Ezekiel 16 is more intense and graphic as it describes God as a husband jealous after his adulterous wife, though the chapter ends in a promise of atonement (16:63). Isaiah 62:4–5 says:

> No longer will they call you Deserted, or name your land Desolate. But you will be called Hephzibah [My Delight is in Her], and your land Beulah [Married]; for the Lord will take delight in you, and your land will be married. As a young man marries a young woman, so will your Builder marry you; as a bridegroom rejoices over his bride, so will your God rejoice over you (NIV).

John intentionally highlighted the "Judean land" in 3:22, and Isa 62 declares that the land itself will be renamed "Married." That Isa 62 highlights the matrimonial aspects of God's relationship with humanity is interesting since the immediate context in Isa 63 also has connections to the narrative at this point.

Isaiah 63:1–6 speaks of the wrath of God as does John 3:36. Then Isa 63:8–9 reads:

> And he said, "Is it not my people? Surely children would not be rebellious? And it was to them salvation out of all their affliction. Not an ambassador, nor a messenger, but the Lord himself saved them, because he loved them and spared them: he himself

ransomed them, and raised them up, and lifted them up all the days of the age.

"He lifted them up"—that's the word ὑψόω from John 3:14. Isaiah 63:9 says that it is not an ambassador or a messenger but the Lord himself who saved them. John has made it clear that John the Baptist was not the light but the witness of the light. The Synoptic Tradition (Matt 11:10; Mark 1:2; and Luke 7:27) connects John the Baptist to the Old Testament tradition of the "messenger" sent before the face of the Lord. In John 3:22–36, John the Baptist must proclaim to his confused disciples what was proclaimed in Isa 63, in the context of the matrimonial move of YHWH, "It is not the messenger, but the Lord himself who saves. Not the friend of the bridegroom, but the bridegroom himself."

Jeremiah 2:1–13 is also relevant to the matrimonial move of YHWH, but we will save discussion of that passage for the next scene in John 4:1–45. What is clear at this point is that John the apostle is painting a picture of Jesus as the messianic Bridegroom-God who brings a new spiritual reality—a new birth—through a fulfillment of the ancient traditions. He is saving any who might believe in him, ransoming them from sin's condemnation, and lifting them up to bestow upon these newborn, spiritual children of God eternal life in his perfect love.

Jesus' Betrothal—John 4:1–45

As we move into the scene of Jesus and the Samaritan woman at the well, I must acknowledge an unpublished article by Rick Johnson, "The Bridegroom in John 4." While discussing the intersection of Robert Alter's type scenes and oral traditional activation during my doctoral studies,[22] Johnson mentioned the connection of Jesus meeting the woman at the well to the type scene of "betrothal at a well" and shared his article with me. He also pointed me to Fehribach's work cited above. Everything in this chapter has grown out of studies catalyzed by that conversation, and it is impossible to fully indicate each space in which Johnson has influenced my interpretation of this passage from John.

In his work *The Art of Biblical Narrative*, Robert Alter discussed the existence of type scenes in the Old Testament,[23] a topic he derived from studying the works on oral tradition from Robert C. Culley and Homeric

22. See also Niditch, *Oral World*, 10, 21.
23. Alter, *Art*, 55–78.

oral traditional scholars.[24] Alter described Old Testament type scenes as "recurrent narrative episodes attached to the careers of biblical heroes" that are "dependent on the manipulation of a fixed constellation of predetermined motifs" occurring "at the crucial junctures in the lives of the heroes, from conception and birth to betrothal to deathbed."[25] Of course, the type scene identified by Alter that is relevant to our discussion is "the encounter with the future betrothed at a well."[26] The type scene looks like this:

1. The groom-to-be travels to a foreign country.
2. He meets a girl or girls at a well.
3. Someone draws water.
4. The girl or girls rush home with news of his arrival.
5. A betrothal is arranged, usually in connection with a meal.[27]

Alter discussed how this type scene applies to the careers of Isaac, Jacob, Moses, Saul, David, Ruth, and Samson.[28] The variations in the scenes from the pattern and/or from hero to hero describe something about the specific hero in the scene. For example, in Exod 2:15, Moses runs away from Pharaoh to Midian and sits down at a well (part 1 above). In 2:16 the seven daughters of the priest of Midian come and draw water (2 and 3 above). In 2:17 the girls are attacked by shepherds, but Moses delivers them and waters their flock. Notice that this part of the story is specific to the episode of Moses meeting *his* bride at a well. In 2:18 the young women go home and report what had happened to their father (4). In 2:20 Moses is invited to eat bread with the father, and he gives Moses Zipporah as a wife (5).

Moses' encounter with his future wife at the well also designated him as a deliverer through the aspects of the story unique to Moses.

Likewise, in Gen 29 Jacob travels to the land of the east (1) and meets Rachel there (2). There is a large stone on the well, and Jacob wrestles the stone off of the well (unique) and waters her flock (3). Rachel runs home and tells Laban (4). Jacob serves Laban for seven years, and finally a feast

---

24. Alter, *Art*, 58–59.
25. Alter, *Art*, 60.
26. Alter, *Art*, 60.
27. Johnson's summary of Alter, *Art*, 62.
28. Alter, *Art*, 63–75.

The Divine Proposal in John

is made for Jacob to marry Rachel (5) (although Laban gives him Leah first!). Much of this scene is clearly unique to Jacob.

Jacob, the trickster who wrestles with God, wrestles the stone from the well and is tricked into marrying a different woman at first! As Johnson said, "Jacob's entire life is characterized by wrestling, from the womb and his birth, through his conflict with Esau to win the birthright and blessing, his dealings with Laban, his nocturnal wrestling with God, and his trouble with his children."[29]

Isaac is absent from his own betrothal scene as Abraham sends a servant to find a wife for Isaac. Rebekah is the active player in that scene, and Isaac will be a passive character most of his life, as Rebekah takes the lead in securing a birthright for Jacob. Saul's betrothal scene is aborted, as is his kingship.[30]

In the biblical oral traditional framework, when a man meets a woman at a well, everyone in that culture immediately expected for the man to meet his wife and for a defining element of the person's character and/or calling to be addressed. We expect to get a glimpse into the person's "significance and destiny."[31]

John's audience would be quite surprised when Jesus, having traveled to a foreign land (Samaria), meets a woman at a well at noon and asks her to draw water. Is Jesus about to get hitched!? Indeed, Jacob also came to a well around noon, and the well at which Jesus sits is described as a well of Jacob in a field Jacob gave. Also, Jesus is traveling for concern of the Pharisees just as Moses had left Egypt for concern of Pharaoh, and the Exodus was just alluded to in the previous section in the Gospel of John. Just like Moses, Jesus rests at the well.[32]

Jesus begins talking with this woman at the well, who had come to draw water (John 4:7), and Jesus asks her for a drink. She will end up running back to the town to announce Jesus. A meal is discussed as Jesus says he has food to eat that the disciples don't know about, but his meal is to do the will of the Father.

The scene is set perfectly. The man is to become the bridegroom, and the woman is to be the bride. How will Jesus' betrothal scene unfold?[33]

29. Johnson, "Bridegroom," 4.
30. 1 Sam 9:11–14.
31. Johnson, "Bridegroom," 4.
32. Johnson, "Bridegroom," 8.
33. Andrew Arterbury argues that Alter mistakenly identified these specific instances of a man meeting his betrothed at a well as a betrothal type scene. Instead,

Jesus asks the woman for a drink. Her response makes perfect sense: "How is it that you, a Jew, ask for a drink from me, a woman of Samaria?"

She did not just say, "How is it that you, a Jew, as for a drink from me, a Samaritan?" The point is not only the distinction between Jews and gentiles, but the nature of their meeting at a well as male and female. Jesus could have been initiating some kind of romantic proposal by such a request at a well. How could he ask such a thing of a *woman* of Samaria since he was a Jew?

Johnson pointed out that the language of this discussion between Jesus and the woman could have been heard with pretty scandalous interpretations at various junctures: "Drinking from a well or cistern is used in wisdom literature as a metaphor of sexual contact (Prov 5:15–18)."[34] After a warning about foreign women, Prov 5:15–18 says, "Drink water from your own cistern, flowing water from your own well. Should your springs be scattered abroad, streams of water in the streets? Let them be for yourself alone, and not for sharing with strangers. Let your fountain be blessed, and rejoice in the wife of your youth" (ESV). Johnson also pointed to Song of Songs, in which the idea of a "sealed fountain" was used to describe virginity. The virgin bride was said to be "a garden fountain, a well of living water" (Song 4:15).[35]

In Jer 2, Israel is spoken of as the bride of YHWH—"I remember the devotion of your youth, your love as a bride, how you followed me in the wilderness, in a land not sown" (Jer 2:2 ESV). Within this context of a bride and her husband, Jer 2:12–13 says, "Be appalled, O heavens, at this; be shocked, be utterly desolate, declares YHWH. For my people have committed two evils: they have forsaken me, the fountain of living waters, and hewed out cisterns for themselves, broken cisterns that can hold no water" (ESV). Jeremiah uses the themes of marriage and waters

---

these specific scenes are part of a larger general type scene of hospitality. His article, "Breaking the Betrothal Bonds: Hospitality in John 4," then argues for an exegetical approach through the lens of hospitality and not betrothal. Arterbury's arguments clearly overlook the unmistakable matrimonial themes of John 2–4, and he unnecessarily reduces the potential for such a scene to reflect two themes simultaneously. Indeed, some of the themes he draws out can be applied (with much insight!) without neglecting the clear connections between the scenes of biblical heroes meeting their betrothed at a well. Much of his application of Greco-Roman literature does not further his overall arguments as the cultures were not connected in the times the ancient well-scenes were developed—Arterbury, "Breaking the Betrothal Bonds," 63–83.

34. Johnson, "Bridegroom," 9.

35. Johnson, "Bridegroom," 10.

to identify the worship of other gods as a sort of adultery (a common theme in Judges, Ezekiel, Hosea, and elsewhere).

Therefore, in this context of a man meeting a woman at a well and asking her to draw water for him, the request could be taken a few different ways. The request could be straightforward—a request for H2O. The request could be received as some sort of initiation of a possible courtship—"What's a girl like you doing at a well like this?" Or, the request could be less honorable—"I'd like to have a drink of your water. And I mean sex."

It is possible that this woman, being mistreated by men throughout her life, would have mistaken the words of Jesus, spoken alone in a field at a well, as a sexual proposal. She replied with a veiled attempt to uncover what Jesus was really saying. "Would a Jewish man really ask for a 'drink' from a woman of Samaria?"

Jesus tells the woman that if she knew who she was talking to, she might actually ask of him. Because he has the ability to give her "living water." The woman would not have had the context to connect "living water" to Jesus' true identity and the reference to Jer 2. That the phrase is used to discuss a bride's sexuality in Song of Songs makes it possible that she could misunderstand Jesus' intentions.

She continues to speak about the water in the well, though a well is not a likely place to find living (flowing) water. She may still be probing to see what this man's motives actually are. She points out that he has no jug and points out that the well is deep. Is this man greater than Jacob who dug the well?

Again, Jesus points to the heavenly interpretation of the water in question. The water he is offering will become a well of water springing up to eternal life. The one who drinks of it will never thirst again.

She says, "Give me this water!"

The ambiguity of the conversation leaves the audience guessing at the woman's interpretation of the situation. But Jesus' response at this point may indicate that she was getting the wrong idea, and he wanted to make his intentions perfectly clear.

"Go, call your husband and come here." She informs Jesus that she has no husband. The audience later discovers that this is a half-truth, and the woman may have left out certain details to leave her romantic availability uncertain.

But Jesus further unveils his clear intentions with his following words. He discloses divinely inspired knowledge of her situation. Jesus knows that she has had five husbands and is now in a relationship with another man who is not her husband.

She acknowledges that Jesus must be some sort of prophet to have access to such information about her life, so she engages this Jewish prophet on a religious matter—which mountain is the correct mountain from which to worship? Who is right, the Jews or Samaritans?

Jesus' reply to her theological inquiry hearkens back to his conversation with Nicodemus. Though Jesus says, "Salvation is from the Jews," his words strongly suggest that the categories of Jew or Samaritan and Moriah or Gerizim are passing away. Jesus says, "The hour is coming and is now here, when the true worshipers will worship the Father in spirit and truth" (4:23 ESV).

At the wedding in Cana, Jesus says, "My hour has not yet come." Here, at a well with this woman, he says, "An hour for proper worship has come." And proper worship is not wrapped up in the works or temples or mountains or religions made my human hands. It is a new spiritual worship from the Father's new spiritual children whom he is seeking through the ministry of the messianic bridegroom.

Indeed, the woman in this betrothal scene is the first to receive an explicit admission from Jesus concerning his identity as Messiah, "I who speak to you am he."

In light of the cultural associations of meeting one's betrothed at a well, it is no wonder that Jesus' disciples are confused that Jesus would be speaking to a woman alone at a well! The woman leaves her jug behind and goes away to tell her town about Jesus.

Johnson points out, "The five elements [of the betrothal at a well scene] are all present, but not all fit the usual expectations."[36] As we saw above, when unique elements arise in the type scene, those elements are meant to point to the unique identity and destiny of those who meet at the well—especially the groom. Jesus indeed journeys to a foreign land (1) and meets a woman (2). That woman runs to tell about the man (4).

However, the woman was not a young woman or girl/maiden—as in the type scene (2). No one draws any physical water (3). There is no material food eaten or an earthly betrothal (5). These variations indicate that Jesus' marriage, like his kingdom, is not of this world (John 18:33–38). The drawn water, representing the future marriage act of the betrothed, is not drawn from any human source. Just as the new birth is not from any

---

36. Johnson, "Bridegroom," 12.

human activity, neither is the receiving of the living water of eternal life from any human activity.

This is a spiritual marriage that is divinely consummated by the giving of the Holy Spirit. The water that is to be drunk is the new wine of the new wedding between God and humanity. It is the water and spirit of the new birth of new spiritual children. The water symbolizes the "Spirit and truth" in which all must worship God now that Jesus' "hour" is arriving.

Right on cue, after the woman runs to tell her "relatives," the disciples invite Jesus to eat. In the type scene, it is time for a betrothal meal. Jesus clarifies what his betrothal meal is. His meal is to do the will of the one who sent him. The betrothal meal that Jesus desires is the will of his Father, and the will of his Father is quickly reflected in the fields that are ripe for harvesting—the people of the town, and all who would hear the gospel of Christ and receive the water he has to give. Jesus' betrothal meal is not just a meat and potatoes and wine type of meal.

Jesus' betrothal meal is a divinely sanctioned destiny-type meal. It is a meal of salvation for all who would believe.

Jesus not only clarifies the type of food for the table, but he also speaks to the time frame of the table for the betrothal meal. He does this in 4:36 by activating Amos 9:13, which reads, "'Behold, the days are coming,' declares the LORD, 'when the plowman shall overtake the reaper and the treader of grapes him who sows the seed; the mountains shall drip sweet wine, and all the hills shall flow with it'" (ESV). Jesus has already produced the wine, and the fields are ripe for the harvest.

As much as Jesus' words in 4:34–38 conjured the promise of restoration from Amos 9:11–15, they may have also referenced Mic 6:15, "You will sow but not reap . . ."—a passage of judgment. The audience may ponder this activation, but its meaning will become clearer at John 20:23, which I will discuss alongside the parallel passages in the following section.

The betrothal meal to which Jesus looks is the eschatological meal when all of God's people will sit with him in shalom and break bread in his presence. And this eschatological marriage feast reflects the consummation of the will of the Father, particularized for Jesus in that moment in the present harvest of this Samaritan town and pointing forward to the growing spiritual family made possible through the divine proposal and rebirth of God's children.

Verses 37 and 38 echo words in Josh 24:13 about the promised land: "I gave you a land on which you had not labored and cities that you had not built, and you dwell in them. You eat the fruit of vineyards and olive orchards that you did not plant" (ESV). Christ's betrothal scene invites humanity into the true promised land of participating with God as his bride, and the saving work is done by the bridegroom himself.

The Samaritan woman, in all of her life's imperfections and misunderstandings, stands as a representative of the bride of Christ, the church. And just as her word brought many to be reborn by Jesus, the bride of Christ is to participate in producing new spiritual children, fulfilling the command from Genesis to be fruitful and multiply as the image of God on earth.

The ideal mate for Christ is his church, which is made up of humans who have wandered so far from the ideal that they need to be saved from the venomous darkness of the world and lifted into the light—baptized, reborn, and indwelled by the Spirit that brings dry bones back to life. And once they are resurrected with their betrothed, they will participate with him in the production of a new spiritual family that represents the kingdom of God on earth.

Jesus sat with the woman at the well in the midst of her shame and sin and cynicism, and he proposed to her in that very place.

He didn't tell her to clean up her life before saying, "I do."

He proposed to her in that place.

She said, "I do" in that place.

We are all the woman at the well.

We all need Jesus to meet us in that place, because we will never escape that place without him. And when he meets us in that place, we discover that we do not need to escape that place at all, because we are reborn as new creatures living under a new law of love. Our wedding redefines us, and so it redefines our presence in that place.

Christ's love transforms that place from a place of shame to a place to which we bring others to meet Jesus and be transformed by his unconditional, unending, incomprehensible love.

We say, "Come with me. Look at this old place of shame and sin. This is where I met Jesus. He'll meet you in your place as well. Come see the one who told me all that I have ever done. Would you like me to introduce you?"

This is the meal of which Jesus desires to partake with us.

Faith without Sight—John 4:46–54

Back in Cana, where water was turned to wine to celebrate a new life for a couple, an official's son is going to be saved from death by Jesus. This is the invitation of the literary tapestry of the divine proposal in John 2:1—4:50. We are all invited to believe, even without sight, and be blessed with new life, salvation from death—just like the Israelites who looked upon the exalted serpent in the wilderness.

The official had heard that Jesus was in Cana, and so he comes from Capernaum to Cana, about sixteen miles as the bird flies, to ask Jesus to save his son. Jesus replies, "Unless you see signs and wonders, you will not believe." Jesus' response sounds very similar to how John set the scene for the conversation between Jesus and Nicodemus—humans believing in Jesus only because of signs.

But the official has no time to discuss the intricacies of faith. His only focus is on the state of his son. He completely bypasses Jesus' remark and doubles down on his request: "Lord, come down before my child dies."

Jesus says, "Go. Your son lives."

Something significant occurs. Without seeing the sign, the human believes in the word of Jesus. John calls him ὁ ἄνθρωπος, "the human." "The human believed the word of Jesus." Nicodemus was called "a certain human" to distinguish him from the other humans who only believed in the signs. This human official seems to be another exceptional character of faith. He believed not only in the signs of Jesus, but he believed in his word.

Sometime the next day, his servants meet him on his way home. He could have made the trip home the same day if he was in a hurry. Perhaps he was traveling home slowly due to his faith in Jesus' words and due to the exertion of reaching Jesus in haste the day before. His servants inform him that his son is recovering.

The official asks the hour in which his son began to improve, and the servants tell him that it was at the seventh hour. The official remembered that that was the same hour that Jesus had told him, "Your son lives." The man and his entire household put their faith in Jesus. F. F. Bruce said, "On the previous day the nobleman had believed Jesus' reassurance; now, together with his household . . . , he believed in Jesus personally, acknowledging him as the sent one of God."[37]

John clearly and intentionally wraps up this section of his Gospel—the inclusio of the two signs performed in Cana. Through the use

---

37. Bruce, *Gospel*, 119.

of repetition and a generous activation of the greater Old Testament and early Christian traditions, John has richly presented Jesus' ministry in terms of marriage, rebirth (as children of God), and salvation from death to eternal life.

John cries out to his audience, calling us to say, "I do."

Do you put your faith in Jesus and find eternal life? Do you put your faith in Jesus and find a new birth from above? Do you put your faith in Jesus and find new living water springing up in your soul? Do you put your faith in Jesus, not just according to the signs and wonders that you expect, but according to his word and according to the proposal of the cross and resurrection as framed by the Law, Prophets, and Writings?

I do.

Repetition of John 2–4 in 19:24b—20:31

In this section I will discuss the parallel nature of John 2–4 and 19:24b—20:31 and interpret John's message behind the deliberate repetition. The parallel framework can be summarized as follows:

2:1–12: Wedding at Cana	19:24b–30: The Cross
2:13–22: Passover, temple cursed	19:31–37: Passover, Jesus' body dies
2:23—3:21: Nicodemus	19:38–42: Nicodemus and Joseph
3:22–36: John's disciples misunderstand	20:1–10: Jesus' disciples misunderstand
4:1–45: Woman at the well	20:11–23: Woman at the tomb
4:46–54: Faith without sight	20:24–29: Faith without sight

These episodes are held together by references to Ps 69, the prophet Zechariah, the presence of Jesus' mother, the presence of Nicodemus, the season of Passover, key words like "hour," the water and wine of the wedding in Cana and the water and blood poured out at Golgotha. They are held together by scenes of confused disciples and a conversation between Jesus and a woman (perhaps both being at some sort of well). They are held together by themes like faith without sight, and they are all wrapped up within the metaphor of the wedding, a new spiritual family, and the love of the bridegroom.

The Divine Proposal in John

The Matrimonial Passover—2:1–22 and 19:24b–37

As John turns to describe the crucifixion scene, he includes much of the familiar traditional gospel material from his own perspective in 19:16–24. He mentions Golgotha, the two criminals on either side of Jesus, and the sign designating Jesus as king of the Jews. He also mentions the soldiers casting lots for Christ's garment, and instead of citing the opening line of Ps 22, he cites the section that discusses this particular event. Then, John turns to material unique to his gospel and relevant to the themes discussed in the Cana inclusio (John 2–4).

For the first time since the wedding in Cana, Jesus' mother appears on the scene. She had attended the wedding event inaugurating Jesus' ministry, and she is present at this divine wedding ceremony—Jesus' hour.

Weddings are all about family. In a wedding ceremony, a new familial reality is formed from two different families. Jesus looks to his mother and the beloved disciple and says, "Woman, behold, your son." And to the disciple he says, "Behold, your mother."

It is interesting that Jesus would entrust his mother's care to John (I assume that John is the "beloved disciple"), considering Jesus had four brothers—James, Joses, Jude, and Simon, as mentioned in Mark 6:3 (Poor Simon! The baby was the only one to not receive a "J" name!).

Why would Jesus, as the firstborn, assign John to care for his mother when she had other sons? Perhaps this is due to the fact that we do not hear about Jesus' brothers believing in him until after his resurrection. After Jesus ascended to heaven, his brothers were with Mary, praying alongside the disciples (Acts 1:14). Later, James became a prominent figure in the church in Jerusalem and authored the book of James, while Jude wrote the book of Jude.

However, during the crucifixion, Jesus' brothers were evidently absent. It seems they might have agreed with the accusations against Jesus of blasphemy and leading Israel astray. As the eldest brother, Jesus would have been responsible for the family following the death of Joseph. His brothers may have felt abandoned as Jesus pursued what they perceived as a blasphemous role as a false Messiah.

If they were to entertain the idea of accepting their big brother as any sort of messiah, they expected Jesus to be a powerful figure, not one who would die on a Roman cross. We actually read something like this in John 7:2–5: "Now the Jews' Feast of Booths was at hand. So his brothers said to him, 'Leave here and go to Judea, that your disciples also may see the works you are doing. For no one works in secret if he seeks to be known openly. If you do these things, show yourself to the world.' For not even his brothers believed in him" (ESV). Their skepticism likely extended to their opinion of their mother, who stood by Jesus, believing in him despite their rejection. His mom, if she believed in him and followed him, may have been just as rejected by the brothers as Jesus.

The shared rejection and struggle of Jesus and Mary at this point in the narrative connects back to the exchange between them at the wedding in Cana. He responded, "What is this matter between you and me?" This phrase typically implies a desire to disassociate oneself from the other party. It questions the relationship and the relevance of the issue between them.

However, twice in the Old Testament, the phrase precedes events that actually connect the two parties in the powerful outworking of God's saving will. In 1 Kgs 17:17–24 the widow says it to Elijah (verse 18) when her son dies. Elijah then cries out to God and the boy is raised. In 2 Kgs 3:13 Elisha asks the king of Israel, "What to you and to me?" Elisha states that it is only for his regard for Jehoshaphat, the king of Judah, that he agrees to inquire of YHWH for water for the armies. While the initial intent of the phrase in these two episodes did, in fact, indicate a disassociation between the parties due to the context of the situations, the parties were later united by the miraculous, relational move of YHWH.

So, when Jesus said this to Mary, on the surface he was questioning the significance of the wine shortage as it related to their relationship and the context of the situation. John points us to the deeper meaning as Mary attends the hour of her son. What did that situation have to do with Jesus and Mary? The wedding proposal of the cross that began at the wedding in Cana had everything to do with Jesus and his relationship with Mary as her firstborn son because that first sign of turning water into wine propelled them to this moment at the cross in which they stand rejected by the rest of their family.

Perhaps Mary understood the weight of that decision at the wedding, which is why she told the servants to obey Jesus. She chose to walk with her son, her savior, to the cross.

Rejected together by their immediate family, they now suffer together at the cross.

They made a decision at the wedding in Cana. They had an idea of what was looming at the end of Jesus' teaching and healing ministry.

And at that wedding, they consciously decided to move forward together toward this moment.

At the wedding Jesus said, "My hour has not yet come." Here at the cross, the hour had arrived.

And at the cross, Mary became "family" with Jesus in a new way, and so did John. As the family of God, we too choose to journey with Jesus to the cross daily. Jesus declared to John, "We're family now. My mom is your mom." This act mirrored a wedding where families merge. In John's eyes, the cross was a wedding event, uniting God and humanity in a committed relationship, like a marriage covenant.

Now, familial realities that were not true have become true. A new spiritual family has been created, and the beloved disciple and Jesus' mother stand as the first representatives of this new reality. John paints a scene at the cross that reflects Jesus' words from the synoptic tradition: "Those who hear my Father's word and does it are my brothers and sisters and mother" (Matt 12:50; Mark 3:35; Luke 8:21).

Directly after the wedding in Cana, we are told that Jesus went to the temple during the Passover season. Now in John 19, on the day of preparation for the Sabbath, when the lamb was to be slaughtered, the incarnate tabernacle is lifted up on the cross. John tells us that Jesus mentions his thirst on the cross in order to fulfill the Scriptures. He is offered sour wine (ὄξος) to drink. This is a clear reference to Ps 69:21 (LXX 68): "They gave me poison (LXX—"gall") for my food, and they gave sour wine (ὄξος) to drink for my thirst." Of course, Ps 69 was also referenced in the scene directly after the presence of Jesus' mother in 2:13-22.

The immediate context of the earlier citation from Ps 69 is stunning in light of the present scene. Psalm 69:7–9 reads, "For it is for you that I have carried reproach; disgrace has covered my face. I am a stranger to my brothers and a foreigner to the sons of my mother. For zeal for your house has consumed me, and the reproaches of those who reproach you have fallen on me." Again, while Jesus is currently a stranger to his earthly brothers, he has instituted a new family through the cross upon which he hangs. And by his grace, his brothers according to the flesh will join him in his new spiritual family before long.

Jesus speaks his last words on the cross: "It is finished." The sign he alluded to back in John 2:19 has begun. "The Jews"[38] have torn down

---

38. F. F. Bruce points out that John uses the term "the Jews" "to denote not the people as a whole but one particular group," such as "the religious establishment in Jerusalem, whether the Sanhedrin or the temple authorities." He also uses it "to mean

"this temple" just as Jesus invited them to do, ushering in the sign that he promised would prove that the day prophesied by Zech 14:20–21 has truly come to pass. There will be no more traders in the house of YHWH. Horses are as holy as high priests, and Tupperware is as holy as the temple basins. No more sacrifices are needed, and all nations are invited to worship in this new temple.

Mark spoke of the curtain of the Holy of Holies being torn from top to bottom, indicating that we no longer need the holy places of the temple to find the presence of YHWH. John also marks the end of the temple symbols through the death of Jesus, as the day prophesied by Zechariah has been fulfilled according to Jesus' sign. High priests and purifying basins are no longer needed.

The Jews did not realize that when they tore down the temple of Jesus' body, they enacted the sign that would tear down the relevance of the temple in which they stood when Jesus first prophesied these very actions. The temple of Jesus' body would be raised back up. The relevance of the old temple would remain torn down.

John explains that since it was the day of preparation and that Sabbath was a high day, the Jews asked for the bodies to be taken down. The soldiers broke the legs of the two criminals to hasten their death, but since Jesus was already dead, they simply pierced his side with a spear. Blood and water came out. The new birth is taking place through the cross. The water and wine of Christ's wedding is poured out. As Eve was taken from the side of Adam, the church is birthed from the one who was pierced for our transgressions.

This also gives rise to fulfilled Scripture for John. The fact that Jesus' bones were not broken reminds him of the Passover lamb slain on the day of preparation (Exod 12:46; Num 9:12).

Also, the prophet Zechariah is referenced in this section that parallels the allusion to Zech 14:20–21 in John 2:16. Zechariah 12:10–11 says:

> And I will pour out on the house of David and the inhabitants of Jerusalem a spirit of grace and supplication. They will look on me, the one they have pierced, and they will mourn for him as one mourns for an only child, and grieve bitterly for him as one grieves for a firstborn son. On that day the weeping in Jerusalem will be as great as the weeping of Hadad Rimmon in the plain of Megiddo" (NIV).

---

the Judaeans as distinct from the Galilaeans, while at other times it has quite a general meaning" (Bruce, *Gospel*, 46).

Verses 12–14 further describe the mourning of the people. Zechariah 13:1 says, "On that day a fountain will be opened to the house of David and the inhabitants of Jerusalem, to cleanse them from sin and impurity" (NIV).

The new day of holiness that Jesus declared through Zech 14 has come to pass in the fulfillment of Zech 12 and 13. Jesus has poured out his blood and water to cleanse the nations from sin and impurity. To invoke Eph 5:26–27, Jesus has sanctified his bride, having cleansed her by the washing of the water with the word so that he might present us to himself in splendor, without spot or wrinkle or any such thing, that we might be holy and without blemish—just like the Lamb, our bridegroom.

John has shown us that Jesus is fulfilling the Law, the Prophets, and the Writings. The story begins with creation (Gen 1:1; John 1:1). God created all of humanity as his very image on earth and as the representatives of his rule and reign—the kingdom of God on earth. God planted humanity as a family on earth in the garden. And even after sin broke things apart and led to brother killing brother and the division of different people groups, ethnicities, races, and cultures, God moved to Abraham (John 8:56–58) and promised that YHWH's relationship with Abraham's family would result in a blessing to all nations. God moved to Moses (John 1:17; 3:14–15) and set his people free from slavery, and established them as a people to represent his rule and reign to all of humanity—the kingdom of God on earth. They were to be a relational, covenant people loving YHWH with all their hearts, souls, and strength and loving their neighbor as themselves. Grace and truth filled God's move toward the world through them.

Jesus fulfilled all of that, uniting us in him through his death and resurrection. He reestablished us as the human family created in him to be united as his image on earth—the representatives of his kingdom on earth bathed in his love, grace, and truth.

John wants us to see Jesus' ministry, especially the cross and resurrection, as a divine proposal to humanity to return to our first love. That means that we are all invited to become a part of the eternal, spiritual family of God.

Spiritual Procreation—2:23—3:21 and 19:38-42

Earlier in the Cana inclusio of John 2–4, after Jesus promised the sign of his death and resurrection as the proof behind his declaration of Zech 14 over the temple, he met with Nicodemus. Right on cue in 19:38-42, after the promised sign has been enacted and Ps 69 and the prophet Zechariah have been activated again, Nicodemus arrives on the scene. While all four gospels mention Joseph of Arimathea, only John places Nicodemus at the scene.[39]

Nicodemus had come to Jesus at night to inquire of Jesus' identity and mission, and Jesus clarified that even Nicodemus needed a miraculous new birth from above, like a valley of dry bones coming to life. Jesus taught Nicodemus that the Son of Man who has both ascended and descended is the only one who can make this happen. And this new birth that only the Son of Man can accomplish, will only happen as the Son of Man is lifted up like Moses lifted up the serpent in the wilderness, that whoever believes in him may have eternal life.

And what stands behind all of this work and effort on the part of the Son of Man who will be lifted up and save people from their sin and rebellion?

Love.

That's where John 3:16-17 lands: "For God loves the world in this way: that he gave his only, unique Son, that whoever believes in him should not perish but have eternal life. God did not send his son to condemn the world but to save it."

And speaking of judgment and condemnation, the judgment that sifts humanity is also all about love. John 3:19 teaches us that "the judgment is this: the light has come into the world, and people have loved the darkness more than the light, for their deeds were evil."

The point of Jesus' conversation with Nicodemus in John 3 is this: we can turn from our adulterous love of the darkness; receive the love of God through his Son, the Son of God and Son of Man; and be saved—reborn from above through the amazing act of love displayed by the Father and the Son! We can abandon adulterous actions of idolatry and the love of darkness, and we can be married to God.

Here in John 19, Nicodemus, with Joseph of Arimathea who procured Jesus' body, takes Jesus to a garden to bury him there with

---

39. Bruce, *Gospel*, 379.

seventy-five pounds of myrrh and aloes. These cultural allusions paint the burial of Jesus as another aspect of the marriage act of God.

Myrrh and aloes appear together only three other times in all of Scripture, and they are always utilized within the context of romantic love. Psalm 45 is designated as a love song, and in it a woman praises her royal lover: "Your robes are all fragrant with myrrh and aloes and cassia" (Ps 45:8 ESV). In Prov 7, Woman Folly cries out to tempt young men away from wisdom: "I have spread my couch with coverings, colored linens from Egyptian linen; I have perfumed my bed with myrrh, aloes, and cinnamon. Come, let us take our fill of love till morning; let us delight ourselves with love" (Prov 7:16–18 ESV).

The final reference to myrrh and aloes is the only place in all of LXX in which we find a Greek root comparable to the word John uses in his gospel.[40] Song of Songs 4:12–15 reads, "A garden locked is my sister, my bride, a spring locked, a fountain sealed. Your shoots are an orchard of pomegranates with all choicest fruits, henna with nard, nard and saffron, calamus and cinnamon, with all trees of frankincense, myrrh and aloes, with all choice spices—a garden fountain, a well of living water, and flowing streams from Lebanon" (ESV). The woman in the Song was a virgin—a garden locked that had never been opened. Jesus was laid in a new tomb in a garden in which no one had yet been placed.

John is the only New Testament writer to indicate that Jesus was buried in a garden tomb. This detail did not matter to the rhetorical purposes of any other gospel tradent. But John intentionally mentioned the garden within the context of an extravagant amount of myrrh and aloes, spices only brought together for romantic intimacy. John is not activating the garden of Eden. The word for garden is not "paradise" but κῆπος, the same word used in Song 4. Indeed, Song 4 is the first time the garden is mentioned in the Song. Shalom M. Paul said:

> The motif of the garden/orchard in Sumerian (giškiri6), Akkadian (kirû), Egyptian (šnw, dd), and Hebrew (גן) love lyrics functions not only as a favorite assignations (with its esthetic and sensual delights and hideaways) for lovers' trysts and *amore alfresco*, but may simultaneously allude to female sexuality and fertility in general...[41]

---

40. Song of Songs 4:14 uses αλωθ, while John uses ἀλόη. Psalm 45 uses στακτή, while Prov 7 does not refer to aloes at all in the LXX.

41. Paul, "Lover's Garden," 272.

Song of Songs 4 highlights the honeymoon night, and our passage cited above is near the climax of the scene of Jesus' marital act. For John, there will never be a more holy display of gentle, selfless, edifying, passionate, perfect love than the cross of Jesus. John paints the death and burial of Jesus as a sort of consummation of God's love for humanity. This is the act of Jesus that will produce spiritual children to worship God in spirit and in truth. God loved the world in this way, that he gave his only, unique Son, so that whoever would believe upon him will not perish but will have eternal life.

Misunderstood Ministries—3:22–36 and 20:1–10

In John 3:22–36, the disciples of John the Baptist misunderstood the purpose of his ministry. Despite John's frequent assertions that he was not the Messiah and that he was not even worthy to tie the Messiah's shoe, as well as his proclamation that Jesus was the Lamb who takes away the sin of the world, his disciples were troubled by the fact that Jesus' ministry was attracting more followers than John's. They had inaccurate expectations about John's role. Right on cue, in the scene paralleling this misunderstanding, John the Evangelist recounts a significant moment of confusion among Jesus' disciples.

Mary Magdalene comes to the tomb on Sunday morning and discovers the stone rolled away and the tomb empty! She runs and tells Peter and the other disciple (whom I will assume is John the Evangelist). Mary's explanation of the empty tomb is a clear sign of her misunderstanding of Jesus' ministry: "They have taken the lord out of the tomb, and we do not know where they have put him!"

Peter and John run to the tomb. John arrives first and looks in. Peter, the one who often seems to leap first and look second, rushes straight into the tomb. All of the burial clothes are there and put in neat order, but the body is nowhere to be seen. John does not believe that Jesus' body is gone until he goes inside himself. When he sees the clothes there, without the body, he believes the words of Mary—someone had taken the body away.

John did not believe in the resurrection at this point. He makes it clear that "they did not yet understand the Scripture that it is necessary for him to rise from the dead" (20:9). The disciples return to their homes.

Just as John the Baptist's disciples did not understand the purpose of his ministry at its most crucial point—the moment when Jesus began to rise in prominence and John began to diminish in importance—Jesus' disciples also did not understand his ministry at the critical moment when he was to rise from the dead.

Living Water—4:1–45 and 20:11–23

Peter and John return to their homes, but Mary lingers at the garden tomb. She stands there weeping. Let the reader remember that John, through his allusion to the Song of Songs, has designated this garden tomb as a well of living water. This garden tomb is the well from which one can draw the living water that Jesus promised the Samaritan woman—the water that will spring up to eternal life. This is the well that will birth spiritual children. Mary stands at this well, weeping.

Just after John the Baptist's disciples misunderstood the baptizer's ministry, Jesus was found at a well with a woman. Now, after John's presentation of Jesus' disciples' misunderstanding of Jesus' ministry, Jesus appears to Mary at the garden tomb.

Angels ask Mary from within the tomb, "Why are you weeping?" She explains her misunderstanding. She still believes that someone has stolen the body. She turns and sees Jesus, but just as the Samaritan woman did not at first know to whom she was speaking, Mary does not recognize her Lord.

Jesus asks her again, "Why are you weeping? Whom are you seeking?"

Thinking that she is speaking to the gardener, she desperately asks for direction to Jesus' body: "If you have taken him, let me know where to! I'll retrieve his body."

Just as the Samaritan woman did not understand the source of living water, Mary cannot see that she is standing before the source of the spring of eternal life.

Jesus speaks her name: "Mary."

And then Mary recognizes him for who he is.

"Teacher!" she cries out.

Just as Jesus needed to separate himself from the Samaritan woman's desire to embrace him in the wrong way, Jesus instructs Mary that now is not the time for the kind of embrace she had in mind. That is not to imply that Mary was seeking a romantic embrace. More simply, Jesus was not present to her in the same relationship as he was before his resurrection, and it was not yet time to fully disclose the nature of this new relationship.

He instructs her to go and tell his brothers (and sisters) that he is ascending to his Father and their Father, to his God and their God.

Just as the Samaritan woman ran to bear witness to her town, Mary goes to bear witness to her community of her interaction with the Lord. The Samaritan woman was the first to hear Jesus' claim to be the Messiah; Mary is the first to see him as the resurrected Lord.

The empty tomb is Jesus' betrothal well. Jesus desires to meet each of us there, to draw his living water, to say "I do" and partake of a divine wedding feast with our Savior.

The evening of the same day that Jesus appeared to Mary at the tomb, he appears to his disciples behind locked doors. He says, "Peace be with you." He shows them the marks of his crucifixion, and they are glad to see him. He repeats his blessing of peace over them, and then he tells them, "Just as the Father has sent me, so I send you." He breathes on them and tells them to receive the Holy Spirit, and he defines his commission over them. They are to proclaim the release and forgiveness of sin.

This scene parallels the aftermath of Jesus' conversation with the woman at the well in chapter 4, when Jesus clarified the betrothal meal he had in mind—to harvest his bride, represented by the people coming from the Samaritan town. There Jesus told his disciples, "I sent you to reap that for which you did not labor." Here Jesus tells his disciples that they are sent to declare God's forgiveness and withholding. As mentioned earlier, while Jesus' words in 4:34–38 conjured the promise of restoration from Amos 9:11–15, they may have also referenced Mic 6:15, "You will sow but not reap . . ."—a passage of judgment.

The apostles are commissioned to proclaim that the light has come to the earth. Any who put their faith in him are not condemned, but whoever does not believe in him stands condemned (3:18). The judgment depends on the reception of the eternal bridegroom. The promise of Amos 9 is at hand, but the judgment of Mic 6 still holds relevance. The apostles are called to announce to all who believe the forgiveness from God, and to all who do not believe the retention of their judgment. To reap a crop they did not labor, and tragically, to sometimes sow for that which they will not reap.

The very breath of Jesus—like the breath of YHWH that gave humanity life, and like the Spirit that brought an army of dry bones to life—quickens the disciples for this ministry.

Leap of Faith—4:46–54 and 20:24–29

Marriage is a leap of faith. Courtship provides some knowledge of the betrothed, and time spent together before the wedding develops intimacy and longing for marriage. However, at the end of the day, neither partner fully knows what they are diving into. The future is unknown, and there is always the possibility that the person we think we are dating is not who they really are.[42]

The final parallel scenes, John 2–4 and 19:24b—20:31, address this issue for those who would answer the divine proposal. Those who believe in Jesus without seeing him are blessed. While experience, logic, historical arguments, and other means of knowing can point us to a general knowledge of Jesus, saying "I do" to Jesus is a leap of faith. It is a relational plunge into a committed relationship. We are committing to an ongoing relational journey with a person, and no one can see the entire journey from the beginning.

The official from John 4:46–54 believed in Jesus' words without seeing his son revived. His faith seemed so sure that he felt no need to rush home. In that earlier scene, Jesus was adamant that there was something powerful in faith beyond the seeing of signs (4:48). In the parallel scene in 20:24–29, Thomas receives a lesson on believing without seeing.

Thomas was not present when Jesus first appeared to the disciples. The disciples told Thomas that they had seen the resurrected Lord, but Thomas would not believe them. He was adamant that he would have to see Jesus with his own eyes and feel the marks of the crucifixion with his own hands and fingers.

While John 2:23–35 and 4:48 seem to imply that Jesus valued faith that went beyond sight, he still accommodated Thomas' felt need to see and feel for himself. When Jesus appears to the disciples again a week later, with Thomas present this time, he invites Thomas to feel the marks of the crucifixion, but in the presence of Jesus, Thomas has no need to touch him. He simply cries out, "My Lord, and my God!"

Jesus affirms Thomas' confession. Jesus is Lord and God. And Jesus tells Thomas, "Because you have seen me you have believed. Blessed are those who do not see and believe." John writes this beatitude as a reflection of what would be the experience for nearly the entire church. We have heard of Jesus' resurrection, but we have not seen the resurrected

---

42. Luckily, I hit the jackpot!

body of Jesus of Nazareth. And we believe. We have taken that relational leap of faith and said to our eternal bridegroom, "I do."

Conclusion of John's Divine Proposal

John's testimony of the crucifixion and resurrection of Jesus is tied directly to his presentation of Jesus as the bridegroom in John 2–4. The presentation in these earlier chapters began with Jesus' *first sign* at the wedding in Cana, tied directly to the Jews inquiry to Jesus as to what *sign* he might perform to prove that the day of Zech 14 was coming to pass. Jesus prophesied about the sign of his death and resurrection. John concluded the Cana inclusio at the end of chapter 4 with the "second *sign*" that Jesus performed in Cana—the unseen healing of the official's son.

In 20:30–31 John informs us that there were many other *signs* he observed that Jesus performed that he did not record in his gospel. He makes sure that we understand that the signs that were written down were carefully chosen in order that we might believe that Jesus is the Messiah, the Son of God, so that through that belief, we might have life in his name.

John wanted us to understand the messianic mission of the Son of God through the illustration he crafted through the signs he chose to share, so that we might believe in Jesus according to the picture of the bridegroom and his new spiritual familial reality and discover the kind of life promised through that sort of messianic ministry.

John deeply wanted us to know the love of Jesus that he had experienced. The love of Jesus softened the heart of this Son of Thunder, so that in his gospel he could only call himself the beloved disciple. In his letters, he could not help but to call on all the churches over which he had influence to love one another, because love comes from God because God is love (1 John 4:7–8).

John, who wanted to call down fire from heaven to destroy a Samaritan town, presented the mission of Jesus through a betrothal scene with a Samaritan woman. His heart softened through the love of his Lord. This transformed apostle was adamant in his teachings about Christ's love to the church.

He believed that if we claim to know God but do not love each other, we are walking in deceit (1 John 4:20). He wanted every church to know that works and toil and endurance and the removal of evil and the testing of truth are not enough to keep an ecclesial lampstand if we forget love

(Rev 2:1–7). He taught that loving each other was the message that had been heard from the beginning (1 John 3:11) and that love must be not in words only but in action and truth (1 John 3:18). The love of Jesus totally transformed John, and he wanted it to transform every aspect of our lives as well.

Indeed, Jerome told in his commentary on Gal 6:10 of John's preaching in his extreme old age. John would have to be carried to church gatherings, and he would muster all his strength to share the same words every time: "Little children, love one another." The disciples and fathers got tired of hearing the same thing from the prestigious apostle! Surely he had greater things to share! They asked him why he always said the same thing. His reply was, "Because it is the Lord's command, and if it alone is done, it is enough."[43]

Jesus taught John that God is love. John was compelled to bear witness to God's historical move to humanity through his friend, Jesus of Nazareth—the Son of God and Son of Man. And John was compelled to bear witness to that move as a divine proposal of eternal matrimony and the establishment of a new kind of spiritual family.

God loves you—right now, just as you are. He longs for you. He delights in you. God demonstrated his own love for you in that while you were yet a sinner, Christ died for you (Rom 5:8). You don't have to rise up to some set of behavioral standards or standards of intellectual belief or understanding in order to be loved. He loved you at your worst—enough to die for you.

When the Son of Thunder stopped trying to perform and allowed himself to be loved, he was transformed. You can stop striving. You can surrender to the love of your bridegroom.

You are cherished. You are wanted. Anyone who confesses that Jesus Christ is Lord, and who believes in their heart that God raised Christ from the dead, will be saved (Rom 10:9). Accepted completely and forever. Washed. Renewed. Purified. Holy. Eternally beloved.

Not because you earned anything, but simply because you said, "I do" to Jesus.

Abide in that love.

---

43. Jerome, *Commentary on Galatians*, 266.

9

Romans 9–11

THERE IS A PATTERN in human behavior. Humans tend to seek their own ways of wisdom instead of God's.[1] Romans 11:25–27 begins, "Lest you be wise in your own conceits, I want you to understand this mystery, brothers ..." (ESV). This is an apt warning for any interpreter of this specific passage. Along with its immediate context of Rom 9–11, this passage has been variously interpreted from the earliest of faithful exegetes.

Jeremy Cohen argues, "From the first centuries of the patristic period through the end of the Middle Ages, Christian theologians and exegetes debated and equivocated over the number and identity of those Jews included in Paul's prophecy, and how and when it would materialize."[2] Some interpreters, like James W. Aageson, refuse to find any final consistency in Rom 9–11, saying, "Quoting Scripture in abundance, Paul embarks on a discussion that is marked by sharp turns, twisted logic, and unrelenting attempts to make sense of the issue at hand"[3] and claiming that "Paul did not pronounce the final word on the subject of Israel, Christ, and the word of God in Rom 9–11."[4]

---

1. Gen 3–11; Job 42; Ps 73; Prov 1; Eccl 1; Isa 40; Jer 51:15–19; Hos 4; Acts 7:51–53, and Rom 1:18–32.
2. Cohen, "Mystery," 281.
3. Porter, *Hearing the Old Testament*, 158.
4. Porter, *Hearing the Old Testament*, 159.

As to Paul's "quoting Scripture in abundance," twenty-five out of Paul's eighty-three citations of the Old Testament in the New, a full 30 percent, are found in these three chapters.[5] And, of course, Rom 9–11 has been a battleground for those holding to a doctrine of single or double predestination, God's sovereignty, human free will, and the relationship between Israel and the church. So, it is with fear and trembling, fully and humbly aware of the warning embedded in Rom 11:25, that I offer a suggestion on the interpretation of Rom 9–11, with a final special emphasis on 11:25–27.

As I take heed of the warning against the human pattern of conceit, I also take notice of the emphasis on God's patterns in Rom 9–11. As we've been noting the tendency for oral cultures to perform their traditions through repetition, we have yet to discuss a certain focus in biblical scholarship on identifying patterns throughout the Bible. The study of God's patterns in Scripture, or *typology*, is one of the four key themes for interpreting the two testaments as one Bible presented by David L. Baker in *Two Testaments, One Bible: The Theological Relationship Between the Old and New Testaments*. Baker says, "The *basis* of typology is God's consistent activity in the history of his chosen people."[6] His citation of von Rad at the beginning of his chapter on typology is especially relevant:

> We see everywhere in this history brought to pass by God's Word, in acts of judgement and acts of redemption alike, the prefiguration of the Christ-event of the New Testament . . . This renewed recognition of types in the Old Testament is no peddling of secret lore, no digging up of miracles, but is simply correspondent to the belief that the same God who revealed himself in Christ has also left his footprints in the history of the Old Testament covenant people. (1952: 36)[7]

God's works reflect themselves, and so they are better understood in comparison. Presenting Goppelt's views, Baker says, "Typology is not a method of biblical interpretation, but a way of thinking. It is an aspect of the New Testament awareness of being part of salvation history."[8]

To all of this might we add: Since oral cultures shared their traditions through performances saturated in repetition, a culture whose

---

5. Longenecker, *Biblical Exegesis*, 92–95.

6. Baker, *Two Testaments, One Bible*, 180.

7. Baker, *Two Testaments, One Bible*, 169; citing Gerhard von Rad, "Typological Interpretation of the Old Testament," *Int* 15 (1961): 174–92; tr. from German, 1952.

8. Baker, *Two Testaments, One Bible*, 173.

traditions retell the consistent and repeating patterns of an unchanging God will certainly represent a tradition saturated in typological tellings. The writers of the New Testament were products of the traditions of the Old Testament. It shaped their vocabulary. It shaped their worldview. It shaped their cognitive constructs. Therefore, the Old Testament, interpreted through Christ, shaped the New. It is wise for interpreters of the New Testament, at least in some way, to seek to enter the typological way of thinking of the New Testament writers, readers, and hearers.

In the following, by critically examining the tradition-activating Old Testament citations in Rom 11:25–27 in light of the typological paradigm of Paul's arguments in Rom 9–11, I argue that the "all Israel" in Rom 11:26 means exactly what it says—*this is the way in which all Israel will be saved*. In other words, if *any* from Israel would be saved, *all* will only be saved in "this way."

Toward this end, I will first define the problem Paul seeks to solve in Rom 9–11 and compare his opening and closing arguments to establish the general context. Then I will demonstrate the typological paradigm of Paul's argument in the body of these three chapters. Finally, Rom 11:25–27 will be analyzed in view of the larger Isaianic and Roman context in order to demonstrate that even as some of Israel is hardened while the fullness of gentiles enter, "all Israel" will be saved even as all the gentiles will be saved—only through the redeemer, Jesus the Messiah. This demonstrates the consistent pattern of God's work in salvation history eliciting the praise in Rom 11:33–36. The praise is in the pattern, because the pattern demonstrates the consistent character of God.

Brief Summary of Paul's Problem and Argument

The basic theological issue of Rom 9–11 is stated in 9:6a—"But it is not as though the word of God has become forfeit." Why is this an issue for Paul? As he laments in 9:1–5, many of his kinsmen, perhaps even most, have not received Jesus as messiah, and his theological teachings thus far in Rom 1–8 do not promise good to those who reject Jesus. Romans 1–8 can broadly be summarized in three sections: (1) Rom 1:1—3:20: There is no distinction between Jew and gentile in that all are under sin and in need of justification; (2) Rom 3:21—5:21: There is no distinction between Jew and gentile in that all can only be saved/justified through faith in Jesus the Messiah; (3) Rom 6:1—8:39: What are the implications of this shared salvation and justification through faith in Jesus the Messiah?[9] According to his teachings from Rom 1–8 then, there is no distinction between Jew and gentile in the need for justification through faith in Jesus (2:11; 2:12–29;[10] 3:9–20; 3:22; 3:30), and, therefore, his kinsmen who do not believe in Jesus the Messiah are outside of the promises of God.

But how can this be? After all, "They are Israelites, and to them belong the adoption, the glory, the covenants, the giving of the law, the worship, and the promises. To them belong the patriarchs, and from their race, according to the flesh, is the Christ who is God over all, blessed forever. Amen" (Rom 9:4–5 ESV). How can this mean anything except that the word of God has failed Israel?

Paul answers this problem with his opening argument, "For not all who are descended from Israel belong to Israel" (Rom 9:6b ESV). Paul will elaborate upon this argument by appealing to God's pattern of behavior in the Old Testament in which (1) the rejection of some people (2) allowed for the establishment of his chosen people (3) for the purpose of offering salvation to all.

This pattern will be the subject matter for the following section. But it may be illuminating to compare this simple opening argument with the beginning of Paul's conclusion of this argument in 11:25–26a: "Lest you be wise in your own conceits, I want you to understand this mystery, brothers: a partial hardening has come upon Israel, until the fullness of the gentiles has come in. And in this way all Israel will be saved . . ." (ESV). Why has the word of God not failed? Because in the hardening of part of Israel the fullness of the gentiles is brought in through Christ, being grafted into the tree of faith with true Israel (11:17–24), who also abides in the tree through faith (11:23). In other words, (1) the rejection of some people (2) allowed for the establishment of his chosen people (3) for the purpose of offering salvation to all.

---

9. For examples of some who follow this structure from different ranges of material, see Harrison, "Romans," 12; Murray, *Epistle*, xxii (though he breaks up the central section somewhat differently); Moo, *Epistle*, 33–34 (Moo breaks the content after 3:20 differently, but his divisions are noteworthy: 3:21—5:21 contain the divisions entitled "Justification by Faith," and "The Hope of Glory," which is clearly the salvation/justification of both Jew and gentile; and 6:1—8:39 contain the divisions entitled, "Freedom From Bondage to Sin," "Freedom From Bondage to the Law," and "Assurance of Eternal Life in the Spirit," which clearly demonstrate implications of salvation/justification); Bruce, *Romans*, 64–65 (Bruce calls the third section "The Way of Holiness"); DeSilva, *Introduction*, 605; Blomberg, *From Pentecost*, 236.

10. Notice that Paul begins to take up the issue of chapters 9–11 directly after his arguments in 2:12–29 but continues to argue for the lack of distinction in 3:9.

Thus, 11:25–27 restates the original argument from 9:6b, summarizes the argument from 9–11, and summarizes much of the content from 1–8: there is no distinction between Jew and gentile in that all need saving from sin, and salvation comes from the deliverer, Jesus the Messiah. The glory is in the revealed mystery that now that most of the Jews have rejected Jesus, though he came to them first, their rejection is leading to gentile salvation, and God is using the gentiles to make Israel jealous and call unbelieving Israel to salvation (11:11–16). God is working in his pattern: (1) His rejection of one people (2) establishes a group of people who (3) operate as the mode of salvation for all. And, even as all were made disobedient without distinction, all will be saved by the deliverer from Zion who removes Jacob's ungodliness, whether Jew or gentile (11:30–32).

Paul's Patterned Argument

After establishing the issue to be discussed in chapters 9–11, Paul launches directly into the first part of his solution in 9:6b–7. The introduction to his argument is this: some are not included as children of Abraham though they are his descendants, and some are not included as Israel though they are descended from Israel. Then verse 8 establishes that it is those who are in line with God's promise who are included. However, it is important to remember that the driving issue is the seeming rejection of Israel by God who promised fidelity to his chosen people. As Rom 3:3 puts it, "What if some were unfaithful? Does their faithlessness nullify the faithfulness of God?" (ESV).

Paul begins to demonstrate God's past pattern of choosing/rejecting some so that all peoples may be blessed (Gen 12:3). Ishmael and his descendants were not included as "children of Abraham" because he was not a child of the promise. Ishmael's line was rejected so that the people of God may be established through the line of promised Isaac and so that all nations, including the nation stemming from Ishmael, may be blessed through the promised line. Esau was not included as being "of Israel" even before birth so that God may establish a people through Jacob based solely on his sovereign choice.

The initial lesson is this: God rejects only so that he can create an avenue for acceptance. This is what he did with his chosen people, and this is now what is happening with those Israelites who are rejecting

Jesus. Their rejection is creating an avenue for the mission to the gentiles. Notice the consistency of this pattern, in that the firstborn served the younger as their rejection established a people of God, and now the rejection of some from Israel, a sort of firstborn of the promises, serves the younger massive gentile mission.

God's choosing a people for his purposes, or *election*, must be distinguished from salvation. Apparently it is possible, through physical lineage, to stem from the chosen and adopted people of God and not be saved, and it is possible to be excluded from God's elect people and be brought in. Paul states, probably as hyperbole, that he wishes he could be cut off from Christ (9:3) for those Israelites who are a part of those chosen (9:4–5; 11:28)[11] but are clearly not justified through faith.

Why would Paul resort to such strong rhetoric if these Israelites are already saved or would be saved because they are identified as members of God's adopted people? It is possible to be part of the elected line of people chosen by God and not be saved. This is consistently portrayed through Rom 9–11—9:27–29; 10:1–4; 21; 11:1–10; 17–24). In contrast, Zipporah, Rahab, and Ruth are stark examples of people who were not of Israel but still entered the promises of God.[12] Esau seemed to finish his life in such a way that he was right with God,[13] and Deut 25:5 allows for the third generation of Edom to enter the assembly of the Lord. Exodus 12:43–51 and Num 15:11–16 explicitly state that any sojourner who

---

11. While Paul does not refer to the Israelites in question as "elect," he does say that theirs is the "adoption." A term that he only uses elsewhere in Rom at 8:15 and 8:23 in no uncertain terms that imply election—especially as much as 8:15 and 8:23 play into the concluding verses of chapter 8. That Paul then, in the very next chapter, refers to the adoption as belonging to these Israelites cannot be quickly dismissed. Romans 11:7 may seem to use the term "elect" to point to salvation, but this is likely referring back to 11:5, to the remnant that is chosen out from the chosen people of Israel. It is the opinion of this author that this is proof that Rom 9–11 can hint at election toward salvation even as the typological pattern Paul argues from implies the need for personal choice for God to rework a person into a vessel of mercy (see explanation of this latter concept below). There is a tension between God's choosing and human free will that must be left unresolved, even while we all fall beneath God's ultimate sovereignty.

12. Especially consider that in a difficult to interpret passage in Exod 4:24–26, the actions of Zipporah, through a ritual of circumcising her son, saved Moses from YHWH who sought to put him to death. Consider that Rahab helped Israel enter the promised land. Consider that Deut 23:3–4 says that no Moabite will ever enter the assembly of the Lord, and yet a Moabite woman, Ruth, became the great grandmother of the great king David and a part of the lineage of the Messiah who is God over all (cf. Rom 9:5)!

13. Blomberg, *From Pentecost*, 253.

desires to be as a native may do so. It is possible for someone who is not a part of the elect people of God to enter the promises.

As he argues the case of the chosen, Paul is not arguing specifically for who is saved. He is arguing that God's promises are consistent with the present rejection of some from Israel because it reflects the pattern of God's past activity of creating an avenue for all to be saved by rejecting some from the chosen line. Not all from the chosen line were God's people, and those who operate as Paul's examples from the Old Testament who were rejected still had the potential to enter the assembly of the Lord—even as Paul prays that some of the currently rejected Jews may be saved (10:1; 11:14) and grafted back into the tree of faith (11:23).

In 9:14 Paul brings up a possible complaint to this line of reasoning and a response—"Is there injustice on God's part? By no means!" By way of a patterned proof of his response ("By no means!") to the complaint, Paul offers God's words to Moses: "I will have mercy on whom I have mercy, and I will have compassion on whom I have compassion" (Rom 9:15 ESV). Once again, Paul is activating for the audience an act of God in the past that served to establish his people. In this instance God had called Israel a "stiff-necked people" (Exod 33:3) with the threat "if for a single moment I should go up among you, I would consume you. So now take off your ornaments, that I may know what to do with you" (Exod 33:35 ESV). Israel removes her ornaments, and Moses goes to intercede for the people. Moses asks for God's presence among the people and that God would "consider too that this nation is your people" (Exod 33:13 ESV). God promises his presence, and so Moses asks to see his glory, perhaps to experience the presence that God has promised. As God answers Moses' request to see him, he also answers Moses' request to consider Israel as his people by saying, "I will be gracious to whom I will be gracious, and will show mercy on whom I will show mercy" (Exod 33:19 ESV).

Paul is likely activating this part of the tradition in order to remind the hearers of this epistle that God, regardless of physical decent among the Israelites, has always held to his sovereignty in applying mercy and compassion. How can the rejection of some from Israel for the salvation of gentiles, which then leads to the salvation of Israelites, be unjust when it merely repeats the pattern of what God has always done—a pattern for which they have worshiped him in the past? And God has always been straightforward with Israel—with those who are "stiff-necked" he retains the right to have mercy and compassion on whomever he desires, and to *stiffen* whom he desires.

Indeed, the same Hebrew word that described the Israelites' necks as *stiff* in Exod 33 is the word that described the end result of Pharaoh's heart as *hard*.[14] And so this leads Paul to remind Israel of how God worked with the hard heart of Pharaoh to bring them out of Egypt and establish them as his people. God did not impose a hardness upon Pharaoh's heart from the outside but used Pharaoh's hard heart to establish his chosen people,[15] and Israel worshiped him for doing so. How is it now unjust for him to do the same with this *stiff-necked* people when he has always retained the right to have mercy and compassion and to harden whomever he wills. It is not unjust. God is hardening some from

---

14. Wünch, "Strong and the Fat Heart," 165–88, demonstrates the three Hebrew words used for the hardening of Pharaoh's heart: חזק—to be strong; כבד—to be heavy; קשה—to be hard. Though God predicted that he would strengthen (Exod 4:21) and harden (7:3) Pharaoh's heart, he only did so after Pharaoh's heart was strengthened (implying it was further resolved in what it already was) or made heavy (implying it was losing its function to operate correctly) on its own four times (7:13, 22; 8:11, 15), after Pharaoh made his heart heavy once (8:28), and after his heart made itself heavy again (9:7). Then God strengthened Pharaoh's heart in 9:12 as he promised in 4:21. Pharaoh made his heart heavy in 9:34, and his heart was strengthened again in 9:35. God makes Pharaoh's heart heavy again in 10:1 and then strengthens his heart in 10:20, 10:27, 11:10, 14:4, and 14:8. God even strengthens the hearts of the Egyptians in 14:17. In 13:5 we see Pharaoh's heart as קשה as God promised in 7:3, though God continues to strengthen it in 14:4 and 14:8. All of this implies, as do other instances of God's hardening, not that God imposes a rejection of himself upon people but that he turns them over to their own rebellion, strengthening their heart to reject him.

Zoccali, "'And So All Israel," 306–7fn41: "See the discussion of 'hardening' (πώρωση) in Nanos 1996:261–64. Though Nanos (wrongly in my view) holds that the hardening envisaged here is temporary, he rightly explains that hardening is 'a strengthening in the course [unbelieving Israel has] chosen for themselves' . . . While God may 'strengthen' them in their chosen course to accomplish his purpose for his people, he does not choose their course for them. They have chosen not to believe; God has 'strengthened' them in this course so that 'salvation [can come] to the Gentiles, to make them jealous.' This is an important recognition, however inexplicable the question of the relationship between human responsibility and divine sovereignty—to the extent that Israel's unbelief is in the first place an integral part of God's redemptive plan—remains to be (cf. 11.33–36!). As with Pharaoh, God's imposition is not upon Israel as *tabula rasa* but upon (like all humanity) a sinful and rebellious people through whom God will freely and unconditionally bring about the greatest good (cf. 9.14–16)—salvation not only for Israel but also the Gentiles. It is according to which that Paul evokes in 11.20–21 the pottery imagery of Jer. 18.1–6, Isa. 29.16 and 45.9 (cf. Wisd. 15.7; Sir. 33.13); see Wright 2001: 640."

For a good discussion of the history of interpreting the hardening of Pharaoh's heart, see McGinnis, "Hardening."

15. G. K. Beale makes a strong argument to the contrary, but he may have underestimated the shifting vocabulary and sequence of narrative. Beale, "Exegetical and Theological," 129–54.

Israel for the sake of the gentiles, and this will lead to the salvation of all Israelites who will receive Christ, fitting perfectly within God's historical pattern of salvation.

This gives rise to the second complaint Paul foresees: "Why does he still find fault? For who can resist his will?" (Rom 9:19). Paul argues that God, as the potter, can make whatever he desires out of his clay, "What if God, desiring to show his wrath and to make known his power, has endured with much patience vessels of wrath prepared for destruction, in order to make known the riches of his glory for vessels of mercy, which he has prepared beforehand for glory . . ." (Rom 9:22–24 ESV). There are several Old Testament passages referring to God as potter,[16] but by far the most expounded illustration is found in Jer 18.

In Jer 18, Jeremiah is told by God to go to the potter's house. As Jeremiah watches, "the vessel he was making of clay was spoiled in the potter's hand, and he reworked it into another vessel, as it seemed good to the potter to do" (Jer 18:4 ESV). God's word to Jeremiah is worth a full citation:

> "O house of Israel, can I not do with you as this potter has done?" declares the LORD. "Behold, like the clay in the potter's hand, so are you in my hand, O house of Israel. If at any time I declare concerning a nation or a kingdom, that I will pluck up and break down and destroy it, and if that nation, concerning which I have spoken, turns from its evil way, I will relent of the disaster that I intended to do to it. And if at any time I declare concerning a nation or a kingdom that I will build and plant it, and if it does evil in my sight, not listening to my voice, then I will relent of the good that I had intended to do to it. Now, therefore, say to the men of Judah and the inhabitants of Jerusalem: 'Thus says the LORD, behold, I am shaping disaster against you and devising a plan against you. Return, every one from his evil way, and amend your ways and your deeds.'
>
> "But they say, 'That is in vain! We will follow our own plans, and will every one act according to the stubbornness of his evil heart'" (Jer 18:6–12 ESV).

Should the overall tradition of the Old Testament be activated by Paul's mention of God as a potter, it would certainly conjure up the theme of God's willingness to change his verdict concerning the judgment of a nation or person should true repentance be offered. Likewise, should a person or

---

16. See Job 10:9; Isa 29:16; 45:9; 64:8.

nation reject God, though he had previously promised good, God has also promised his ability to reshape vessels of honor into vessels of destruction.

Craig Blomberg, though arguing for single predestination, says, "The asymmetry between verses 22 and 23 [of Rom 9] is striking: (a) God prepares the vessels of mercy, but the vessels of wrath are simply 'prepared' (the Greek could even be translated 'have prepared themselves') for destruction; and (b) the vessels of mercy are prepared 'in advance,' whereas no such qualifier attaches itself to the vessels of wrath."[17] In light of Blomberg's analysis and the almost certain allusion to the Old Testament theme of potter and clay, which is dominated by Jer 18, it seems as if Paul is reminding the Jews that, while God may be bearing in patience with them as vessels of destruction—vessels whose spoiled clay may be of their own doing—his patience represents his desire to reshape them into the vessels of mercy that he had prepared them beforehand to be. But the warning remains—will they be wiser than their ancestors who followed their own vanity and stubbornness?

In other words, the answer to "Who can resist his will?" is "You *are* resisting his will in your own stubbornness! Stop suppressing the truth! Submit to the potter and be remade!" This interpretation does not deny the absolute and total sovereignty of God any more than does Jer 18. It simply argues that Scripture makes room for God's sovereignty to both provide for and transcend human free will.

Strengthening the argument for interpreting this potter/clay section through the lens of Jer 18 are Paul's words in 2 Tim 2:20–21 that use the same vocabulary (vessels for honorable and dishonorable use) as Rom 9:21.[18] In 2 Tim 2:20b–21, Paul declares that a great house may have some vessels "for honorable use, [and] some for dishonorable. Therefore, if anyone cleanses himself from what is dishonorable, he will be a vessel for honorable use, set apart as holy, useful to the master of the house, ready for every good work" (ESV). The categories of clay—honorable/dishonorable, destruction/mercy—in both Jeremiah and Paul are described in Scripture as being reversible, determined by the vessels themselves, even as they rest in the sovereign hand of the potter. Therefore, the pattern continues from Jeremiah to Paul—God holds out his hands in patience

---

17. Blomberg, *From Pentecost*, 254.

18. Blomberg, *From Pentecost*, 254. Brindle also points out that "Romans 2:4 states that God's patience and kindness are intended to lead sinners to repentance. And Ephesians 2:3 shows that those who were 'children of wrath' can become believers." Brindle, "Prepared by Whom," 139.

to a people who are resisting in their stubborn hearts. God's outstretched hands long to remake these people into vessels of mercy from vessels of destruction. And God is sovereign in the process, using both their *hardness* and their faithfulness for his glory and the salvation of "all."

Once again, Paul's argument leads to another display of God's pattern in salvation history, and Paul will intentionally activate the larger tradition for his rhetorical purposes. During Hosea's day, God called Israel "Not My People" and "No Mercy" (Hos 1:6–9). But he promised that one day he would call them "My People" and have mercy on them (2:23). Just as he can reshape a rebellious lump of clay into a vessel of honor, he can reidentify "Not My People" as "Beloved Sons of the Living God." And in this case, Paul also teaches that this past move of God is not just presented as a potential pattern for present-day Israel; it is repeated for present day gentiles (9:24), as they are now called "My People." Perhaps Paul also meant for the context of Jer 18 to apply to gentiles, since they are "a nation" turning from its evil way.

Finally, Paul reminds his hearers that God promised in the past to save a remnant, and a remnant is still saved from within Israel. The typological remnant pattern is repeated, demonstrating God's faithfulness and the success of his word. Paul then proceeds to summarize his argument up to this point in 9:30–32 and to project toward chapters 10 and 11. The content of his summary is expected by the hearer at this point—gentiles who are righteous have their righteousness by faith, and Jews who do not have righteousness lack it because they sought it as if it were based on works.

In chapter 10, Paul acknowledges that the Law was given to provide life for Israel. In 10:5, Paul refers to Lev 18:1–5, in which God promises that should someone practice his statutes "he shall live by them." When the Law was given to Israel, it was clear that should they keep it, the Law would bring them life. But Israel missed the mark when they thought that their own effort in the Law could establish their position before God.

Toward the point of Israel's misinterpretation of their efforts' efficacy, Paul provides a brilliant argument activating both Deut 34 and Ps 107. In 10:6–8 Paul acknowledges the truths of Deut 34—the word is very near, in your mouth and in your heart, and it is not too difficult to keep and thereby avoid the curses of Deuteronomy. That does not mean, however, that human effort earns salvation from God. Psalm 107 tells of men who trusted in their own strength to brave deserts, darkness, seas, and even their own sin, only to fail and require salvation from God. The Law is good and was given to keep Israel in the life that God desired for her, but her efforts would never earn her a place before YWHW. That position was always given through grace, and Israel would always need God to save them from their own efforts. Just as humans cannot navigate the seas of sin that toss them between the heavens and the abyss, they cannot effect the death and resurrection of Christ so as to earn salvation for themselves.

In Christ, the word that is now close to our hearts and in our mouths, the word that brings life, is found in Rom 10:9–10: "Because if you confess in your mouth the Lord Jesus and believe in your heart that God raised him from the dead, you will be saved." For Paul, this simply reaffirms what he has been driving home: "For there is no distinction between Jew and Greek; the same Lord is Lord of all, bestowing his riches on all who call on him. For everyone who calls on the name of the Lord will be saved" (Rom 10:12–13 ESV). By referencing Isa 28:16 and Joel 2:27 in this context, Paul explicitly declares that confessing that Christ is Lord is how both Jew and gentile are to call upon the name of YHWH for salvation—the same Lord is Lord of all.

In verses 14–21, Paul demonstrates that there is no excuse for the Jews who have rejected Jesus. The gospel has been preached to them through the prophets (as in Isa 52 and 53 and elsewhere). As Jesus said in the parable of the rich man and Lazarus, "They have Moses and the prophets. Let them hear them" (Luke 16:29 ESV). Jesus said in that parable that should some from Israel neglect to hear Moses and the prophets, they would also reject the word of one who rose from the dead. Faith for all comes through the word of Christ, and the word has been proclaimed in the Law, the Prophets, and the Writings. And Christ has fulfilled it all.

Paul cites Ps 19 in 10:18 to make the point, much as he did in Rom 1, that faith in God has been proclaimed from the beginning through creation itself. Then, Paul references Isa 65, God's response to Israel's request from Isa 63:15—64:12. Israel called for God to return in mercy, to rend the heavens and come down, to restore the clay as the potter. God declares that he came and said, "Here am I, here am I," but they did not return to him. God holds his arms out to "a disobedient and contrary people" (Rom 10:21 ESV; cf. Isa 65:2).

Romans 11:1–10 then reaffirms the concept of a remnant of Israel as proof that God has not rejected Israel. Israelites like Paul have been saved by the Jewish Messiah! Once again Paul uses the language of *hardening* from the Old Testament. The discussions on the subject above also apply here—God's hardening is not an imposition of an external rejection upon an individual but more of a handing over of the rebellious hearts already present (much as God did to those discussed in Rom 1:18–32—see especially 1:24; 1:26; and 1:28).[19] Indeed, 11:8 is taken from two Old Testament texts: (1) Deut 29:4, amongst a passage that actually recalls God's faithfulness (29:5–9) and presents a call for Israel to be established as the people of God (29:10–13) along with whoever is not standing among them that day (29:14–15); and (2) Isa 29:10, a verse that follows the words, "Astonish yourselves and be astonished; blind yourselves and be blind!" This passage is shortly followed by another reference to the potter and clay in 29:16.[20] Isaiah 29 also ends with the promise of Jacob seeing the work of YHWH's hands in his midst and finding sanctification and understanding (29:23–24). This is especially notable, since it has been shown that Isa 29:16 was linked to Jer 18:6b in the targums by verbal parallels, suggesting that they were read alongside each other by the greater tradition.[21]

Paul then references Ps 69 in verses 9 and 10 in reference to their "darkened eyes." Again, the context of this reference ends with those who see God's work, seek him, and have revived hearts. In these passages, Paul has demonstrated that the Law (Deut 29), the Prophets (Isa 29), and the Writings (Ps 69) have spoken to Israel and warned them about hard hearts, blind eyes, and stopped up ears. Those same Scriptures call them out of those states of stupor, promising salvation and renewed intimacy with YHWH. God always hardens so that he might establish intimacy with people, and those who are hardened are not excluded from the potential of being saved (11:13–14; 23).

In Rom 11:11–24 Paul first argues that Israel has not stumbled just to fall, but to (1) bring gentiles to salvation so that (2) gentile faith will bring Jews to faith (11:11–16). He then uses the image of a cultivated olive tree to demonstrate that Israel's stumbling is being used for the purpose of grafting the gentiles—wild olive branches—into the cultivated tree of faith. This argument denies gentiles any sort of supersessionism, for being engrafted is an opposite of superseding. Paul says that the Jews may still be grafted in

---

19. Perhaps this is also Paul's point in 1 Cor 5:5: "You are to deliver this man to Satan for the destruction of the flesh, so that his spirit may be saved in the day of the Lord" (ESV).

20. Though Craig A. Evans points out these passages within the quotation, he fails to acknowledge the context of these passages which brings nuance into the interpretation. Evans, "Paul and the Hermeneutics," 567. Read Isa 29:10–16 to get a feel of the immediate context. It is no small matter that this passage of hardening points to another potter/clay passage, likely conjuring the same conclusions as Rom 9:20–24.

21. Reasoner, "Redemptive Inversions," 400.

again, so it is evident that though they are presently rejected,[22] salvation for them is still possible. The purpose of chapter 11 at this point is to humble the gentiles into appreciating the roots of their faith so that they would have a heart for the salvation of those branches who made a way for their engrafting. They have not superseded Israel, but they have become partakers of the same tree of faith, even as wild olive branches.

It is easy to see why 30 percent of Paul's OT citations are found in these three chapters—he argues stringently that God's actions among the Jews and gentiles of his day are concurrent with the pattern of God's character, just as it has been written. It is not as if the word of God has failed! Indeed, it is being repeated. Paul is now prepared to conclude his argument in 11:25–36.

All Who Are Saved—An Analysis of Rom 11:25–27

The last major Old Testament citation within the citation-rich section of Rom 9–11 is found in 11:26–27.[23] Throughout these three chapters Paul has activated the traditions of the Old Testament for rhetorical purposes in order to demonstrate that God's present work among the Jews and gentiles does not represent a failure of his words to Israel but instead represents a consistent pattern of God found within his word, and Paul will now utilize a composite citation from Isaiah to wrap up his argument.[24] As stated above, this passage reinforces what Paul has already said—(1) part of Israel has been hardened, (2) this serves to bring in the gentiles, (3) this process makes a way for all to be saved. The following analysis of this citation will demonstrate that the best way to understand "in this way all Israel will be saved" is essentially, *The revealed mystery of God is that part of Israel was hardened to bring in the gentiles, and this process of hardening part of Israel to bring in the gentiles is now the process in which all Israel must be saved.* How marvelous are his ways!

The citation in 11:26–27 comes mostly from Isa 59:20–21 and Isa 27:9 and almost directly from the LXX. Note the following comparison:

---

22. Somehow, unbelieving Jews are presented as being both not elect (11:7) and still beloved for the sake of their forefathers as regards to election (11:28).

23. There are allusions to Isaiah and Job in 34–35, but the concluding hymn is "undoubtedly" "Paul's own composition." Seifrid, "Romans," 678.

24. It is fascinating that so many commentators and interpreters see Paul introducing a brand new concept of a future salvation for "all Israel" at the end of this massive rhetorical project of Paul in Rom 9–11.

First, the differences between Paul and the LXX are highlighted:

Romans 11:26b–27a
ἥξει ἐκ Σιὼν ὁ ῥυόμενος,
ἀποστρέψει ἀσεβείας ἀπὸ Ἰακώβ.
καὶ αὕτη αὐτοῖς ἡ παρ' ἐμοῦ διαθήκη,

Romans 11:27b
ὅταν ἀφέλωμαι τὰς ἁμαρτίας αὐτῶν.

Isa 59:20–21 LXX
καὶ ἥξει ἕνεκεν Σιων ὁ ῥυόμενος
καὶ ἀποστρέψει ἀσεβείας ἀπὸ Ιακωβ.
καὶ αὕτη αὐτοῖς ἡ παρ' ἐμοῦ διαθήκη,

Isa 27:9 LXX
ὅταν ἀφέλωμαι αὐτοῦ τὴν ἁμαρτίαν,

The Redeemer will come **from** Zion, will turn away ungodliness from Jacob, and this is my covenant with them: When I take away **their sins**.

And the Redeemer will come **for the sake** of Zion **and** will turn away ungodliness from Jacob, and this is my covenant with them . . . When I take away **his sin**.

Highlighted below are the significant differences between the MT and LXX of Isa 59:20–21.

Isa 59:20–21 MT
וּבָא לְצִיּוֹן גּוֹאֵל וּלְשָׁבֵי פֶשַׁע בְּיַעֲקֹב נְאֻם יְהוָה׃
וַאֲנִי זֹאת בְּרִיתִי אוֹתָם אָמַר יְהוָה

Isa 59:20–21 MT
And a redeemer comes **to Zion and to those who turn from transgression in Jacob**, this is a declaration of YHWH. As for ME, this is My covenant with them, says YHWH . . .

Highlighted below are the significant differences between the MT and LXX of Isa 27:9.

Isa 27:9 MT
לָכֵן בְּזֹאת יְכֻפַּר עֲוֹן־יַעֲקֹב וְזֶה כָּל־פְּרִי הָסִר חַטָּאתוֹ בְּשׂוּמוֹ ׀ כָּל־אַבְנֵי מִזְבֵּחַ כְּאַבְנֵי־גִר מְנֻפָּצוֹת לֹא־יָקֻמוּ אֲשֵׁרִים וְחַמָּנִים

Isa 27:9 MT
Therefore, by this the iniquity of Jacob will be atoned for, **and this is the full fruit of the removal of his sin**: when he makes all the alter stones like smashed chalk. The Asherahs and incense alters will not stand.

Isa 27:9 LXX
διὰ τοῦτο ἀφαιρεθήσεται ἡ ἀνομία Ιακωβ, καὶ τοῦτό ἐστιν ἡ εὐλογία αὐτοῦ, ὅταν ἀφέλωμαι αὐτοῦ τὴν ἁμαρτίαν, ὅταν θῶσιν πάντας τοὺς λίθους τῶν βωμῶν κατακεκομμένους ὡς κονίαν λεπτήν· καὶ οὐ μὴ μείνῃ τὰ δένδρα αὐτῶν, καὶ τὰ εἴδωλα αὐτῶν ἐκκεκομμένα ὥσπερ δρυμὸς μακράν.

Isa 27:9 LXX
Because of this the lawlessness of Jacob will be taken away, and **this is his blessing, when I take away his sin**, when they make all the stones of the alters broken into pieces like fine dust. And their trees will not remain, and their idols will be cut down just as a far away thicket.

There are significant differences between the LXX and the MT and between the LXX and Paul. By far, the most significant difference is in the alteration of the redeemer's movement. In the LXX the redeemer comes *on behalf* of Zion. In the MT the redeemer comes *to* Zion. Yet in Paul the redeemer comes *from* Zion. No other readings are significant for understanding Paul's usage here.[25] Mark A. Seifrid says that "Paul's unique use of the preposition ἐκ ('from') is likely intentional," and "Paul's reading is probably theologically motivated, since his entire citation of the text is highly interpretive."[26] In the ongoing discussion among scholars concerning the identity of "all Israel," it is exceptionally relevant that Paul intentionally shifts the redeemer's movement away from "for the sake of Zion" or "to Zion" to "from Zion." The focus on the redeemer's movement is not for the sake of Zion, or to Zion, but from Zion.

If Paul was simply making a statement about the future of Israel, this shift would be unnecessary and counterproductive. To maintain a future focus on ethnic Israel in this passage Seifrid (and others) says that Zion must here be "the heavenly Zion."[27] By Seifrid's account Paul is injecting a significant amount of new information and new theology into this concluding citation of Rom 9–11. Suddenly, Paul is no longer talking about the present interaction between Jews/Israel and gentiles and the present faithfulness of God, but he is talking about the later coming of Christ. In this interpretive scheme Paul inserts the concept of heavenly Zion to proclaim the new theological truth that somehow, when Christ comes from the heavenly Zion in the second coming, some sort of miracle will occur in which a large number of Jews, representing "all Israel," will be saved. That is quite a lot of new and provocative information to drop inside a single concluding composite citation with no following elaboration.

Indeed, Moo points out that it is normal for Paul to conclude each part of his argument in 9–11 with a composite citation,[28] and it is noteworthy that Paul never adds a totally novel idea in these conclusions. If a new idea seems to be brought up, such as the remnant in 9:25–29 or the jealousy brought upon the Jews by gentiles in 10:18–20, these *new ideas* are in line with the argument at hand and are elaborated on later in the ongoing argument—the remnant in 11:1–10 and Jewish jealousy

---

25. Seifrid, "Romans," 674—There is a reading from *1QIsaiah*, "'al ṣiyyôn," but it is irrelevant to this discussion.

26. Seifrid, "Romans," 674.

27. Seifrid, "Romans," 673.

28. Moo, *Romans*, 727.

in 11:11–16. There is no other correspondence to this future theology of Israel from Paul.

Seifrid points to Ps 14:7 and 53:6 that speak "of the Lord sending forth from Zion 'the salvation of Israel' . . . of the Lord 'turning back the captivity' of his people . . . and of the resultant rejoicing of Jacob."[29] Seifrid's point is well made here—the Old Testament does speak of God moving *from Zion* to rescue *his* people. However, this move is not from a heavenly Zion but from an earthly Zion, to rescue Israel from an earthly exile. Of course, Paul could draw on earthly realities from Israel's past to make statements about her heavenly future, but there may be another way to interpret Paul's alteration of the direction of the redeemer's movement that is more consistent with Paul's message in Rom 1–11.[30]

Christopher R. Bruno points out that ἐκ Σιών occurs ten times in the LXX,[31] and only one of these occurrences is in Isaiah—Isa 2:3. Bruno argues, in accordance with the criteria presented in Richard B. Hays's book *Echoes of Scripture in the Letters of Paul* that Isa 2:3 should be considered a referent in Rom 11:26.[32] Bruno argues that the inclusion of Isa 2:3 as an allusion or citation fits five out of the seven criteria, especially the criterion of thematic coherence which will be discussed below.

I have already maintained that Paul argued for God's faithfulness to Israel in Rom 9–11 utilizing the Old Testament to activate the traditions of Israel for the rhetorical purpose of demonstrating God's consistent activity in his work of salvation. The conclusions of Paul's argument can be summarized: (1) God rejected part of Israel in accordance with his character and past actions with other people—for the salvation of all; (2) therefore, Israel's rejection makes way for the gentiles to be saved, (3) and then, the gentiles' salvation can act to make Israel jealous and receive salvation. In light of the ability for oral traditional cultures to activate aspects of their tradition through words and phrases, what might Paul's composite citation of three Isaiah passages in 11:26–27 have to say to Paul's arguments thus far?

Isaiah 59 concludes a section in Isaiah that begins in 56:1.[33] The section begins with a command to do righteousness and keep justice

---

29. Seifrid, "Romans," 674.

30. See also Christopher R. Bruno's refutation of the "heavenly Zion" position: Bruno, "Deliverer from Zion," 126–28.

31. Bruno, "Deliverer from Zion," 123—though he leaves out Ps 13:7 LXX.

32. Bruno, "Deliverer from Zion," 123–25.

33. See Oswalt, *Isaiah*, 56–59.

and with a promise that even the eunuch and foreigner who do these things will be joined to God's people. This has echoes in Rom 2:12–29. Soon, however, the section turns grim, demonstrating that God's people are not able to keep God's commands. The climax of this theme is in Isa 59:9–15a, which is "one of the more poignant statements of human sinfulness and fallibility in the entire Bible."[34] This has echoes in Rom 3:1–20. Isaiah 59:15b–21, the section of Isaiah from which Paul quotes in Rom 11:26–27, reveals that "God will come and do for his people what neither they nor anyone else can do for them."[35] He will, through his arm, which Oswalt identifies as the servant of 53:1,[36] defeat the enemy—the sinners in Israel. In the MT, God is doing this for "those who turn from transgression in Jacob," but in the LXX, which Paul quotes, the redeemer simply comes for the sake of Zion and removes Jacob's ungodliness. In any case, 59:1–15a has made it clear that "he is not coming here to vindicate the righteous . . . No, he has come to do what the people, sinners and righteous alike, cannot do, namely, defeat the power of evil in their lives."[37] And just as this section began with inclusion of obedient gentiles (56:3–8), it ends promising worldwide recognition of YHWH (59:19). All of these themes are clearly comparable to the interpretations of Rom 1–11 discussed to this point.

Isaiah 2:1–5, like 59:15b–21, turns from a context of grim status to promise. Whereas Isa 1 speaks of the desolate country and a religion that burdens God, Isa 2:1–5 declares that Zion will be so exalted that all the nations come to her, because "*out of Zion* shall go the law, and the word of the LORD from Jerusalem" (Isa 2:3b ESV). Paul's entire argument in Rom 9–11 is that God's word—the word that comes *out of* Zion—has not failed Israel. Gentiles are flowing in to receive the *torah* of faith. Indeed, Paul says that "Christ is the end of the law for righteousness to everyone who believes" (Rom 10:4 ESV). So, the word that matters—the *instruction* of faith—is Christ. And this Word has not failed.

After citing the first part of Isa 59:21, modifying it with Isaiah 2:3, it would have seemed natural for Paul to continue on with 59:21. After all, 59:21 and following declares that the covenant is the Spirit of God given to his people, and his very word that he placed on their lips with the promise that it would never depart from their lips or their descendants'

34. Oswalt, *Isaiah*, 629.
35. Oswalt, *Isaiah*, 636.
36. Oswalt, *Isaiah*, 636.
37. Oswalt, *Isaiah*, 636.

lips. This would neatly fit into Paul's words on the Spirit in Rom 8 and the unfailing word of God in 9–11, and perhaps he intended this context to be activated. But instead of citing the rest of 59:21, Paul inserts a section from 27:9—when I take away your sins.

Isaiah 27 also concludes a section within Isaiah, a section which is often called "Isaiah's Apocalypse," Isa 24–27.[38] Isaiah 24:4–5 is curious in that it charges that the earth withers because the people of the earth, without distinguishing between Jew and gentile, have disobeyed the laws, violated the statutes, and broken the everlasting covenant. Again, this is strangely reminiscent of arguments from earlier in Romans (1:18—3:20). In Isa 25, LXX, God destroys not the "foreign city" (MT) but the "city of the impious," (25:2) and not only "all peoples" but all "ἔθνος" are invited to the feast that God prepares (6). In the MT, God swallows up death forever and wipes away tears for all people and takes away the reproach from his people. In the LXX, death is said to have triumphed at first, but God wiped away every tear and removed disgrace from all the earth from the people.

The LXX is much more universal in tone. In both the MT and LXX, those who persist in their pride, represented by Moab, are brought low (10–12). Isaiah 26 celebrates God's peace in submission and dependence. It declares God's salvation of the city, declaring that any nation/people that keeps the faith may enter. And it declares that God's dead will live—their bodies will rise (18)—before promising that God will come to punish people for their sin and slay Leviathan (26:20—27:1). Isaiah 27 is difficult to follow in the LXX. Verses 1–5 seem to display a level of disorientation with the "vineyard" and "strong city." Though the vineyard elicits singing and the city is strong, the city is besieged with falling walls, and the vineyard is watered in vain. There seems to be a move in the text to seek salvation not from within the city or from within the vineyard but simply in God (4–5). Verse 6 declares that Jacob will bud and blossom, and 7–8 asks if he will be killed by the spirit of God's wrath. All of this, whatever else it means, seems to imply a lack of confidence in the older relics of faith in God. Jacob, no longer trusting in the strong city or the vineyard, stands on the edge of being consumed by God's *hard* spirit of wrath. It is into this context that Isa 27:9 declares, "Because of this the lawlessness of Jacob will be taken away, and this is his blessing, when I take away his sin, when they make all the stones of the alters broken into

---

38. Oswalt, *Isaiah*, 280.

pieces like fine dust. And their trees will not remain, and their idols will be cut down just as a far away thicket."

This implies both God's gracious move and Jacob's obedient/faithful response, as Jacob no longer seeks refuge in the fortified city, or in the vineyard (representing national Israel—see Isa 5) but in God alone. Interestingly, desolation still awaits (10–11), and during that day the hearer is charged to gather the sons of Israel one by one until the day when the lost will be brought back into Jerusalem.[39]

Whatever else may be argued about the Isaianic context of Paul's composite citation with which he concludes the formal argument in Rom 9–11, some things are clear. The Isaianic context clearly emphasizes the inclusion of the gentiles and a struggle of maintaining covenant, laws, or simply a right place before God in obtainable things like willpower, strong cities, and vineyards. God is always the gracious hero, and humanity is always called to active response. Each portion of the citation has its own echoes with Romans, but as a composite one can clearly see the essentials of the Roman theology: (1) There is no distinction between Jew and gentile, in that all are under sin and in need of justification; (2) There is no distinction between Jew and gentile, in that all are saved/justified through faith (and Paul would definitely identify the saving arm of God, the word of God, and the redeemer as Christ); (3) There is even some representation of the implications of this shared salvation/justification through faith in Jesus the Messiah—rising from the dead, peace, wiped away tears, and communion with God and his people.

While the Isaianic context engages the theology of Rom 1–8 (which is the same theology as 9–11), the final form of the citation, as mentioned earlier in the paper, summarizes the argument of 9–11. The following may help to see the flow of Rom 11:25–27:

---

39. It must be admitted that the mention of the "great trumpet" in 27:13 LXX could make a case for bringing a future orientation into Paul's citation. However, in light of the rest of the contextual evidence of Rom 1–11 and the Isaiah passages, this is not a strong enough argument to bring in such a foreign concept into Paul's flow of thought at this point.

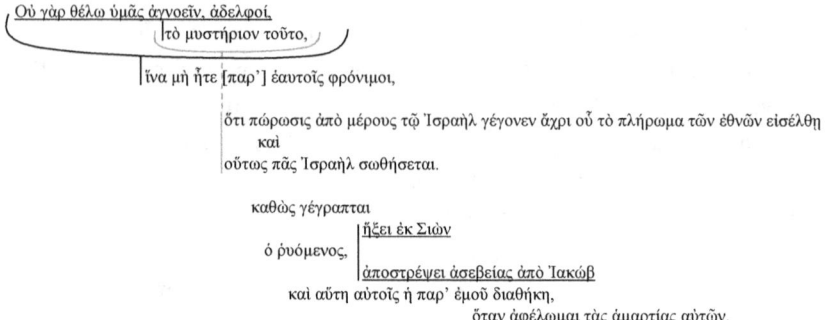

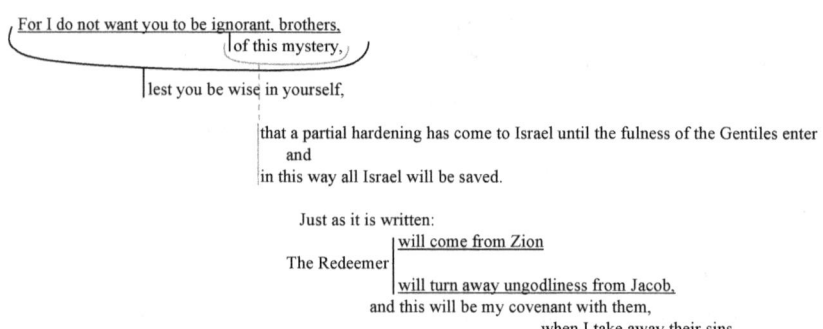

At least since 11:13, Paul has been speaking directly to the gentiles. The purpose of Paul's declaring "this mystery" is to keep them from being wise in themselves—perhaps from seeing themselves as having superseded the Jews. John Goldingay rightly identifies the mystery: "The *mystērion* about Israel is God's decision to make Israel's unfaith the way of opening up the gospel to the gentiles and then to make gentile faith the way of winning Israel back to faith."[40] The gentiles are being called by Paul, who is on the gentile mission, into the Jewish mission.

40. Goldingay, *Biblical Theology*, 257. Moo says the mystery has three components: (1) "a hardening has come partly on Israel"; (2) "until the fullness of the Gentiles comes in"; (3) "and in this way all Israel will be saved" (Moo, "Romans," 716). And yet then Moo continues to complicate the issue by trying to make these three components mean something somewhat alien to Paul's line of argumentation.

When Paul writes "just as it is written," that does not connect back to "in this way," but instead it serves to summarize and support the entire statement that Paul just made, which is itself a summary of Paul's entire argument. The future orientation of the citation does not require a future fulfillment (see Rom 15:9). Paul is seeking to attach Old Testament authority to his statement about the mystery, even as he would like to encapsulate his argument up to this point. Christopher Zoccali, citing Fitzmyer as support, says that "the 'covenant' referred to here is for Paul the 'Jeremianic new covenant,' which he believes is fulfilled in his gospel, is widely agreed upon."[41] Along the lines of a new covenant perspective, it does seem that as Paul deletes the "and" from Isa 59:20 LXX, he puts more emphasis on the covenant aspect of the citation. Paul has, in a way, already presented Jesus as ὁ ῥυόμενος (the deliverer) when he identified Jesus as the one who saves (ῥύομαι) him from his body of death (7:24–25).

To summarize, Paul writes a composite citation from Isaiah that undergirds all of the theology of salvation from Rom 1–11, declaring that Jesus, the redeemer and word of God who comes out of Zion, reinstates the covenant with Israel in the new covenant, now explicitly including gentiles, by taking away all of their sin, both Jew and gentile.

There is nothing new or alien to everything that Paul has been saying since chapter 1. There are no mysterious ways, doubled covenants, superseding peoples, or future miracles of salvation. There are only Jews and gentiles who have sinned and fallen short of God's glory, who must receive Christ in faith and be justified, for there is no distinction. This is all in line with the unfailing promises of God.

Conclusion: The Praise Is in the Pattern

Emperor Claudius expelled much of the Jewish population from Rome in 49 CE, and Claudius then died in 54, his death inviting Jews to return.[42] Paul writes Romans right around 57 CE,[43] just after Jews, including Jewish believers like Priscilla and Aquila (Rom 16:3), would have returned. And so, whereas the earlier letter of Galatians[44] dealt with a more Jewish

---

41. Zoccali, "And So All Israel," 294. David Baker also links this citation with Jer 31:34 (38:34 LXX). Baker, *Two Testaments, One Bible*, 262.

42. Moo, *Romans*, 4–5.

43. Moo, *Romans*, 3.

44. See Blomberg, *From Pentecost*, 117–19, for a fair treatment of the dating of Galatians.

church that sought to Judaize gentiles, Romans is likely written to a predominantly gentile church that may have been disregarding or even belittling their Jewish heritage. Perhaps this is why circumcision is not as much of an issue in Romans, as are liberal practices of eating what may not be clean (Rom 14). Therefore, Paul writes to the church in Rome to correct gentile pride and facilitate Jew/gentile unity by explaining his gospel, and to make contact for his intended future visit. He hopes that the church in Rome will connect with him in the gospel message so that she might partner with him in his ongoing missionary endeavors. Should the gentiles and Jews in the church in Rome heed Paul's words in Rom 1–11 (and indeed 12–16), these goals would surely be accomplished.

Paul's Gospel is thoroughly Christ-centered. Justification is found in faith in Christ alone. Jew and gentile operate on a level playing field—there is no distinction in their need for Christ in the mode of receiving him, or in the results of receiving him. Furthermore, gentiles are encouraged to remember their Jewish roots and practice their faith as a mission to unbelieving Jews. Indeed, the gentile believers may have needed help from their Jewish brethren in order to pick up on the nuances of Paul's activated arguments—something Phoebe would certainly have been qualified to aid with as well. Should the church heed Paul's words and enter into such a community, they would naturally grow in affection and *koinonia* with the apostle and grow in expectation of participating in his mission founded on the glorious mystery of God; there is a partial hardening on Israel paving the way for gentile salvation so that gentile faith can lead Jews to salvation.

In other words, as the rest of chapter 11 unfolds, unbelieving Jews, in regard to the gospel, are currently enemies of God for gentiles' sake, but are still beloved in regard to election (Rom 11:28)—though they have been cut off, they are still natural branches! Even in their unbelief they are working as God's chosen people to bless all nations, "for the gifts and the calling of God are irrevocable" (Rom 11:29 ESV). Gentiles were disobedient but are now receiving mercy because of Jewish disobedience so that disobedient Jews may now receive mercy through gentile mercy—all have been consigned to disobedience so that all may have mercy (11:30–32). It is this consistent pattern of God that now elicits doxology in 33–36:

> Oh, the depth of the riches and wisdom and knowledge of God!
> How unsearchable are his judgments and how inscrutable his ways!
> "For who has known the mind of the Lord,

or who has been his counselor?"
"Or who has given a gift to him
that he might be repaid?"
For from him and through him and to him are all things. To him be glory forever. Amen.

God's sovereignty is graciously ruling over human free will, as hard as humans may become, to bring about salvation, and his character shines throughout history in a pattern of sovereign grace. All praise is due him. The praise is in his unchanging character, and so the praise is in the pattern.

10

A Multiform Tradition and Performance

I HAVE ARGUED THAT the analysis of biblical texts has traditionally applied modern textual assumptions anachronistically to ancient oral cultures. Recent studies of oral traditions and the texts they utilize and/or leave behind have challenged the methodologies and conclusions of those old analyses and so require new perspectives on the old proficiencies in critical approaches to the Bible, as well as new approaches in the areas of interpretation and proclamation of the message of the biblical tradition. I have argued that the most immediate shift in exegesis requires the acknowledgment and interpretation of various forms of repetition, including the ability for smaller parts of any given performance to activate various elements of the greater tradition for rhetorical purposes.

In this final chapter I will discuss two other approaches that should be considered in exegeting and proclaiming the greater tradition behind the Bible in light of its oral traditional origins. First, I will discuss exegetical realities of a Bible with no original text.[1] Toward that end I will present two examples of how we might approach the varied textual traditions of the Bible as a multiform authoritative biblical tradition: (1) by engaging multiple witnesses of a specific passage or book of Scripture, and (2) by investigating the activation of the greater tradition represented

---

1. There may be some "original texts" for parts of the Bible, especially in reference to the letters sent by Paul and the apostles to specific audiences. See my discussion at the beginning of chapter seven.

by multiple textual witnesses. Second, I will discuss performance criticism and the performance of the biblical traditions today.

A Bible with No Original Text

Scholars often presumed that biblical texts originated from singular authors who may have processed oral traditions into cohesive, authoritative texts intended for exact replication. While copying errors produced various manuscript families, scholars believed that through the analysis of a multitude of manuscripts, one could trace back to an original authoritative textual document. Once a critical text approaching the hypothetical original document was in hand, then the holy words could be mined for systematic theological data along the lines of modern pursuits of exact historical and philosophical truths. Such "mining" for data might include source and redaction criticism employed to discover earlier sources of the text and reveal the rhetorical effects of the history of the growth of the text, and it might include form criticism, employed to discover oral forms that predated the textual traditions and represent earlier states of the material before it was all organized into a new unified presentation.

Even the most nuanced approaches to the interplay of orality and textuality believed that authoritative texts had evolved from a rich tapestry of oral and written traditions within the community. These traditions were believed to have stemmed from community events, needs, and experiences, cultural influences, and/or creations by individuals and were occasionally compiled into new written documents. Singular authors or editors, such as Ezra for the Torah or a disciple in the line of Isaiah for the book bearing the prophet's name, eventually codified these oral and written traditions into a final textual form. This "final form" became the authoritative text for copying.

Even in this more nuanced understanding, textual critics attempt to trace manuscript strains back to an "original" final form, a concept that by oral traditional standards likely never existed until the Masoretic era.[2] The Masoretic tradition can hardly be considered an ancient final form

---

2. Carr said of ancient scribes, "Though scribes certainly inclined toward overall preservation (albeit with memory variants, harmonizations/coordinations, and a general trend to expand rather than abbreviate), they did not yet treat the texts in the same way that, say, the later Masoretes did. To presuppose otherwise is to project anachronistically into other periods a form of textual transmission that is not characteristic of them" (Carr, *Formation*, 114).

in comparison to the earlier textual witness of a multiform tradition. The very concept of a "final form" is a more recent notion to the historical faith community.

What we actually have in the textual tradition are various creative performances, written to be performed. Without its original audience and performer, the written text stands as a fossilized version of the performance it represents.

Redaction critics seek to trace the editorial process of the source traditions of the "final form" (a hypothetical document greatly predating the Masoretes) despite the fact that no certain final form exists for study and likely never did exist. Furthermore, the written sources they presuppose never existed within the linear, text-centered constructs from which the modern critics have operated. The purposes of the traditions that did exist do not align with modern, Western, post-Enlightenment philosophical pursuits of data.

Likewise, form critics, from their own modern mindsets, analyze imperfect representations of nonexistent final forms in order to trace hypothetical genres of oral tradition and their cultural origins according to cultural realities that never existed within the oral traditions under investigation. Oral traditions do not normally collect unconnected forms of stories, law codes, poetry, songs, and cultic instructions to weave together a historical reality that never actually occurred in any meaningful way.

In other words, recent studies in orality and textuality challenge old presuppositions of the texts of the Bible, offering a more nuanced understanding of texts left behind by oral traditional cultures. I suspect that this newer approach argues for a more fluid traditional reality than many scholars and pastors will be comfortable with but also a more stable tradition than scholars and pastors on the other extreme will want to acknowledge.

From the perspective of recent developments in the study of oral traditional cultures, seeking an authoritative original text is misguided. Each performance is a valid partial presentation of the greater community-held tradition. Multiple "originals" likely coexisted, offering a broader representation of a broader tradition of understanding and interpretation.

This different understanding of the use of *text* in the biblical tradition should certainly reshape the purposes of critical approaches to the Bible. Perhaps form criticism can aid in understanding each performance by analyzing its components as forms of activation for the originating culture, but form-critical scholars must reassess assumptions about oral tradition. Gunkel's notion of fireside stories is outdated, and the idea of disconnected forms of various natures being brought together in an almost absolute and novel creative act cannot be assumed. The goal of redaction criticism to understand the rhetorical purposes of the performances we have in hand would remain, but assumptions of the "growth" and "editorial process" of the community would require drastic revision.[3]

Of course, what is most important for the purposes of this book is to investigate how the existence of multiform authoritative presentations might affect the interpretation and proclamation of Scripture. If multiple textual witnesses that have been left behind of the biblical tradition were accepted as representations of the tradition at large, then multiple textual traditions might need to be consulted for a more holistic understanding of the ancient faith tradition. As I acknowledged in chapter four, the application of the concept of a multiform inspired textual tradition requires much further investigation. In what follows, I will only engage the topic as far as I believe is prudent in light of what I have argued to this point.

I will discuss the benefit of reading a book of the Bible through multiple textual traditions by discussing the multiform performance of Habakkuk and then provide an example of activation through multiple textual traditions in the use of Hab 2:3–4 in Heb 10:37–38.

Exegeting from Multiple Textual Traditions

The Masoretic Tradition as the Basis for Comparison

In my survey of the variations in the textual tradition of the book of Habakkuk as seen in Codex Lenigradensis, Codex Vaticanus, 1QpHab, 8Hev12gr, Ms 86, Ms Or 2211, Ms 7a1, and Codex Amiatinus, I assumed a general sense of priority for the Hebrew textual tradition of the performance. In light of my discussion just above, I confess that in many ways this assumption is arbitrary and/or anachronistic—the oral traditional culture likely saw little to no "priority" of any performance. If any performance was actually accepted by the community, it was likely held to be authentic without measure of prioritization. On the other hand, the prophet almost certainly proclaimed and/or wrote his performances in Hebrew, and so it seems fair to assume any performance in another language depended at one time on a translation from a chronologically

---

[3]. Carr has led the way in this sort of application in *Formation*.

"original" Hebrew performance even if chronological priority did not require any other sort of prioritization by the original traditional culture.

It is notable that 1QpHab and Mur XII followed the MT very closely, and 8Hev12gr reflected a Greek translation that very closely reflected the MT. So, whether or not the Hebrew performance found in the MT had any sense of priority, there did seem to be some value in some circles of the tradition in preserving the performance of Habakkuk represented by something like the MT.

However, we should not overstate the importance of the MT in the early community of faith. Some of Jesus' use of the Old Testament passages quoted by him in the Gospels depends on the LXX performance of the tradition.[4] Even as late as the writing of the New Testament, Paul's use of Hab 2:4 reflects more the Syriac of Ms 7a1 in Rom 1:17 and Gal 3:11, with the lack of any pronoun attached to the "faith" by which one will live. The MT refers to "his" faith, while the LXX specifies it as "my" faith. As will be discussed below, Heb 10:37–38 presents a unique composite performance of the text, along with a reference to Isa 26:20. Paul's multiform use of passages from Isaiah in Rom 11:26–27, as discussed above, is another example illustrating the fact that the New Testament tradents had a more multiform approach to their use of the Old Testament.

It does not seem that Paul or the New Testament tradents preferred the Hebrew performance of the text but utilized whatever acceptable performance suited their rhetorical needs—or they just took creative liberties to offer their own performance of the text—often crafting a composite reference from multiple traditional sources! Indeed, even as late as the translation of the Vulgate, earlier performances seemed to possess at least some validity as Codex Amiatinus often assimilates various elements of the earlier versions.[5]

---

4. See Longenecker's discussion, *Biblical Exegesis*, 45–50.

5. See for instance the discussion on the activation from the word רִיב in Hab 1:3 in chapter five above. Here is a summary of some important variations of the first verses of Habakkuk from my examination: V (Codex Amiatinus—the representative of the Vulgate) offers a performance that, while highly influenced and inflated by G (Vaticanus), is closer in its final form to the structure and message of M (MT). What is found in 1:2–4 is typical. V follows G in 1:2 in clarifying the personal suffering of the prophet and then adds "while I hurt." Then in 1:3, V follows G in identifying justice behind the tradition but does not follow G in discussing a corrupt judge. Therefore, in this initial section, V reflects some of the variants of G, but holds closer to the final structure and message of M, even as V adds some of its own nuances.

Similarly, V blatantly conflates G and M in 1:5 only to follow M largely thereafter through verse 10. In verse 11, V offers a unique reading—the strength of the Chaldeans'

At any rate, while the Hebrew performance likely had little to no priority for the ancient community, the MT stands as the base text for most of the current believing community. It is logical for the MT to stand as the "home base" of sorts to which compare the other versions. So, hopefully without disqualifying my arguments above, for the sake of discussion, I will continue within my somewhat plausible, albeit possibly tenuous, assumption of some sort of chronological priority of a Hebrew "original" represented by the MT in the following discussion of the various ancient traditions of performing Habakkuk. The MT seems noticeably stable from my work in comparing Codex Lenigradensis, 1QpHab, 8HevXIIgr, and Mur XII as it relates to Habakkuk.

Summary of the MT Performance of Habakkuk

The performance of MT can be summarized as follows.[6] In 1:2–17 the book opens with Habakkuk's lament concerning the rampant evil and injustice he witnesses around him in Judah. He cries out to YHWH, questioning why divine justice seems absent and the instruction of YHWH is paralyzed as violence and wrongdoing prevail. Habakkuk's role here is that of a desperate observer, overwhelmed by the moral decay of his society and perceiving YHWH as unresponsive.

YHWH does respond. However, his response is startling and shifts the narrative dramatically. YHWH announces the rise of the Chaldeans, a ruthless and unstoppable force that he has raised up as an instrument of judgment. This revelation broadens the scope of Habakkuk's concern from local injustices to the seeming injustice of a larger, more terrifying, international divine plan.

The Chaldeans, described in vivid terms, dominate this section, and YHWH is depicted as actively orchestrating these events, while Habakkuk and his people are relegated to passive observers. Habakkuk

---

god is reflected in the change and fall of the wind. V does not ask why God looks upon those who live in iniquity, but why he does not. Both questions, however, question the inactivity of God. For the other versions, God looks and does nothing. For V, God does not even look. In the face of iniquity and wickedness, the prophet experiences only shear silence. YHWH simply does not regard the wicked. Like S (the Syriac translation as found in Ms 7a1), V highlights the immediacy of the Chaldean activity in proclaiming the past worship of his instruments of domination and his ongoing merciless use of them for death, and the ongoing idolatry stands in opposition against the eternity of YHWH.

6. For an exhaustive discourse analysis of Habakkuk, see Fuller, *Discourse Analysis*.

acknowledges YHWH's eternal nature and past deeds but is troubled by the use of the Chaldeans, whom he describes as excessively cruel and inhumane. The prophet complains that the Chaldeans are idolators, worshiping their tools of warfare and subjugation. It seems inconceivable to the prophet that the Chaldeans should be set loose to continually slay nations.

In Hab 2:1–6 the prophet adopts a posture of watchful expectation, waiting for YHWH's response. This section marks a shift from active questioning to passive anticipation, indicating Habakkuk's willingness to receive further revelation.

YHWH's reply begins with a call for patience and faith. He instructs Habakkuk to write down a vision and to wait for its fulfillment, emphasizing that though the vision may seem delayed, it will surely come to pass. This message contrasts the arrogance and insatiability of the proud man (certainly representing the Chaldeans) with the faithfulness of those who wait on YHWH. The divine response reassures Habakkuk that the proud and wicked will ultimately face judgment, shifting the focus from immediate injustices to the ultimate certainty of divine retribution.

Habakkuk 2:6 begins a section containing five woes that dominate the structure and message of the rest of Hab 2. The rhetorical structure of the woe oracles has already been summarized in chapter five of this book. Suffice to say at this point that this series of oracles pronounces woes upon the evildoer, likely focusing on the Chaldeans, progressively shifting focus from specific wrongdoings to a broader condemnation of idolatry and arrogance.

These oracles highlight the futility of human pride and the inevitability of divine justice, as woes one through three culminate at 2:14 with a vision of YHWH's glory filling the earth, and as woes four and five culminate at 2:20 as YHWH is stationed securely in his temple against the breathless idols of the world's idolaters. All the earth is called to be silent before him. This section serves to expand the narrative from the fate of individual evildoers, beginning with the violent in Judah and escalating to the violent Chaldeans, to a universal proclamation of divine sovereignty and justice. The oracles highlight the futility of idolatry and the certainty of divine justice, culminating in a vision of YHWH's glory filling the earth.

As can be seen from this overview of Hab 1–2, a reoccurring theme in Habakkuk is the incremental broadening of Habakkuk's view of YHWH's realm of justice, discipline, and covenant faithfulness.

The final chapter is a psalm of Habakkuk in which he recounts YHWH's past mighty deeds and expresses awe at God's power over nature and nations. Habakkuk moves from fear to faith, ultimately trusting in YHWH's protection and justice. This section is dominated by references to YHWH's supreme authority, portraying him as the master of creation and history and as the ultimate, indomitable divine warrior. Habakkuk moves from commanding YHWH to save to a posture of humble trust and patient expectancy of divine deliverance.

The final words that the prophet sings represent some of the most powerful words of trust in and devotion to YHWH in all of Scripture.

> I heard and my belly trembled.
> My lips quivered at the sound.
> Rottenness enters my bones, and at my very foundations, I tremble;
> I who wait for the day of trouble to go up to the people who will invade us.
> When the fig should not blossom, nor fruit be on the vines;
> The produce of the olives deceived, and the fields yield no food;
> The flock cut off from the fold and there be no herd in the stalls;
> Yet in YHWH I will exult. I will rejoice in the God of my salvation.
> YHWH is my Lord, my strength.
> And he set my feet like the deer, and he makes me tread on my high places.[7]

The Performance of Habakkuk by Codex Vaticanus

The tradition of the Septuagint represented by Codex Vaticanus (referred to as G in what follows) varies significantly with the MT (represented by Codex Leningradensis and henceforth referred to as M). G's shift can be seen as early as the second verse when G utilizes the passive participle to make explicit the suffering of the prophet. In verse 3, G translates "violence" as "ungodliness" and utilizes the word again for "wicked" in verse 4. Also contrary to M, as discussed earlier in chapter 5 of this book, G describes a judge receiving bribes in verse 3. Those who are identified as ungodly are those who oppress the righteous causing the law to be broken and judgment to go out perverted through bribery. In verse 5, G defines the audience commanded by God to "behold," "watch," "and marvel" as "despisers"—reading בוגדים instead of בַגּוֹיִם. YHWH then commands them to "be ruined" because God is doing something the

---

7. Hab 3:16–19.

despisers would not believe if someone declared it—he is raising up the Chaldeans. Therefore, quite clear in G is that Hab 1:5–17 speaks of the Chaldeans as an instrument of YHWH against the despisers.

Then in verse 9, G makes a declaration not found in the other witnesses—"An end will come to the ungodly, those having opposed them face to face." This is a great shift from M. In 1:5–11, M only refers to those who are to watch, and perhaps be judged by, the Chaldeans. Verse 6 contains the only first-person pronoun referring to God in M. In M, the rest of verses 6–11 describe the Chaldeans. The phrase in verse 11b, "and guilty is the one whose strength is his god," likely speaks of the Chaldeans, whose "judgment and dignity proceed from himself." However, the phrase could also operate as a foil to the righteous who lives by faith. In other words, "Whoever worships their own strength instead of placing their faith in God will be found guilty, and, therefore, be subject to the terrors of the Chaldean threat." Perhaps the ambiguity is intentional.

At any rate, G has so restructured chapter 1 that all required threats against the ungodly of Judah have already been given well before 11b—in verses 5 and 9. The refrain of the ruin and end of the ungodly has been sounded. Instead of a threat in 11b, the first-person singular voice of the prophet interrupts the description of the Chaldeans and their arrival, proclaiming a promise of a shift in the spirit of God from which he will provide some sort of atonement. This is the strength to the prophet's God.

While the overall message of 1:1–11 of G is quite similar to that of M in that the issue raised by the prophet in 1:2–4 will be addressed by God through the raising up of the Chaldeans (1:5–11), G is more explicit as to the prophet's personal suffering and makes more explicit that the Chaldean move is an instrument of judgment against those discussed in 1:2–4. G then emphasizes the promise of God's shifting of the wind/spirit to bring atonement. This is described as the power of God (1:11).

In 1:12–17 G varies from M's framing questions, moving from acknowledging the strength of God (in the atonement following the judgment of the ungodly of Judah by the hands of the Chaldeans) to once again questioning his activity. Upon the stated truth of the strength of God, and upon the rhetorical question of his eternity, the prophet declares, "Surely we will not die," and then declares the purpose of this reply.

The prophet declares that YHWH has appointed (perfect tense) the Chaldean nation to be judged, and he has formed (aorist tense) the prophet to reprove his corrective measure. Habakkuk asks, If God's eyes are too pure to look upon evil and toil of sorrow, why does he look upon the despisers—the disobedient of Judah—and will he remain silent while the righteous are swallowed by the Chaldeans due to the disobedience of the ungodly of Judah?

Verses 14–17 then provide a case of the evil nature of the Chaldeans' activities as a reproof of God's corrective measure. The end for the ungodly comes as humans are made to be like fish of the sea, brought up by the Chaldean hook. G asks if the Chaldeans' movements will be eternal even as is YHWH.

In G, Hab 1:5–11 is a direct answer to the question in 1:2–4—God is going to move against the ungodly in Judah by raising up the Chaldeans. Verses 1:12–17 is a reproof of God's use of the Chaldeans for the discipline of his people, even in light of a promised shift of spirit and atonement. G offers a more personal performance as the prophet's own pain is mentioned, and he and the other actors are named and discussed more often—the judge, the despisers (v. 5), the ungodly (v. 9), my God (v. 11), formed me (v. 12). Generally, the chapter still grows from an immediate situation before the prophet, to an international situation, and to a creation-wide situation, though the situation is more intentionally placed before the prophet.

In summary, in Hab 1:1–11, G offered a uniquely nuanced reading that clarified the communal breaking of covenant in Judah by those who were twice called "ungodly" in 1:2–4. G then identified those who were commanded to watch, marvel, and be ruined—the despisers. And these despisers were differentiated from the instrument God was raising up—the Chaldeans. The most natural interpretation equates the despisers of 1:5 with the ungodly of 1:3 and 1:4.

YHWH's description of the Chaldeans in G is similar to the other versions until verse 9, at which point G takes a major shift in declaring that an end will come to the ungodly, those having opposed them face-to-face. Because of these ungodly despisers, YHWH will gather captives from the Judahites like sand, mock rulers, and overthrow strongholds. Then, he will change the spirit/wind, pass through, and in some way make atonement. Habakkuk declares, "This is the strength to my God."

In Hab 1:12–17, G first establishes God's eternity and commitment to his people. Upon the fact of God's eternity, holiness, and ultimate protection of the lives of his people, the prophet declares the Chaldean nation is appointed for judgment, and that YHWH has formed the prophet to reprove God's disciplinary move through the Chaldeans. Therefore, in verses 13–17, the prophet does just that—he critiques and reproves the discipline of God that is to come to pass through the Chaldeans. God is critiqued for looking at the despisers of Judah and allowing the righteous in Judah to be swallowed by God's discipline of the ungodly.

Then the prophet laments that humanity is in such a state of divine justice. They are drug up and slain like fish who have no ruler. G concludes the first chapter with a question for God—will he allow the Chaldean nation to continue in idolatry, worshiping their instruments of domination and unsparingly killing nations? If God is going to use the evil of the Chaldeans to bring an end to the ungodly of Judah, will he allow the evils of the Chaldeans to then continue in the place of Judah's evil?

YHWH's answer comes to the prophet. In G, YHWH promises that the Chaldean nation is certainly coming. The coming of the Chaldeans is so certain and ordained by God that should "he" draw back, YHWH would not be pleased with him, but in the midst of this impending disaster, hope exists for life for the righteous in the faithfulness of God. Just as certain as the arrival of the Chaldeans is the arrival of the vision of the end, seemingly described throughout the rest of Hab 2 as the end of all idolatry—the proud man will fail.

While 2:5 of G seems to continue discussing the Chaldeans through the identification of "the proud man," it may also intend to contrast the "despiser/ungodly" with the righteous who will live from God's righteousness as it employs the term "despiser" in parallel with the proud man. Perhaps G intended to group both the ungodly of Judah and of Babylon in the third term it used—a boastful man. At any rate, though the coming Chaldean nation will certainly accomplish God's intentions, no boastful man will accomplish his own purposes. The boastful man, in any context, is like death, always consuming and never satisfied. All that he plunders for himself becomes chains that weigh him down and invite the survivors of his violence to rise up and despoil him.

Other than peripheral translational variations, G closely follows the woe patterns of M. G's "beetle" in 2:11 and "caves" in 2:15 seem to be simple translational issues, and the choices of "you destroyed" in 2:10 and "foul outpouring" of 2:15 seem to be interpretive translational choices. While these variants may change the meaning of a statement, they do not shift the overall function of the statements from the meaning of the woes themselves. One notable variant is the use of G's loaded word "ungodliness" in 2:17. In the end, the ungodliness of the ungodly will overshadow them as YHWH's sovereignty is manifested. YHWH will reverse the glory of the ungodly.

G's major variation from M occurs in 1:2—2:5 in that it makes consistent translation choices which clearly depict the ungodly despisers of Judah as the catalyst of the terrifying discipline of God through the raising up of the Chaldeans. The pain of the prophet is more personal, and the sin of the community more specific (the abandonment of the covenant and bribed judges).

The ungodly of Judah are as certain to come to their end as the Chaldean nation is surely to come, and it is clear that only the purposes of God will be fulfilled. He is not exalting the evil purposes of the Chaldeans over the evil purposes of the ungodly of Judah. Indeed, he will even bring atonement to his people. The prophet has been formed to reprove the discipline of YHWH brought through the Chaldeans, and YHWH validates the prophet's concerns while broadening the prophet's perspective to the eternal nature of God and the surety of YHWH's established eschaton—the vision of the judgment of every boastful man is certain. Even in the midst of such terrible trials, the righteous will live from YHWH's faithfulness. YHWH is in his temple, and all the earth should be silent before him.

Indeed, from G's perspective, the devastating arrival of the Chaldeans is a sign of God's faithfulness to his word. Habakkuk's faith can actually increase due to the unthinkable discipline dished out by the unholy nation. When the devastation arrives, he can be even more sure of the coming promised atonement and vision. If God is faithful in his word concerning the arrival of the Chaldeans, he will be faithful concerning the arrival of the promised atonement and vision. After all, they are all guaranteed to arrive with equal certainty. And, in addition to all of this, Habakkuk has been informed that he was raised up for the very purpose of questioning God's move through the Chaldeans so that God's universal justice could be acknowledged. Every corner of human pride and ungodliness will be exposed, and the position of the proud will be reversed. Habakkuk chapter 3 will further draw out the theme of the reversal of the pride of the wicked.

G divides the first section of Hab 3:1-13 into three subsections: 3:2-3a; 3b-9a; and 9b-13. The first subsection following the psalm's title in 3:1 (3:2—3:3a) begins with the only perfect tense verb in the entire chapter—*I have heard*. Throughout the rest of this section, the text shifts back and forth from the aorist and future tense. In this section, the prophet's responses to his having heard the report are in the aorist—*I was terrified, I considered, I was astonished*. God's activity is then declared in the future—*you will be known, you will be acknowledged, you will be revealed, you will remember, God will come*. The verbal structure seems to imply that the prophet's activity of having heard the report governs the chapter. His response to the report was terror, followed by amazement once he had considered the work of God.

Read in the context of chapters 1–2, Habakkuk confesses his response to the report of God's raising up of the Chaldeans followed by a proclamation of future hope. Indeed, this section seems to summarize exactly what the prophet experienced in the first two chapters. He heard from God, stood astonished, but also received words of hope: an end of the ungodly, atonement, life for the righteous ones through God's faithfulness, and a vision of God's universal justice and sovereignty. Perhaps the phrase "between two living creatures you will be known" (3:2) refers to the mercy seat and harkens back to the atonement of Hab 1:11. The declarations that God will be acknowledged and revealed demonstrate a faith in the vision from chapter 2 of God's sovereignty over all nations and idols. The language of Habakkuk's troubled soul closely echoes Ps 6:1–3, which asks God for relief from his wrath, and the rest of Ps 6 seeks salvation from evil foes. Finally, Hab 3:3a promises a move on the part of God that will be reminiscent of his great miraculous works from the exodus.

G is much less focused on God as the actor of terrifying deeds and more focused on the results themselves and on God's redemptive work. This focus began even in the first section when God is not told to "revive it," nor is it declared that God "will make it known." Instead, the passive is utilized to say that God *will be known, acknowledged*, and *revealed*. In verse 4, "covering of his might" is not present, but he *appointed a mighty love from his strength*. Perhaps this refers to the atonement from chapter 1 which was described as the strength of the prophet's God. In verse 5, God does not have "pestilence" and "plague" proceeding before and after him but a *word*. In verse 6, the results may be intensified in that the nations *melt away* and the hills *were dissolved*, but the passive tense still focuses more on the results than on the actor. In that these aorist verbs are situated within declarations concerning the future, they should likely be taken as ingressive aorists, which would imply that these future events are already beginning to unfold. At least, it is clear that the performance shifts from the future and the aorist in order to paint the picture of the future move of God in a way that emphasizes the certainty of its occurrence.

This section paints God's move as a divine warrior, mounted on horses, dissolving hills, and melting nations as he declares the direction of his wrath—it is not toward the waters but *against the scepters*, representing God's opposition against the authority of earthly rulers like the Chaldeans. This emphasis of God's wrath directed toward earthly authorities will dominate the rest of the chapter and finally connect back to the themes of Habakkuk in G from chapters 1–2.

G's final subsection within 3:1–13 (9b–13) demonstrates unique translation choices that emphasize YHWH's move against human authority and pride. In 3:10, G speaks of *people* seeing God and suffering birth pains as opposed to "mountains." The abyss does not lift his hands, but attention is drawn to her *pomp*. YHWH will cast death upon the heads of the lawless and leave their necks in bonds, demonstrating the move from pomp and authority to enslavement.

In 3:19 G points back to 1:9 and 1:15 through the use of the keyword συντελέιαν. The shift in G at 1:9 has been discussed thoroughly above, as G declared the coming "end" (συντελέιαν) of the ungodly. At 3:15 G used the word again to highlight that the end that was promised to come to the ungodly is an event that affects not only them but all of humanity. Thus, the ungodly are seen to swallow the righteous, in that all of humanity suffers the chastisement of the ungodly. At 3:19, G ignored the clear allusions to 2 Sam 22 and Ps 18 [17], allusions acknowledged by Targum Jonathan (Ms Or 2211) and the Peshita (Ms 7a1), and used the word συντέλειαν, for which no visual stimuli can be demonstrated. Though Codex Amiatinus did not seem to highlight the allusions to 2 Sam 22 and Ps 18, it still contained connections due to similar translational choices for the similar Hebrew phrases. On the other hand, G produced the unique *he will set my feet to consummation* (συντελέιαν). The negative *end* for the ungodly parallels the positive *consummation* for the faithful. The ungodly will come to an end, but, even while it may seem that all of humanity suffers because of the ungodly, God will set the feet of the faithful, represented by the prophet, to consummation.

As G closes Hab 3, YHWH divides the heads of rulers, transforming their high and lofty state into a state of the poor who eat in secret, continuing the unique theme of the reversal of human authority and pride begun in 3:9 with the phrase *against scepters*.

In G, the prophet does not wait for trouble to come upon the invading nation, but he rests in the day when he is associated with his fellow exiles. Why does he find rest in a day such as that? His rest comes in the knowledge that the authority and pride of rogue nations will be reversed. After all, YHWH will set his feet to consummation on the same day when an end will come to the ungodly (1:9). And even his complaints concerning the use of the Chaldeans has been acknowledged by God. Indeed, YHWH raised him up for the very purpose to question the justice of such an act. The arrival of his exile is the firstfruits of the fulfillment of God's promises to him—promises that will culminate in the end of the ungodly and a consummating atonement for the faithful.

Therefore, Hab 3 in G rehearses the prophet's experience—his hearing of YHWH's work of raising up the Chaldeans in response to his initial complaint (1:2–11); his reproval of this discipline from YHWH (1:12–17); and his receiving of the answer that YHWH's eternal nature will summon the pride of all nations to reverence (2:1–20). YHWH's initial reply to Habakkuk in 1:5–11 declared the coming of the Chaldeans, but it also promised an end to the ungodly, and that God would change the wind, pass through (activating a Passover or sorts?), and make atonement.

Likely, G intended the hearer of 1:9–10 to understand that it might actually be God who gathers captives like sand, toys with human rulers, and mocks fortresses. He reverses the state of the mighty. Habakkuk reproves God's discipline, since it swallows up the righteous along with the ungodly like fish brought up by a hook. The Chaldeans, who are supposedly the instruments of YHWH, commit idolatry in worshiping their instruments of war.

God replies to this reproof promising the Chaldean invasion is surely coming, but in the end, God will accomplish his purposes through the vision that rises to the end. YHWH's righteous ones will live by his faithfulness. This is followed by a series of woes that depict the reversal of human delusions of grandeur and idolatry in the face of YHWH's eternity. Because of this exchange of words with YHWH, Habakkuk knows that the day of famine and exile brought on by the Chaldeans is actually a fulfillment of the promise of YHWH's eternal nature, and therefore, evidence for hope in the future fulfillment of YHWH's promise of salvation. YHWH will bring the prophet to the day of consummation—an end for the ungodly. Even after the inevitable defeat before the Chaldeans, God will place him upon the heights to conquer in YHWH's song.

It is quite possible that the nuances brought out in Vaticanus's presentation of the tradition of the LXX were actually traditional understandings of the interpretation of Habakkuk and the performance simply drew out what was already accepted by those who first received the performance of the prophet. For example, while the MT does not mention *atonement*, the tradition at large may have held a traditional understanding and interpretation of Habakkuk to include such a move from God—such as the traditional inclusion of *robbery* at Hab 2:11 in Or 2211 and 1QpHab. The church might benefit from exploring the tradition of understanding and interpretation that stood behind the authoritative performances of the prophet Habakkuk.

Considering the alternative performance of the LXX as represented by Vaticanus, we can glean specific principles that may have only been hinted at by the MT. For instance, while the MT certainly demonstrates that Habakkuk felt the freedom to question the move of God and God did not rebuke the prophet for his reprovals, Vaticanus presents Habakkuk questioning the justice of God even after the promise of atonement! Indeed, he is even formed for that very purpose. While we wait for the second advent of Christ, we are not condemned by God when we raise questions of justice in the face of the pain and suffering we experience in this life. Indeed, God may have raised us up for this very purpose—to point out that the pain and suffering in this world is not God's ultimate desire. Even the violence and pain inherent in discipline itself is contrary to the telos—the heart and goal—of heaven. Shalom is the ideal, and even godly discipline reflects a reality contrary to shalom. As his representatives, we are formed to reprove the arrival of evil while we await Christ's return.

In light of this performance's highlight of the prophet's purpose of rebuking the discipline of YHWH, the performance presents a more holistic view of God's activity. Habakkuk serves to highlight that YHWH's use of the Chaldeans does not overlook the facts of the Chaldeans' own guilt before God. Habakkuk *is part* of YHWH's disciplinary plan! YHWH raises Habakkuk up as a part of God's holistic disciplinary and redemptive plan in order to proclaim the universal justice of God over all nations and his desire to rescue any who would humble themselves and surrender to YHWH in faith. God moves through the ungodly Chaldeans to judge the ungodly of Judah, and he moves through Habakkuk to proclaim his universal justice and purposes of redemption even in the midst of this terrifying disciplinary use of an evil nation.

The performance of the LXX as represented by Vaticanus contained the greatest overall variation from among the versions I analyzed, but the other versions offered noticeable variation as well. For instance, Ms 7a1's performance (henceforth referred to as S) explicitly equated the insolence of the Babylonians with the insolence of the Judeans at 1:6, reflecting other creative choices of the translation from Hab 1:2–4. G does not connect the evil of the Chaldeans and Judahites until 2:5. Perhaps

S brought forward in its performance of the tradition what it knew was present later in G and what may have been implied by the language of M in 1:4 and 1:13.

The Performance of Habakkuk by Ms 7a1

Seemingly, S has worked with the performances of the traditions it had before it—likely M, G, and Targum Jonathan (T)—to craft a performance of its own. S equates the insolent ones of Judah with the insolence of the Chaldeans, as YHWH answers the prophet's plea from 1:2–4 by saying something like, "The insolent one is being raised up to dumbfound the insolent. Look how frightening he is!"

Verse 12 of S flows naturally from verse 11: "And his strength is convicted by his god, because you are from the beginning, O Lord my God, the Holy One." As in G, this leads to the second complaint on behalf of the prophet: "If you're so holy, are you without law? You set *him* as an instrument of judgment, and you formed me to reprove him!" The prophet is not raised up to reprove the move of God but the Chaldeans themselves. He is stuck between a rock and a hard place—living in the midst of those receiving the discipline of YHWH from the Chaldeans while being raised up to reprove the Chaldeans.

When S asks, "Why do you look upon the insolent and are silent as the wicked swallow the righteous?" the performance has so structured the argument that both the evil Judahites of 1:2–4 and the Chaldeans described in 5–11 are identified. The righteous are swallowed by the impending punishment of the insolent by the insolent ones whom God is raising up to punish them. The Chaldeans are seen as presently gathering people like fish and already rejoicing and worshiping their nets. The ongoing insolence argues against the one who is from the beginning. Again, while the tradition is presented creatively, the overall message and flow of sins and sufferings from specific and local instances to the general and global remain. Many of the differences are simply highlights of nuances already present in other parts of other performances, including M.

S brings a nuance to the text not found as explicitly in the other versions. YHWH acknowledges immediately that those whom he is using to discipline his people are just as evil as those he is disciplining. This word choice also serves to highlight just how far the insolent of Judah have fallen—they are immediately comparable to the Chaldeans! However, the Chaldeans' god will convict the Chaldeans' strength, because only YHWH is from the beginning. While YHWH set the Chaldean nation as an instrument of judgment, he has also formed the prophet to reprove that nation. The prophet asks why God looks upon the insolent—the Chaldeans and the evil of Judah—and remains silent while these wicked ones swallow the righteous. By the end of chapter 1 in S, the immediacy of the Chaldeans' barbarity and idolatry stand stark against the eternity of YHWH while highlighting just how far Judah has fallen.

S does not vary in its message in chapter 2 in any significant way.

In Hab 3, S largely follows the verbal patterns of G in that it utilizes the perfect when G gives the Greek perfect or aorist, and S utilizes the imperfect or participle when G gives the future. A few inconsistencies occur in this pattern. S gives the perfect for *the mountains saw you and shook* in verse 10, and, most importantly, S gives a unique imperative at the end of 3:2—*In anger, remember your compassion.*

Since this unique imperative concludes the introduction of the song in verse 2, one would expect it to drive this section. Indeed, S presents YHWH as remembering his compassion in the protection and salvation of his people. S gives this psalm of Hab 3 the heading "Concerning the One Who Wandered," which is a fitting title for a prayer on behalf of those who need compassion in the face of YHWH's anger. God's coming from Paran is declared as a glorious event that covered the heavens with splendor and the earth with his praises. His brilliance will abide in the city that he holds in his hands, and he will set his power in the surrounding countryside.

Apparently, S trusts YHWH to guard his people safely in his city by executing his power in the surrounding areas. In this work of God, death goes before him and a winged creature (bird) at his foot. Since S was clear in Hab 1 that both the wicked of Judah and the Chaldeans are equally insolent, this prayerful prophecy of Habakkuk in chapter 3 highlights the importance for God's elect people to petition God to remember his compassion in the midst of his justice.

As God measured the earth, he saw that the people lied, and therefore the landscape was destroyed. The tents of foreigners shook. God's anger is so apparent that even the waters seem to be impacted. God has mounted his horse like a warrior, and the arrows of his bow will be sated in his glorious word. However, rivers, as opposed to being recipients of or staging areas for wrath, will be agents of restoration. God executes his wrath while remembering compassion.

In a refrain found in verses 10–13, the mountains shake at God's sight, and the abyss lifts his voice and hands at the downpour of waters that passes over. Sun and moon stand still until they follow the flashes of God's arrows and the brilliance of his spears. In anger, God treads the earth and threshes peoples in order to save his people and his anointed by cutting off the head of the wicked. God executes his wrath while remembering compassion for his people.

In the final section of Hab 3, S limits its assimilation of the versions, perhaps due to the difficult Hebrew in the section and the increasing paraphrastic nature of T. It is equally possible, however, that S simply presents an intentional fluid and unique performance that is also faithful to the stable universal tradition.

Verse 14 continues the focus of the previous section, as God shows mercy to the poor by breaking the heads of ferocious rulers. The prophecy cleaves to the prophet and shows him the day of tribulation, which comes upon the people. S concludes by saying that even in famine, the prophet will rejoice and be glad in YHWH. After all, S has demonstrated YHWH will answer the imperative from the beginning of the chapter—in anger, he will remember his compassion.

His wrath brings salvation and preserves the poor. He sends forth waters to heal. YHWH is the prophet's very strength, and he raises the prophet up to sing his praises. In light of the unique presentation of the tradition in Hab 1—the identification of both the wicked from Judah and the Chaldeans as equally insolent—the theme of YHWH remembering his compassion in his anger is appropriate. If God is to act in saving his people, the prophet's only hope is that YHWH remember his compassion in his anger.

The performance of the Syriac in this manuscript, therefore, emphasizes the need of God's people for YHWH's compassion as he judges the nations. While the righteous will certainly live by faith, S emphasizes that saving faith is defined as trust in the compassion of YHWH to forgive those who do not walk in their insolence but in surrender to God. This theme is certainly embedded within M and G, but the performance of S invites the preacher to receive this interpretation as a central understanding of the message of Habakkuk by the ancient faith community. This message should be proclaimed explicitly to a current faith community who is interested in receiving the inspired move of YHWH through Habakkuk.

The Performance of Habakkuk by the other Versions

As to the other versions, for brevity's sake, I will repeat what I already discussed in chapter 3 of this book. The Barberini version of Hab 3 varied from the other performances as it presented God's move of judgment against the singer's enemy as a sudden and devastating event. The concluding words of the psalm declare, "Having been swift, it ceased." In contrast to Vaticanus, Barb promises the suffering of God's people to be short and his victory over her enemies sudden.

Amiatinus seemed to play more with the eternal nature of YHWH, and the paraphrastic interpretation of the Targum in 2211 emphasized Torah obedience. Not enough was present in the Nahal Hever scroll to determine major shifts except that, just like 1QpHab, it seemed to largely follow the MT.

Those versions that draw out different nuances than what is made explicit in the MT, bear witness to the faith community's tradition of interpretation and reception of the inspired message from YHWH through the prophet. Those nuances deepen our understanding of the tradition at large and may even direct us to other specific messages not clearly stated in the MT—such as Vaticanus's holistic look at YHWH's approach to the sin of Judah, their discipline at the hands of sinful Chaldeans, the mention of atonement, and the global reversal of the proud by YHWH.

Intertestamental Activation from Multiple Textual Traditions: An Example from Hab 2:3–4

Again, some of the textual variants represented by various manuscripts and ancient translations may not represent error of translation or corruption of the tradition but simply a different representation of the true tradition that the faith community would have received.[8] The wide variation represented by the citations of the Old Testament in the New Testament gives credence to the fact that the believing community did not seem to see any particular textual tradition as the only word-for-word holy representation of the true tradition.[9] Therefore, when there are

---

8. For the idea of any given manuscript potentially representing a faithful presentation of the tradition, see Person, *Deuteronomic History*, 75–77; Niditch, "Oral Tradition," 44; Lemmelijn, "Text-Critically," 131, 152–56; Person, "Text Criticism," 201–7.

9. For discussion on the lack of stable textual tradition of the Old Testament represented in the New Testament from outside the perspective of oral tradition studies see McLay, "Biblical Texts," 38–58.

variants between ancient witnesses of the textual tradition, perhaps the goal should not be to seek a critical text by determining which witness is "best." Instead, since both witnesses might have been seen as a valid representation of the tradition, both can be studied in order to gain a wider perspective on what may represent the fuller received tradition of the faith community.

For example, Hab 2:3–4 varies greatly between the MT and the LXX:

MT	LXX
3. For still the vision is for the appointed time and pants to the end.	3. For still the vision is for an appointed time, and it will rise to the end
And it will not lie. It will not tarry.	and not for nothing. If he should tarry,
Wait for it. For it will surely come.	wait for him, because he will surely come
It will not delay.	and by no means delay.
4. Behold, his soul swells up. It is not upright in him. But [the] righteous by his faith will live.	4. If he draws back my soul is not pleased in him. But the righteous from my faith will live.

The LXX seems to imply that it is not the vision that will not tarry, but the Chaldean nation. The pronoun, αὐτόν, is masculine while ὅρασις is feminine. Therefore, the command, "wait for it/him," cannot have the vision as its object. Syntactically, the most straightforward translation of G is, "If he should tarry, wait upon him, because he who is coming will come, and is by no means delayed." That this problem exists is demonstrated by Tov's comment in the reconstruction of ὅρασις in the text of 8HevXIIgr. He said, "On the other hand, [αὐ]τόν later in the verse should probably refer to this noun, so that a masculine noun may be expected here . . . However, the same problem obtains in the LXX, so that the problem of grammatical agreement may have been overlooked by both the LXX and R."[10] If one does not follow Tov in believing the versions simply ignored the bad grammar (an assumption based on the expectation of a textual tradition of stability with variation due to human error), then an intelligible translation and interpretation of the tradition as it stands must be attempted.

Cleaver-Bartholomew said only two options exist for the identity of the coming one: YHWH's representative or messenger, or YHWH

---

10. Tov, *Greek Minor Prophets Scroll*, 92–93.

himself.[11] These choices were so limited because Cleaver-Bartholomew focused on the eschatological themes and uses of the text of Hab 2:2–3, and so he only looked forward to Hab 3 for contextual help. This seems to be a poor approach of applying meaning to a text. While a passage can certainly find a fulfillment and/or clarification of its intended meaning from what follows, the immediate meaning of the text should also make sense from what preceded it.

The closest previous masculine singular subject is "the one reading them," but that connection does not make much sense. If this is truly an answer given to Habakkuk's reproof of God's discipline, then the most natural contextual interpretation is to understand the coming one to be the Chaldean nation—he who seemingly will cast his net and through it all spare not to kill nations. Following the context of 1:1–17 and 2:1–2, the best option for "he who is coming" is surely the Chaldean nation. This is a great shift in meaning from the MT to the LXX in Hab 2:3.

In verse 4 the LXX moves the ownership of the word "soul" to God. *God's soul* is not pleased in the Chaldean nation should he draw back. On the other hand, in the MT someone's soul is not said to draw back, but it swells up and is not upright in him. In the LXX the righteous will live from God's faith, or faithfulness. In the MT [the] righteous one will live by his own faith.

Instead of arguing that one text, or one part of one of the texts, represents the faithful tradition and another does not, the full textual witness should be explored. The witness as a whole declares that a swelled soul that is not upright does not please God. A righteous person will live by his faith in God. Furthermore, the faith of a righteous person stems from the faithfulness of God. Even if something as horrible as the Chaldean invasion is certain to occur, the promises of God are equally certain. The righteous person trusts in God even in the face of calamity because God is trustworthy. Faith prevents the righteous from swelling up and falling way from God. This approach is further supported by the quotation of Hab 2:3–4 in Heb 10:37–38:

> 37. For still in a very short while the one who is coming will come and not delay.
>
> 38. But my righteous one from faith will live. And if he draws back, my soul is not pleased with him.

---

11. Cleaver-Bartholomew, "One Text," 6.

The first part of verse 37 is a small citation from Isa 26:20 LXX. In the context of Hebrews the author connects the tradition of Hab 2:3–4 to a passage in Isaiah that "orients the proclamation to the day of the Lord, especially as a day of Judgment, but also as a day in which the people of God are protected."[12] While the original prophecy of Habakkuk concerned God's use of the Chaldeans as an instrument of judging his people, the coming vision was given as a source of hope in light of impending judgment. Hebrews projects the prophets' words to the return of Jesus and the judgment promised on that day in order to encourage the audience of Hebrews to not "draw back" to their old ways of worship. Hebrews reverses the order of the phrases in Hab 2:4 to put greater emphasis on the righteous one who lives by faith. Indeed, in Hebrews it is not simply *a* righteous one, or *the* righteous one, but *God's* righteous one.

The audience of Hebrews is encouraged to remember that Jesus is returning soon, and that promise also attends a reality of judgment. It is only through faith that they will be found as God's very own righteous ones. If they draw back, God will not be pleased with them.

Interestingly, in 1QpHab the Qumran community also projected this passage toward the last days, which it states will be very long, encouraging the community to remain faithful to the teachings of the Teacher of Righteousness who received the vision written on the tablets in Hab 2:2.[13]

The full textual witness reminds the believing community that times of judgment are real. They surely come. The Chaldeans will surely come—wait for him. God's vision of the last days will not delay—wait for it. Jesus is returning in a very short while—expect him. Be ready. God is faithful. He is trustworthy. The believer would do well to not swell herself up and draw back. She can place her faith in God because he is faithful, and she will find herself counted among God's righteous ones who will surely live. And God's soul is pleased with his righteous ones who trust him and live. This sounds suspiciously similar to what the one who fulfilled the Prophets said in places like Mark 13:32–37.

Of course, there should be much caution in the approach of accepting multiple textual witnesses as faithful tradents of the biblical tradition. Some textual witnesses may not be faithful representations of the faith community. As a starting point, at the very least, the LXX can be consulted to investigate the greater witness to the tradition.

---

12. Guthrie, "Hebrews," 982.
13. Cook, "Commentary," 84–85.

There is no room for extensive elaboration, nor do I have the expertise to helpfully elaborate in an extensive way, but perhaps text-critical studies such as Bénédicte Lemmelijn's in her article, "Text-Critically Studying the Biblical Manuscript Evidence: An 'Empirical' Entry to the Literary Composition of the Text,"[14] can be modified to help determine if any given text is faithful to the full textual tradition and so worthy to be determined a part of it and so applied to discover the fuller meaning of the whole.

She argues for text criticism as a starting point for further critical study. The first step involves selecting and collecting the textual material to be studied—this requires an informed consideration of which witnesses to the tradition should be evaluated at all. Utilizing the accepted material, objective data can be mined by analyzing variants through what she calls a synoptic survey. Then the variants are registered and described followed by an evaluation. Then, the variants can be utilized for literary (redaction) criticism according to her understanding of the source material and its purposes.

Extensive modification of the model is necessary because while Lemmelijn's methodology does not seem to accept the traditional concept of an "original text," it still seems to expect a growth process of the text that stands in contrast to recent studies in oral traditional cultures. While her methodology does not take into account theories of orality discussed in this work, should her method be refashioned with these theories in mind, it might produce a working model for analyzing different textual witnesses. Specifically, I would suggest the gathering of early individual manuscripts of various traditions instead of critical texts (as she uses for the LXX) in her example. Then, as I did in my study of Habakkuk, we should investigate the rhetorical effects of variants in the entire presentation of each specific manuscript.

While Lemmelijn argues against the pursuit of a *Urtext*, she still seemed to be preoccupied with discovering an original presentation or performance of a tradition—such as the plague narrative of Exod 7:14–11:10 that she discussed in her article. Her methodology would need to be significantly adjusted for the possibility of multiform authoritative performances. Any further evaluations of her model and suggestions for adjustments toward my suggested purposes are beyond my area of expertise. Further studies for specific approaches to create boundaries for which performances should be accepted are certainly needed.

14. Lemmelijn, "Text-Critically," 129–64.

Performing the Text

General Remarks on Performance Supported Exegesis

David Rhoads pointed out that no one would be considered a valid critic of Shakespeare without ever seeing a play.[15] One does not study Bach merely by staring at the notation. To experience the meaning of script and notation one needs to experience their performance. If the biblical texts were originally written to be performed and experienced through performance, then perhaps they should be treated similarly today. Certainly, the texts should be analyzed as works intended for performance, and we might gain new insights by experiencing these ancient texts through modern performances should the methods behind such performances adhere to the exegetical perspectives already outlined up to this point.

Peter Perry designated the approach described by Rhoads above as a representative of a third wave in the first version of biblical performance criticism (BPC).[16] However, he also acknowledges its ongoing relevance to the current version of BPC as he discusses the possible interpretive nuances of the centurion's words in Mark 15:39.[17] Perry's ponderings of the interpretive possibilities of this passage's performance points to my major critique of certain approaches to exegeting orality in light of modern performance.

The words of Foley again find relevance:

> Since modern fieldwork has shown that textuality and oral traditions not only co-exist but interact, and since the chief criterion of how verbal art works is the language or register within which it morphs and through which it communicates, the role of textuality is certainly no reason to deny oral traditional roots. *Better to remain agnostic about scenarios for which we have no primary, irrefutable evidence,* and *at the same time to take full account of the oral traditional structure and expressivity of such works.*[18]

We have no scenarios for theatrical performances of the biblical tradition, nor do we have evidence that the statement of the centurion was open for this kind of interpretive approach. Perry leaves no doubt that the biblical tradition was certainly performed through the public vocalization, often

---

15. Rhoads, "Performance Criticism," 27.
16. Perry, "Biblical Performance Criticism," 3.
17. Perry, "Biblical Performance Criticism," 9–10.
18. Foley, "Plenitude and Diversity," 109 (emphasis added).

through an audible reading of a text accompanied with an explanation of the tradition:

> Moses is portrayed in Deuteronomy as retelling the story of the exodus from Egypt while the Israelites stand on the bank of the Jordan River ready to enter Canaan (Deut 9:1). The book of Proverbs imagines parents repeating its wisdom to their children (e.g., 1:8). Singers and musicians practice psalms to sing in the courts of the Jerusalem Temple (1 Chr 25). Ezra the scribe reads the scroll of the Law of Moses to the people gathered in the restored walls of Jerusalem, and Levites help further teach and explain it to the audience (Neh 8). Luke depicts Jesus standing to read from an Isaiah scroll before sitting to teach (Luke 4). Matthew and Luke describe Jesus teaching similar words in two locations, a Sermon on the Mount and a Sermon on the Plain (Matt 5–7; Luke 6: 17–49). Acts portrays Paul and other apostles summarizing the history of Israel, climaxing with Jesus, to people gathered in synagogues (e.g., Acts 13:16–41). Paul asks that his letters be read to all believers in Thessalonika (1 Thess 5:27). John expects the book of Revelation to be read aloud, likely to many audiences (Rev 1:3). These examples suggest the ways in which almost all the biblical material functioned in communication events.[19]

Before applying performance methodologies that are not represented—for which we have no primary, irrefutable evidence—we should apply the more representative methodologies I outlined in earlier chapters "to take full account of the oral traditional structure and expressivity of such works."

In this case, before performing the passage containing the centurion's words, work should be done on the rhetorical purposes of Mark's use of repetition between the water baptism of Jesus and the baptism of the cross, as discussed earlier in chapter 7. After such an analysis, any interpretation of the centurion's words as insincere would certainly be ruled out. His words parallel the voice of the Father from Mark 1:11.

Hypothetical methodologies of modern performances of the text must not breach what can likely be discovered through the application of more substantial theories of the structure and rhetorical approaches of oral traditional cultures.

As another example of the misapplication of exegesis stemming from modern biblical performance, West discussed an aspect of the

---

19. Perry, "Biblical Performance Criticism," 1.

narrative of the binding of Isaac from Gen 22:1–19 that may be overlooked in silent reading. Once the angel stops Abraham from sacrificing Isaac, what becomes of the knife intended to slaughter Isaac? In an independent, silent reading of the story the knife is likely forgotten once the tension is broken by the provision of the ram, but in acting the narrative out the most natural way for an actor playing the part of Abraham to release Isaac from being bound on the altar is to use that very knife to set him free. Thus, "by using the knife to cut Isaac free, the knife is transformed from an instrument intended to cause death and destruction to an instrument of life and liberation."[20] This could even reflect the cross of Jesus itself!

Perhaps Abraham really did use that very knife to set Isaac free. And the message received from such an interpretation is hardly contrary to the biblical message as a whole. Indeed, the theme of reversal from death and destruction to life and liberation is certainly a biblical theme worth acknowledging at every applicable intersection. The theme certainly reflects the connotations of the word, ὑψόω, discussed in chapter 8. However, in his evaluation of my dissertation at this point, Stephen von Wyrick pointed out:

> It appears presumptive to come to this conclusion since biblical Hebrew uses four separate words for "knife."[21] The word in Gen 22 and in Prov 30 refers to a knife designed for slaughtering, while there are three other words for a knife not used for slaughtering and which Abraham may have had on his person as well as the knife dedicated for slaughtering. Can "performance" become a tool that leaves an improper interpretation for the audience. Think of how many people interpret the crossing of the Yam Suph in light of Cecil B. DeMille's performance of the *Ten Commandments.*[22]

Indeed, we must be cautious to not become the very thing we are critiquing. While I have been arguing that the Bible has been studied through anachronistic projections of modern text culture, we can overcorrect and begin to study the Bible through anachronistic projections of modern performance culture. As Judges warned us, we can become the very thing

---

20. West, "Art of Biblical Performance," 18–19.

21. "מַאֲכֶלֶת—specifically for cutting or butchering to make small: Gen 22:6, 10; Judg 19:29; Prov 30:14 (pl); שַׂכִּין—knife: Prov 23:2; תַּעַר—penknife, razor: Jer 36:23; חֶרֶב—a knife made of flint used for circumcision: Josh 5:2, 3" (Wyrick's footnote).

22. Wyrick, comment on dissertation, 2022.

we are trying to correct. As Romans warned us, we can be wise in our own eyes and so overlook the meaning of the overlap of the ancient and current move of God.

West seems to advocate for the performance of biblical narratives through an ensemble of actors, and he downplays the absolute lack of evidence from within the text or from extra-biblical material that Israel had such performances.[23] West even seems to argue that ancient Israel would cast a person to play the role of YHWH. It seems unlikely that the community that guarded the NAME so carefully and who was forbidden to make images of God would cast a human to play such a role. West's argument that Genesis's description of humanity as being made in the image of God justifies humans acting as YHWH is unconvincing.

The acts of performance recorded in the Bible, such as Exod 24:7, Deut 31:9–13, Neh 8:1–12, and Luke 4:16–20, seem to suggest a singular reader as performer. To West's point, the examples from the Old Testament listed above are readings of the Law and not of the biblical narratives that his study discusses. However, it is certainly unclear if the narratives of Torah were separated in genre and performance by ancient Israel. It is a far different performance for a reader to say "The LORD said thus" than for an actor to perform as YHWH. The latter does not seem likely.

This is not to say that the public performance of a text is without merit. Indeed, even studying the text as a verbal performance, written to be read aloud to an audience, can aid in interpretation through the imagined impact the performance would have had on the original audience. Jeanette Matthews investigates the impact of performing Habakkuk in her dissertation, "Performing Habakkuk: Faithful Re-Enactment in the Midst of Crisis."[24] Matthews pointed to Hab 1:1–4, at which point the audience receives a bit of a surprise, as Habakkuk, designated as a prophet in verse 1, is expected to declare that he has heard a word from YHWH and then deliver it. Instead, the prophet cries out that YHWH is not listening to *him*! Even so, the audience expects to watch the event play out from afar as the prophet speaks to God without necessarily acknowledging the crowd.

But Hab 1:5 shifts the scene immediately with a second-person plural indicative: "*Look* to the nations!" An audience that hears a second-person plural indicative, seemingly announced at them from the

---

23. See West's discussion on *Resistance to the Narratives as Drama* in "Art of Biblical Performance," 64–69.

24. Mathews "Performing Habakkuk," 191, 269–70.

performer, instead of a word from God to the prophet, would certainly be affected. Suddenly the audience, feeling personally addressed by the performance, is drawn into the drama to participate in the experience and be personally transformed alongside the prophet.

As the following section of Habakkuk, beginning in 1:12, shifts back to a second-person singular, perhaps those in the audience, now fully involved, would see themselves as joining in the criticism of YHWH's plan and so be primed to journey with the transformation of Habakkuk from lament, through fear, and into faith.

Performance criticism seems to hold great potential in honoring the nature of the texts and in producing intriguing insights to their meaning and application for the believing community. However, if the anachronistic application of the text-based, Western approach to biblical studies of the past can teach the scholarly community anything, it should be to move forward slowly in the application of new critical insights.

I have thoroughly enjoyed Max McLean's performance of the book of Mark and the more recent performance of the Jesus tradition in Dallas Jenkins's *The Chosen*.[25] Such performances can certainly evoke powerful responses to the biblical tradition that may be lost in a sermon or commentary, even if the sermon or commentary is informed in matters of the Bible's oral traditional origins. Indeed, if a performance is based on exegetical methodologies derived from the theories and examples in this book, it could bridge the gap between ancient and modern faith communities in new and exciting ways!

Performing Ecclesiastes as a Whole

One final example of exegeting the oral text is offered as it relates to the text as performed. While a community's metanarrative may be activated by the performance of only one short narrative unit, some works may have been intended to be performed as a whole. Such a case may be made for the book of Ecclesiastes. In his presentation, "Ecclesiastes: Finding

---

25. Of course I acknowledge that *The Chosen* takes exceptional liberties with the tradition. Some are helpful, such as the dialogue that draws out the connection of Jacob's ladder to Nathaniel's conversation with Jesus in 1:43–51 in Season 2, Episode 2. However, the discussion of shepherds and swaddling clothes in its depiction of the Christmas story is not as biblically and historically grounded. Many of the liberties of the show, just like creative liberties in any sermon I have ever heard or given, must be taken with a grain of salt.

Meaning in a Meaningless World," at B. H. Carroll Theological Institute's 2019 spring colloquy, Tremper Longman III argued that there are two voices in Ecclesiastes—the voice/message of Qohelet in Eccl 1:12—12:7 and the voice/message of the frame narrator in Eccl 1:1–11 and 12:8–14.[26] The frame narrator provides his "son" (12:12)[27] with Qohelet's message, essentially saying, "This is a voice you need to hear" but qualifying the voice of Qohelet with the final message: "Fear God. Obey the commandments. Live in the light of the future judgment."

If Longman's perspective is correct, then any truth interpreted from Eccl 1:12—12:7 is incomplete unless it addresses the instructional intention of the frame narrator, which culminates in 12:8–14. Should everyone "eat and drink and take pleasure in all his toil"? Is this "God's gift to man"? (Eccl 3:13). This is only true as long as it can be applied in the fear of God, obeying the commandments in light of the future judgment.

Qohelet's voice is not "Scripture" apart from the voice of the frame narrator. And the frame narrator's voice only has its full meaning when it is seen as the voice of a wise father giving instruction to a son in light of the message of Qohelet—acknowledging a layer of wisdom in Qohelet's voice. The meaning of Ecclesiastes is not discovered in any single section of the work but in the presentation of the whole. Qohelet's voice about the world's meaninglessness rings true enough to be heard, but it should never shout louder than the impending trumpet blasts of God's final judgment. Any sermon or sermon series on Ecclesiastes must present the full message represented by both voices performed in the text. One may even find a way to perform the entire book, or at least a rendition of it, casting both a wise father/narrator and a skeptic Qohelet.

---

26. See also Longman's discussion of Ecclesiastes in Longman, *Fear of the Lord*, 26–42.

27. See Prov chapters 1–7 as an example of the prevalence in biblical wisdom tradition of instruction given to a son.

Final Words

A Performance for our Modern Tradition of Exegesis

THE STORIES WE BELIEVE drive us. We play our role in whatever plot line our soul accepts, and the more we play that role, the more we believe in the story, and the better we get at playing our part. Soldiers do not fight for a list of names in the Senate. They fight for a story they believe is worth fighting for. That story might be a narrative about their country, the righteousness of the battle, or the life they might have after their time in the military. But it is the story that drives them. Cults do not take control over a soul through the sharing of data but by acclimating acolytes to a story. The stories we believe determine our engagement with reality. The stories we believe become our identity.

    Students of Scripture choose to skate a treacherous line in the story of life. The inspired words of Scripture ground humanity's story in a garden temple,[1] planted by the creator God as humanity's home. He named the garden "Delight." Created as the very image of God's rule and reign and love and creativity on earth, humanity was placed inside Delight as a holy priesthood of creation to keep and guard her. God would come and walk with his beloved priests in Delight, sharing sweet fellowship.

    There were two trees in the midst of Delight, and one of them was off-limits to the priests. It was the tree of the knowledge of good and evil. That was God's tree. He alone, as the creator and sustainer of all things, can truly know and determine what is good and what is evil. Actually, it is deeper than that. The definitions of good and evil all depend upon the identity of God. And so, as long as God's priest and priestess walked in intimacy with him, they were always growing deeper in abiding in his benevolence—always moving further away from evil. Even Delight

---

1. Wenham, "Sanctuary Symbolism," 19–26.

reflected the story of God's loving identity to the priests as they kept and guarded her.

God's beloved image was free to abide in Delight in loving intimacy with each other and with God, trusting fully in their relationship with him as their daily guide to guarding and keeping Delight. But Eve was deceived into believing that she could be like God on her own, knowing and determining what was good and evil apart from God. It seems as though Adam, who was with her, may not have been deceived (2 Tim 2:14) yet he also ate. Sometimes we cannot make sense of the insanity of rebellion against God and his garden of Delight.

Before they launched their assault against God's fruit, they had walked in intimate knowledge of their purpose in creation. They were tending to Delight, reflecting the loving kingdom of the creator on earth. God had planted Delight. The priesthood communed with him as his royal priests as they tended to his garden. It was a sublime story. But they began to believe a different plot line. They believed they could attain godlikeness on their own terms. They grasped for a divine identity of their own.

Suddenly, instead of walking openly in their intimate purposes without shame, they then knew how to know apart from God. Knowing apart from God separated them from God. They were naked and ashamed. They discovered that knowing apart from God drove distance between them as well. They hid from God and covered themselves up from each other. She wanted to own him. He wanted to rule over her (Gen 3:16).[2]

Delight was lost. The temple garden no longer had a priesthood who was safe to guard her. God drove the fallen priesthood out of Delight but not before first accommodating their new knowledge apart from him. He covered their newfound shame according to their new knowledge apart from him. This would not be the last time he moved to humanity according to their own knowledge apart from him in order to draw them back into his presence.

---

2. The Hebrew phrase in Gen 3:16, וְאֶל־אִישֵׁךְ תְּשׁוּקָתֵךְ, is only reflected two other times. It appears in the very next chapter at 4:7, וְאֵלֶיךָ תְּשׁוּקָתוֹ, indicating that sin desires Cain the same way Eve's offspring will desire men—not a healthy longing but an unhealthy desire to consume the other. However, in Song 7:10 the phrase appears again, modified with a different preposition: וְעָלַי תְּשׁוּקָתוֹ. The woman sings, "And his desire is for me," not "against me." When husband and wife approach each other in godly love, they can once again taste flavors of God's intentions for humanity. They can partake of a reverse of the curse.

As the story goes, the entire line of the fallen priesthood now struggles with the enticing plot line of abandoning the gift of simply existing as the image of God in intimate trusting relationship with him. Instead, they strive to attain godhood for themselves—determining for themselves what is good and evil. This struggle reverberates as we try to be wise in our own eyes—as in the cycle of the judges, in the legalistic approach of the Law discussed in Romans, and in the vanity of Qohelet's observations. We are all tempted to pursue knowledge apart from God. The narrative of fallen humanity assumes that life is about knowing good and evil. But the primordial plot line consisted of walking in relational intimacy with God, who is goodness and in whom abides not even a shadow of evil.

Make no mistake, there was knowledge to be known in the garden of Delight. The priest and priestess knew the name of every animal. They knew their purpose. They knew the prohibition of eating the fruit of the tree of the knowledge of good and evil. Most importantly, they knew God and they knew each other. And they were growing in that most important knowledge before they made "knowledge apart from God" their god.

The inspired words of Scripture proclaim to us today, as we live and breathe in this chapter of that same story, that no matter what we think we know, we know in part (1 Cor 13:9). We are all capable of pursuing knowledge. We are all capable of gaining knowledge. But, perhaps more often than not, this knowledge puffs up the divisions between us and God (1 Cor 8:1). It is the love of God as displayed in Delight that builds up everything that is eternal and true. If anyone pursues the knowledge of the fallen fruit, no matter how much knowledge they possess, they do not yet know as they ought to know (1 Cor 8:2). But if they learn to walk in love as the priest and priestess first did in Delight, then just like the original priesthood in the first scenes of the true story of humanity, they will be known by God (1 Cor 8:3). We can be married to God again through Christ's divine proposal. We can be known by our eternal bridegroom.

There is a fine line between the two types of knowledge—the knowledge that puffs up and divides and the knowledge led by love toward being known. Students of Scripture often skate this treacherous line. We want to know fully so that we can know how to be fully known. But we are always in danger of crossing over and making certain aspects of knowledge the end instead of the means. We can possess knowledge in order to take control of life, to grasp equality with God like Adam and

Eve. All too often, we find ourselves learning to know apart from God. We let knowledge divide us—from God and from each other.

The hero of our story did not give in to that temptation. Though he was in every way the God of creation, literally equal with God, he did not consider godlikeness something to be seized and usurped (Phil 2:6). His purpose was not to wield knowledge to be served by it and to find power through it. His purpose was to offer himself to be known by God and others through the service of humble love (Mark 10:45). Indeed, while being the exact nature of God, he emptied himself to become a servant to all (Phil 2:7). He became human. He stepped into the image of God, the priesthood of all creation, and he walked in the original way of the holy priesthood—in the presence and knowledge of the Father (Heb 4:14—5:10). He died the death of our usurpation of godlikeness to bridge the gap we had formed by striving to know apart from God (Rom 6:23). Now, in him, we can be known by God, and in his love and grace, learn to truly know ourselves and others; we can even abide in the intimacy of the Trinity and make Christ known to the world (John 17:20–23).

As I have surveyed biblical scholarship, I have often felt as if I caught scents of the fruit of the tree of the knowledge of good and evil behind some of the words I read. Pursuits to possess as opposed to inquiries toward intimacy. A lust for novelty. A stacking of books to build a tower to heaven. It is the scent I am still trying to leave behind. Jesus is still washing the scent from my feet.

The story of the Western pursuit of knowledge can reflect the sin of trying to control our lives by building up our own opinions about what is good and evil. Our desire to know fully and perfectly can stem from a desire to be like God within terms we control, and that pursuit can limit our experience of being known by God through submission to him. Oh, how I pray that I might not fall into temptation. Lord, have mercy. Christ, have mercy.

I am thankful in so many ways for the Western culture in which I have been raised. I am thankful for the legacy of a pursuit for objective truth that drives me to expend my means to obtain truth and never sell it (Prov 23:23). In my joy, I desire to sell all that I have to purchase the field in which I have discovered the great treasure (Matt 13:44). I *know* the treasure is there. I *know* something of the treasure's identity and worth. I *know* it is worth the price of purchase, and I *know* that no price is worth its selling.

I *know* that God's word proclaims to me that knowledge will pass away and that faith, hope, and love will abide (1 Cor 13). I believe that to be objectively true. I want to grow to know in such a way that I honor that truth. It has been helpful for me to grow in my knowledge that knowledge will pass away. Knowledge itself is not the enemy. Knowledge in loving submission to God is good. We can know the truth, and the truth will set us free as we abide in Christ and his word (John 8:32).

The Renaissance, the season of rationalism, and the age of Enlightenment gave a new voice to the ancient deficient plot line of the fallen priesthood—a voice that has driven the modern Western world for many hundreds of years. The story has taken some plot twists here and there. Some have tried to jump ship. But the story still owns the souls of many of us.

The story bequeathed to us in the Western pursuit of knowledge has often reflected more of Adam and Eve's grasping for ownership of their identities and ownership of the world as opposed to Jesus' demonstration of a pursuit of the truths of faith, hope, and love. The Western pursuit often looks less like the Word becoming flesh to give his life as a ransom for many and more like flesh seeking to be like God on humanity's own terms. It often looks like knowing apart from God. The Western pursuit can drive us further east of Eden.

Some modern scholarly approaches to the Bible have sought to subject the Scriptures to the cultural assumptions of a post-Enlightenment age of human reason. We have tried to squeeze the nature of the word into the box of post-Gutenberg humanistic knowledge. But the inspired word is not the text. The text is not the fullness of our story. We cannot enslave the story of the creator within the cage of linear print.[3] The texts we have are the abiding tradents of the inspired word of God, and if we will let them be what they were and listen to them within their own ontological identities, we can hear the ancient traditions of our own ontological identity activated for us to walk in as the new royal priesthood of our creator through Christ our Lord.

The word should not be proclaimed merely as knowledge to be analyzed, discussed, and argued over but instead as a communal identity to be lived out. The Bible is not just a text to be studied, but it is a tradition of identity that is to be re-proclaimed and reenacted in the community of faith. We still hear these ancient traditions through the voice

---

3. To borrow a phrase from Finnegan, *Where is Language*, 55.

of our ancient community of faith. Let us not recast their ancient voices into modern epistemological molds. Let their voices speak. Hear them through the abiding Holy Spirit who connects us all to the story of Jesus. And let us live that story out today together.

May the Spirit of the Living God use this work to lead Christ's church, as well as others who may be open to his words, to experience the biblical traditions as our communal identity, and may we actualize that ancient identity today for his glory and our joy.

Bibliography

Acker, Nick. "How Should the Reader Run: Implications of Orality and Textuality in the Transmission and Message of the Habakkuk Tradition as Seen in Important Witnesses to the Text." PhD diss., B. H. Carroll Theological Institute, 2022.
Albright, William F. "Some Oriental Glosses on the Homeric Problem." *American Journal of Archaeology* 54 (1950) 162–76.
Allen, Joseph Henry, and J. B. Greenough. *Allen and Greenough's New Latin Grammar for Schools and Colleges*. Boston: Ginn and Co., 1903.
Alter, Robert. *The Art of Biblical Narrative*. New York: Basic Books, 2011.
Amodio, Mark. *Writing the Oral Tradition: Oral Poetics and Literate Culture in Medieval England*. Notre Dame, IN: University of Notre Dame Press, 2004.
Arterbury, Andrew E. "Breaking the Betrothal Bonds: Hospitality in John 4." *Catholic Biblical Quarterly* 72 (2010) 63–83.
Bahnsen, Greg L. *Always Ready: Directions for Defending the Faith*. Edited by Robert R. Booth. Nacogdoches, TX: Covenant Media, 2011.
———. "Apologetics." Covenant Media Foundation. https://www.cmfnow.com/mp3/apologetics.
Baker, David L. *Two Testaments, One Bible: The Theological Relationship between the Old and New Testaments*. 3rd ed. Downers Grove, IL: InterVarsity, 2010.
Bakker, Egbert J. "Activation and Preservation: The Interdependence of Text and Performance in an Oral Tradition." *Oral Tradition* 8.1 (1993) 5–20.
Balogh, Csaba. "Review of *A Discourse Analysis of Habakkuk* by David J. Fuller." *Journal of Semitic Studies* 66.2 (Autumn 2021) 31–34.
Barber, Karin. *The Anthropology of Texts, Persons and Publics*. New York: Cambridge University Press, 2007.
Barr, James. *Comparative Philology and the Text of the Old Testament*. Oxford: Oxford University Press, 1968.
Barthelemy, Dominique. *Ézéchiel, Daniel et les 12 Prophètes*. Critique textuelle de l'Ancien Testament. Tome 3. Göttingen: Vandenhoeck und Ruprecht, 1992.
Beale, G. K. "An Exegetical and Theological Consideration of the Hardening of Pharaoh's Heart in Exodus 4–14 and Romans 9." *Trinity Journal* 5 (1984) 129–54.
Biakolo, Emevwo. "On the Theoretical Foundations of Orality and Literacy." *Research in African Literatures* 30.2 (Summer 1999) 42–65.

Billingham, Val. "Review of *Performing Habakkuk: Faithful Re-enactment in the Midst of Crisis* by Jeanette Mathews." *Colloquium* 45.1 (May 2013) 110–13.

Block, Daniel I. *The New American Commentary, Vol. 6: Judges, Ruth*. Nashville: B&H, 1999.

Blomberg, Craig L. *From Pentecost to Patmos: An Introduction to Acts through Revelation*. Nashville: Broadman and Holman, 2006.

Bock, Darrel L. "Luke." In *The NIV Application Commentary*. Grand Rapids: Zondervan, 1996.

Boda, Mark J. "Freeing the Burden of Prophecy: Maśśā' and the Legitimacy of Prophecy in Zech 9–14." *Biblica* 87 (2006) 338–57.

Botha, Pieter J. J. "The Gospel of Mark, Orality Studies and Performance Criticism: Opening Windows on Jesus Traditions." *Religion & Theology* 25 (2018) 350–93.

Brindle, Wayne A. "Prepared by Whom? Reprobation and Non-Calvinist Interpretations of Romans 9:22." *Criswell Theological Review* 12.2 (Spring 2015) 135–46.

Brownlee, William H. *The Midrash Pesher of Habakkuk*. Missoula, MT: Scholars, 1979.

———. *The Text of Habakkuk in the Ancient Commentary from Qumran*. Philadelphia: Society of Biblical Literature and Exegesis, 1959.

Bruce, F. F. *The Gospel and Epistles of John*. Grand Rapids: Eerdmans, 1983.

———. "Habakkuk." In *An Exegetical and Expository Commentary on the Minor Prophets, Vol. 2*, edited by Thomas Edward McComiskey, 831–96. Grand Rapids: Baker, 1993.

———. *Romans*. Tyndale New Testament Commentaries. Edited by Canon Leon Morris. Grand Rapids: Eerdmans, 1989.

Bruno, Christopher R. "The Deliverer from Zion: The Source(s) and Function of Paul's Citation in Romans 11:26–27." *Tyndale Bulletin* 59.1 (2008) 119–34.

Bultmann, Rudolf. *History of the Synoptic Tradition*. Peabody, MA: Hendrickson, 1963.

Carr, David M. *The Formation of the Hebrew Bible: A New Reconstruction*. Oxford: Oxford University Press, 2011.

———. "Orality, Textuality and Memory: The State of Biblical Studies." In *Contextualizing Israel's Sacred Writings: Ancient Literacy, Orality, and Literary Production*, edited by Bryan B. Schmidt, 161–73. Atlanta: SBL, 2015.

———. *Writing on the Tablet of the Heart: Origins of Scripture and Literature*. Oxford: Oxford University Press, 2005.

Carruthers, Mary. *The Book of Memory: A Study of Memory in Medieval Culture*. 2nd ed. New York: Cambridge University Press, 1992.

Cathcart, Kevin J., and Robert P. Gordon. *The Targum of the Minor Prophets*. Aramaic Bible. Vol. 14. Edited by Kevin J. Cathcart, Michael Maher, and Martin McNamara. Collegeville, MN: Liturgical, 1990.

Ceriani, Antonio Maria. "Praefatio." In *Translatio Syra Pescitto Veteris Testamenti ex codice Ambrosiano, sec. fere VI photolighographice edita*, 7–8. Milan: Bibliotheca Ambrosianae Mediolani, 1883.

Chazelle, Celia Martin. *The Codex Amiatinus and Its "Sister" Bibles: Scripture, Liturgy, and Art in the Milieu of the Venerable Bede*. Leiden: Brill, 2019.

Chilton, Bruce D. *The Glory of Israel: The Theology and Provenience of the Isaiah Targum*. Journal for the Study of the Old Testament Supplement Series. Vol. 23. Edited by David J. A. Clines, Philip R. Davies, and David M. Gunn. Sheffield, England: JSOT, 1982.

Cleaver-Bartholomew, David. "One Text with Two Interpretations: Habakkuk OG and MT Compared." *Proceedings* 28 (2008) 1–13.

Clover, Carol J. "The Long Prose Form." *Arkiv för nordisk filologi* 101 (1986) 10–39.

Bibliography

Cohen, Jeremy. "The Mystery of Israel's Salvation: Romans 11:25–26 in Patristic and Medieval Exegesis." *Harvard Theological Review* 98.3 (2005) 247–81.

Collins, John J. "Prophecy and History in the Pesharim." In *Authoritative Scriptures in Ancient Judaism, Vol. 141*, edited by Mladen Popović, 209–26. Supplements to the *Journal for the Study of Judaism*. Leiden: Brill, 2010.

Cook, Edward M. "A Commentary on Habakkuk." In *The Dead Sea Scrolls: A New Translation*, edited by Michael O. Wise, Martin G. Abegg Jr., and Edward M. Cook, 79–88. San Francisco: HarperSanFrancisco, 2005.

Crenshaw, James L. *Samson: A Secret Betrayed, A Vow Ignored*. Atlanta: John Knox, 1978.

Cross, Frank Moore. "Prose and Poetry in the Mythic and Epic Texts from Ugarit." *Harvard Theological Review* 67 (1974) 1–15.

Culley, Robert C. "An Approach to the Problem of Oral Tradition." *Vetus Testamentum* 13 (1963) 8–125.

———. *Oral Formulaic Language in the Biblical Psalms*. Toronto: University of Toronto Press, 1967.

———. "Oral Tradition and Biblical Studies." *Oral Tradition* 1 (1986) 30–65.

———. "Oral Tradition and Historicity." In *Studies on the Ancient Palestinian World: Presented to Professor F. V. Winnett*, edited by J. W. Wevers and D. B. Redford, 102–16. Toronto: University of Toronto Press, 1972.

———. "Oral Tradition and the OT: Some Recent Discussion." *Semeia* 5 (1976) 1–33.

———. "Orality and Writtenness in the Prophetic Texts." In *Writings and Speech in Israelite and Ancient Near Eastern Prophecy*, edited by Ehud Ben Zvi and Michael H. Floyd, 45–64. Atlanta: SBL, 2000.

Culpepper, R. Alan. "Luke." In *The New Interpreter's Bible*, Vol. 9, edited by Leander E. Keck, 3–490. Nashville: Abingdon, 1995.

Delnero, Paul. *The Textual Criticism of Sumerian Literature*. Boston: American Schools of Oriental Research, 2012.

DeSilva, David A. *An Introduction to the New Testament: Contexts, Methods & Ministry Formation*. Downers Grove, IL: InterVarsity, 2004.

Dewey, Joanna. "The Gospel of Mark as an Oral/Aural Narrative: Implications for Preaching." *Currents in Theology and Mission* 44.4 (October 2017) 7–10.

———. "Mark as Interwoven Tapestry: Forecasts and Echoes for a Listening Audience." *Catholic Biblical Quarterly* 53.2 (April 1991) 221–36.

Dorson, Richard M. "Introduction: Folklore and Traditional History." In *Folklore and Traditional History*, edited by R. Dorson, 7–9. The Hague, Paris: Mouton, 1973.

Drew, Paul. "Precision and Exaggeration in Interaction." *American Sociological Review* 68 (2003) 917–38.

Dubois, Thomas A. "Oral Tradition." *Oral Tradition* 18.2 (October 2003) 255–57.

Dundes, Alan. *Holy Writ as Oral Lit: The Bible as Folklore*. New York: Rowman & Littlefield, 1999.

Eddy, Paul Rhodes. "The Historicity of the Early Oral Jesus Tradition: Reflections on the 'Reliability Wars.'" In *Jesus, Skepticism & the Problem of History: Criteria & Context in the Study of Christian Origins*, edited by Darrell L. Bock and J. Ed Komoszewski, 145–63. Grand Rapids: Zondervan Academic, 2019.

———., and Gregory A. Boyd. *The Jesus Legend: A Case for the Historical Reliability of the Synoptic Jesus Tradition*. Grand Rapids: Baker Academic, 2007.

Engnell, Ivan. "The Traditio-Historical Method in Old Testament Research." In *A Rigid*

Scrutiny: Critical Essays on the Old Testament, edited and translated by John T. Willis, 3–16. Nashville: Vanderbilt University Press, 1969.

Evans, Craig A. "Paul and the Hermeneutics of 'True Prophecy': A Study of Romans 9–11," *Bíblica* 65 (1984) 560–70.

Fehribach, Adeline. *The Women in the Life of the Bridegroom*. Collegeville, MN: Liturgical, 1998.

Finnegan, Ruth. "Introduction; or, Why the Comparativist Should Take Account of the South Pacific." *Oral Tradition* 5.2 (1990) 159–84.

———. "'Oral Tradition': Weasel Words or Transdisciplinary Door to Multiplexity?" *Oral Tradition* 18.1 (March 2003) 84–86.

———. *Where Is Language? An Anthropologist's Questions on Language, Literature and Performance*. London: Bloomsbury Academic, 2015.

Floyd, Michael H. "Prophecy and Writing in Habakkuk 2, 1–5." *Zeitschrift für die alttestamentliche Wissenschaft* 105.3 (1993) 462–81.

———. "'Write the Revelation!' (Hab 2:2): Re-imagining the Cultural History of Prophecy." In *Writings and Speech in Israelite and Ancient Near Eastern Prophecy*, edited by Ehud Ben Zvi and Michael H. Floyd, 103–43. Atlanta: SBL, 2000.

Foley, John Miles. "Editing Oral Epic Texts." *Journal of American Folklore* 100.398 (1987) 465–93.

———. "Editor's Column." *Oral Tradition* 18.1 (March 2003) 1–2.

———. *How to Read an Oral Poem*. Chicago: University of Illinois Press, 2002.

———. "Introduction." *Oral Tradition* 1.1 (January 1986) 7–9.

———. "Plenitude and Diversity: Interactions Between Orality and Writing." In *The Interface of Orality and Writing: Speaking, Seeing, Writing in the Shaping of New Genres*, edited by Annette Weissenrieder and Robert B. Coote, 103–18. Eugene, OR: Cascade, 2015.

———. "Selection as *Pars Pro Toto*: The Role of Metonymy in Epic Performance and Tradition." In *The Kalevala and the World's Traditional Epics*, edited by L. Honko, 106–27. Helsinki: Finnish Literature Society, 2002.

France, R. T. *The Gospel of Matthew*. The New International Commentary on the New Testament. Grand Rapids: Eerdmans, 2007.

Fromm, Hans. "Kalevala and Nibelungenlied: The Problem of Oral and Written Composition." In *Religion, Myth and Folklore in the World's Epics: The Kalevala and Its Predecessors*, edited by Lauri Honko, 93–114. New York: Mouton de Gruyter, 1990.

Fuller, David J. *A Discourse Analysis of Habakkuk*. Studia Semitica Neerlandica. Vol. 72. Boston: Brill, 2020.

Garland, David E. *Luke*. Exegetical Commentary on the New Testament. Grand Rapids: Zondervan, 2011.

———. *A Theology of Mark's Gospel*. Grand Rapids: Zondervan, 2015.

Gelston, Anthony. "Introduction." *Twelve Minor Prophets*. Biblia Hebraica BHQ, edited by Anthony Gelston, vol. 13, 5*–10*. Stuttgart: Deutsche Bibelgesellschaft, 2010.

———. *The Peshitta of the Twelve Prophets*. Oxford: Clarendon Press, 1987.

———. *The Twelve Minor Prophets*. Biblia Hebraica Quinta. Edited by A. Schenker. Vol. 13. Stuttgart: Deutsche Bibelgesellschaft, 2010.

Gevirtz, Stanley. *Patterns in the Early Poetry of Israel*. Chicago: University of Chicago 1963.

Giles, Terry, and William J. Doan. *Twice Used Songs: Performance Criticism of the Songs of Ancient Israel*. Peabody, MA: Hendrickson, 2009.
Gillard, Frank D. "More Silent Reading in Antiquity: Non Omne Verbum Sonabat." *JBL* 112.4 (Winter 1993) 689–94.
Goldingay, John. *Biblical Theology: The God of the Christian Scriptures*. Downers Grove, IL: InterVarsity, 2016.
Graham, William A. *Beyond the Written Word: Oral Aspects of Scripture in the History of Religion*. New York: Cambridge University Press, 1987.
———. "Summation." *Oral Tradition* 25.1 (2010) 231–38.
Green, Joel B. *The Gospel of Luke*. The New International Commentary on the New Testament. Grand Rapids, MI: William B. Eerdmans, 1997.
———. "Jesus and a Daughter of Abraham (Luke 13:10–17): Test Case for a Lucan Perspective on Jesus' Miracles." *Catholic Biblical Quarterly* 51 (1989) 643–54.
Greenspoon, Leonard J. Review of *The Greek Minor Prophets Scroll from Naḥal Ḥever (8ḤevXIIgr): (The Seiyal Collection I)*, by Emanuel Tov. *AJS Review* 18.1 (1993) 137–40.
Gunkel, Hermann. *Genesis*. Translated by Mark E. Biddle. Macon, GA: Mercer University Press, 1997.
Gunn, David M. "Narrative Patterns and Oral Tradition in Judges and Samuel." *Vetus Testamentum* 24 (1974) 286–317.
Guthrie, George H. "Hebrews." In *Commentary on the New Testament Use of the Old Testament*, edited by G. K. Beale and D. A. Carson, 919–95. Grand Rapids: Baker Academic, 2007.
Hagner, Donald A. "Matthew 1–13." In *Word Biblical Commentary*. Dallas: Word, 1995.
———. "Matthew 14–28." In *Word Biblical Commentary*. Dallas: Word, 1995.
Hale, Thomas. "Oral Tradition in the Context of Verbal Art." *Oral Tradition* 18.1 (March 2003) 91–92.
Halpern, Baruch. "The Assassination of Eglon: The First Locked-Room Murder Mystery." *BR* 4.6 (Dec 1988) 32–41.
Harper, Joshua. *Responding to a Puzzled Scribe: The Barberini Version of Habakkuk 3 Analysed in Light of the Other Greek Versions*. London: T&T Clark, 2015.
Harrison, Everett F. "Romans." In *The Expositor's Bible Commentary Volume 10*, edited by Frank E. Gaeblelein, 1–171. Grand Rapids: Zondervan, 1976.
Harrison, R. K. *Introduction to the Old Testament*. Peabody, MA: Hendrickson, 2004.
Harvey, John D. *Listening to the Text: Oral Patterning in Paul's Letters*. Grand Rapids: Baker, 1998.
———. "Orality and Its Implications for Biblical Studies: Recapturing an Ancient Paradigm." *Journal of the Evangelical Theological Society* 45.1 (March 2002) 99–109.
Havelock, Eric A. "Oral Composition in the Oedipus Tyrannus of Sophocles." *New Literary History* 16.1 (Autumn 1984) 175–97.
Hayes, John H. "The Songs of Israel." In *The Hebrew Bible Today: An Introduction to Critical Issues*, edited by Steven L. McKenzie and M. Patrick Graham, 153–71. Louisville, KY: Westminster/John Knox, 1998.
Hays, Richard B. *Echoes of Scripture in the Gospels*, Waco, TX: Baylor University Press, 2016.
Hendel, Ronald S. *The Epic of the Patriarch: The Jacob Cycle and the Narrative Traditions of Canaan and Israel*. Atlanta: Scholars, 1987.

Holbek, Bengt. "Introduction." In *Principles for Oral Narrative Research* by Axel Olrik, translated by Kirsten Wolf and Jody Jensen, xv–xxvi. Indianapolis: Indiana University Press, 1992.

Holdrege, Barbara A. *Veda and Torah: Transcending the Textuality of Scripture.* Albany, NY: SUNY, 1996.

Honko, Lauri. "Epics Along the Silk Road: Mental Text, Performance, and Written Codification." *Oral Tradition* 11 (1996) 1–17.

———. "Introduction: Oral and Semiliterary Epics." In *The Epic: Oral and Written*, edited by L. Honko, J. Handoo and J. M. Foley, 9–30. Mysore, India: Central Institute of Indian Languages, 1998.

———. "Text as Process and Practice: The Textualization of Oral Epics." In *Textualization of Oral Epics*, edited by L. Honko, 3–54. New York: Mouton de Gruyter, 2000.

———. *Textualizing the Siri Epic.* Helsinki: Academia Scientiarum Fennica, 1998.

Horsley, Richard. "Oral Tradition in New Testament Studies." *Oral Tradition* 18.1 (March 2003) 34–36.

Irwin, Bonnie D. "Frame Tales and Oral Tradition." *Oral Tradition* 18.1 (March 2003) 125–26.

Jerome, Saint. *Commentary on Galatians, Titus, and Philemon.* Notre Dame, IN: University of Notre Dame Press, 2010. https://archive.org/details/stjeromescommentoooojero.

Johnson, John W., Thomas A. Hale, and Stephen Belcher, eds. *Oral Epics from Africa: Vibrant Voices from a Vast Continent.* Bloomington, IN: Indiana University Press, 1997.

Johnson, Lee A. "Review of *Performing Habakkuk: Faithful Re-enactment in the Midst of Crisis* by Jeanette Mathews." *Catholic Biblical Quarterly* 76.3 (July 2014) 532–34.

Johnson, Rick. "The Bridegroom in John 4." Unpublished manuscript, 199?.

Kaufmann, Walter, ed. and trans. *The Portable Nietzsche.* New York: Penguin, 1982.

Kelber, Werner H. "Oral Tradition in Bible and New Testament Studies." *Oral Tradition* 18.1 (March 2003) 40–42.

Kelley, Page H., Daniel S. Mynatt, and Timothy G. Crawford. *The Masorah of Biblia Hebraica Stuttgartensia.* Grand Rapids: Eerdmans, 1998.

Kirkpatrick, Patricia G. *The Old Testament and Folklore Study.* Sheffield: JSOT, 1988.

Kitchen, K. A. *On the Reliability of the Old Testament.* Grand Rapids: Eerdmans, 2003.

Kittel, Gerhard. *Theological Dictionary of the New Testament: Volume IV.* Grand Rapids: Eerdmans, 1974.

Kittel, Gerhard, Gerhard Friedrich, and Geoffrey W. Bromiley, eds. *Theological Dictionary of the New Testament: Abridged in One Volume.* Grand Rapids: Eerdmans, 1985.

Knezevich, Ruth. "Rethinking Individual Authorship: Robert Burns, Oral Tradition, and the Twenty-First Century." *Oral Tradition* 26.2 (2011) 627–34.

Knight, Douglas A. Foreword to *Oral World and Written World* by Susan Niditch, 1–7. Louisville: Westminster/John Knox, 1996.

———. *Rediscovering the Traditions of Israel: The Development of the Traditio-Historical Research of the Old Testament, with Special Consideration of Scandinavian Contributions.* 3rd ed. Atlanta: Scholars, 2006.

Ko, Grace. *Theodicy in Habakkuk.* Milton Keynes, UK: Paternoster, 2014. Kindle.

Köstenberger, Andreas J. "John." In *Commentary on the New Testament Use of the Old Testament*, edited by G. K. Beale and D. A. Carson, 415–512. Grand Rapids: Baker Academic, 2007.

Lasor, William Sanford, David Allan Hubbard, and Frederic William Bush. *Old Testament Survey: The Message, Form, and Background of the Old Testament*. 2nd ed. Grand Rapids: Eerdmans, 1996.

Lemaire, André. "Levantine Literacy Ca. 1000–750 BCE." In *Contextualizing Israel's Sacred Writings: Ancient Literacy, Orality, and Literary Production*, edited by Bryan B. Schmidt, 11–45. Atlanta: SBL, 2015.

Lemmelijn, Bénédicte. "Text-Critically Studying Manuscript Evidence: An 'Empirical' Entry to the Literary Composition of the Text." In *Empirical Models Challenging Biblical Criticism*, edited by Raymond F. Person Jr. and Robert Rezetko, 129–64. Atlanta: SBL, 2016.

Lewis, C. S. *The Abolition of Man*. New York: Harper One, 2001.

Lied, Live Ingeborg. "2 Baruch and the Syriac Codex Ambrosianus (7a1): Studying Old Testament Pseudepigrapha in Their Manuscript Context." *Journal for the Study of the Pseudepigrapha* 26.2 (2017) 67–107.

Liefeld, Walter L. "Luke." In *The Expositor's Bible Commentary Volume 8*, edited by Frank E. Gaeblein, 795–1059. Grand Rapids: Zondervan Publishing House, 1984.

Long, Burke O. "Recent Field Studies in Oral Literature and Their Bearing on OT Criticism." *Vetus Testamentum* 26 (1976) 189–98.

Longenecker, Richard N. *Biblical Exegesis in the Apostolic Period*. Grand Rapids: Eerdmans, 1999.

Longman, Tremper, III. *The Fear of the Lord Is Wisdom: A Theological Introduction to Wisdom in Israel*. Grand Rapids: Baker Academic, 2017.

Lord, Albert B. "Formula and Non-Narrative Theme in South Slavic Oral Epic and the OT." *Semeia* 5 (1976) 93–106.

———. "Patterns of Lives of the Patriarchs from Abraham to Samson and Samuel." In *Text and Tradition: The Hebrew Bible and Folklore*, edited by Susan Niditch, 7–18. Atlanta: Scholars, 1990.

Louw, Johannes P., and Eugene A. Nida, eds. *Greek-English Lexicon of the New Testament: Based on Semantic Domains*. 2nd ed. New York: United Bible Societies, 1988.

Lust, Johan, Erik Eynikel, and Katrin Hauspie. *Greek-English Lexicon of the Septuagint*. 3rd ed. Stuttgart: Deutsche Bibelgesellschaft, 2016.

Mak, Chelsea D. "Rehearsing Mythic Memory: Cultural Memory, Intertextuality, and the Sitz im Leben of Habakkuk's Prophecy." Master's thesis, Ambrose Seminary, 2017. https://apnts.whdl.org/sites/default/files/resource/academic/EN_Thesis_Mak_Rehearsing_mythic_memory_0.pdf?language=en.

Marshall, I. Howard. *The Gospel of Luke*. The New International Greek Testament Commentary, edited by I. Howard Marshall. Grand Rapids: Eerdmans, 1978.

Martin, Gary D. *Multiple Originals: New Approaches to Hebrew Bible Textual Criticism*. Atlanta: SBL, 2010.

Martin, M. "The Babylonian Tradition and Targum." In *Le Psautier: ses origines, ses problèmes littéraires, son influence*, edited by Robert de Langhe, 425–51. Louvain: Publications Universitaires, 1962.

Mathews, Janette. "Performing Habakkuk: Faithful Re-Enactment in the Midst of Crisis." Ph.D. diss., Charles Sturt University, 2010. https://illuminate.recollect.net.au/nodes/view/926.

McCarthy, Carmel. *The Tiqqune Sopherim and Other Theological Corrections in the Masoretic Text of the Old Testament*. Orbis biblicus et orientalis. Vol. 36. Göttingen: Vandenhoeck & Ruprecht, 1981.

McClister, David. "'Where Two or Three Are Gathered Together': Literary Structure as a Key to Meaning in Matt 17:22—20:19." *Journal of the Evangelical Theological Society* 39.4 (1996) 549–58.

McConnell, Taylor. "Oral Cultures and Literate Research." *Religious Education* 81.3 (Summer 1986) 341–55.

McGinnis, Claire Mathews. "The Hardening of Pharaoh's Heart in Christian and Jewish Interpretation." *Journal of Theological Interpretation* 6.1 (2012) 43–64.

McLay, R. Timothy. "Biblical Texts and the Scriptures for the New Testament Church." In *Hearing the Old Testament in the New Testament*, edited by Stanley E. Porter, 38–58. Grand Rapids: Eerdmans, 2006.

Miller, Joseph C. "The Dynamics of Oral Tradition in Africa." In *Fonti Orali: Antropologia e Storia*, edited by B. Bernardi, C. Ponti, and A. Triulzi, 75–101. Milan: Angeli, 1978.

———. "Introduction: Listening for the African Past." In *The African Past Speaks: Essays on Oral Tradition and History*, edited by J. C. Miller, 1–59. Hamden, CT: Archon, 1980.

Miller, Robert D. "The Performance of Oral Tradition in Ancient Israel." In *Contextualizing Israel's Sacred Writings: Ancient Literacy, Orality, and Literary Production*, edited Bryan B. Schmidt, 175–96. Atlanta: SBL, 2015.

Miller, Shem. *Dead Sea Media: Orality, Textuality, and Memory in the Scrolls from the Judean Desert*. Boston: Brill, 2019.

Mills, Margaret A. "Domains of Folkloristic Concern: The Interpretation of Scriptures." In *Text and Tradition: The Hebrew Bible and Folklore*, edited by Susan Niditch, 231–41. Atlanta: Scholars, 1990.

Mitchell, Ella P. "Oral Tradition: Legacy of Faith for the Black Church." *Religious Education* 81.1 (Winter 1986) 93–112.

Moo, Douglas J. *The Epistle to the Romans*. The New International Commentary on the New Testament. Edited by Gordon D. Fee. Grand Rapids: Eerdmans, 1996.

Mulroney, James A. E. "A Stone Shall Cry Out from a Wall: Studies on the Translation Style of Old Greek Habakkuk." Ph.D. diss., University of Edinburgh, 2014.

Murray, John. *The Epistle to the Romans*. The New International Commentary on the New Testament. Edited by F. F. Bruce. Grand Rapids: Eerdmans, 1965.

Niditch, Susan. *Folklore and the Hebrew Bible*. Minneapolis: Fortress, 1993.

———. "Hebrew Bible and Oral Literature: Misconceptions and New Directions." In *The Interface of Orality and Writing: Speaking, Seeing, Writing in the Shaping of New Genres*, edited by Annette Weissenrieder and Robert B. Coote, 3–18. Eugene, OR: Cascade, 2015.

———. *Judges: A Commentary*. Louisville: Westminster John Knox, 2008.

———. "Oral Register in the Biblical Libretto: Towards a Biblical Poetics." *Oral Tradition* 10.2 (1995) 387–408.

———. "Oral Tradition and Biblical Scholarship." *Oral Tradition* 18.1 (March 2003) 43–44.

———. *Oral World and Written Word: Ancient Israelite Literature*. Louisville: Westminster/John Knox, 1996.

———. *A Prelude to Biblical Folklore: Underdogs and Tricksters*. Urbana, IL: University of Illinois Press, 2000.

———, ed. *Text and Tradition: The Hebrew Bible and Folklore*. Atlanta: Scholars, 1990.

Nielsen, Eduard. *Oral Tradition: A Modern Problem in Old Testament Introduction*. London: SCM, 1954.

Niles, John D. *Homo Narrans: The Poetics and Anthropology of Oral Literature*. Philadelphia: University of Pennsylvania Press, 1999.

Nissinen, Martti. *Prophets and Prophecy in the Ancient Near East*. 2nd ed. Atlanta: SBL, 2019.

Oswalt, John N. *Isaiah*. The NIV Application Commentary. Edited by Terry Muck. Grand Rapids: Zondervan, 2003.

Oyler, Elizabeth. "The Heike in Japan." *Oral Tradition* 18.1 (March 2003) 18–20.

Park, Chan. "Korean P'ansori Narrative." *Oral Tradition* 18.2 (October 2003) 241–43.

Paul, Shalom M. "A Lover's Garden of Verse: Literal and Metaphorical Imagery in Ancient Near Eastern Love Poetry." In *Divrei Shalom: Collected Studies of Shalom M. Paul on the Bible and the Ancient Near East 1967–2005*, 271–84. Culture and History of the Ancient Near East 23. Leiden: Brill, 2005.

Payne, Philip B., and Paul Canart. "The Originality of Text-Critical Symbols in Codex Vaticanus." *Novum Testamentum* 42.2 (2000) 105–13.

Pender-Cudlip, Patrick. "Oral Traditions and Anthropological Analysis: Some Contemporary Myths." *Azania* 7 (1972) 3–24.

Pentikainen, Juha. "Oral Transmission of Knowledge." In *Folklore in the Modern World*, edited by R. Dorson, 237–52. The Hague: Mouton, 1978.

Perry, Peter. "Biblical Performance Criticism: Survey and Prospects." *Religions* 10.2 (2019). https://www.mdpi.com/2077-1444/10/2/117/pdf. Accessed through https://www.biblicalperformancecriticism.org.

Person, Raymond F., Jr. "The Ancient Israelite Scribe as Performer." *Journal of Biblical Literature* 117.4 (Winter 1998) 601–9.

———. *The Deuteronomic History and the Book of Chronicles: Scribal Works in an Oral World*. Atlanta: SBL, 2010.

———. "The Problem of 'Literary Unity' from the Perspective of the Study of Oral Traditions." In *Empirical Models Challenging Biblical Criticism*, edited by Raymond F. Person Jr. and Robert Rezetko, 217–37. Atlanta: SBL, 2016.

———. "Text Criticism as a Lens for Understanding the Transmission of Ancient Texts in Their Oral Environments." In *Contextualizing Israel's Sacred Writings: Ancient Literacy, Orality, and Literary Production*, edited by Bryan B. Schmidt, 197–215. Atlanta: SBL, 2015.

Person, Raymond F., Jr., and Robert Rezetko. "Introduction." In *Empirical Models Challenging Biblical Criticism*, edited by Raymond F. Person Jr. and Robert Rezetko, 1–35. Atlanta: SBL, 2016.

Polak, Frank H. "Oral Substratum, Language Usage, and Thematic Flow." In *Contextualizing Israel's Sacred Writings: Ancient Literacy, Orality, and Literary Production*, edited by Bryan B. Schmidt, 217–38. Atlanta: SBL, 2015.

Porter, Stanly. *Hearing the Old Testament in the New Testament*. Grand Rapids: Eerdmans, 2006.

Quick, Laura. "Recent Research on Ancient Israelite Education: A Bibliographic Essay." *Currents in Biblical Research* 13, no. 1 (2011) 9–33.

Raggazoli, Chloé. *Scribes: Les artisans du texte de l'Égypte ancienne (1550–1000)*. Paris: Les Belles Lettres, 2019.

Ranković, Slavica. "Who Is Speaking in Traditional Texts? On the Distributed Author of the Sagas of Icelanders and Serbian Epic Poetry." *New Literary History* 38 (2007) 293–307.

Ready, Jonathan L. *Orality, Textuality, & the Homeric Epics: An Interdisciplinary Study of Oral Texts, Dictated Texts, and Wild Texts*. Oxford: Oxford University Press, 2019.

Reasoner, Mark. "The Redemptive Inversions of Jeremiah in Romans 9–11." *Bíblica*, 95.3 (2014) 388–404.

Rhoads, David. "Performance Criticism: An Emerging Methodology in Biblical Studies." https://www.sbl-site.org/assets/pdfs/rhoads_performance.pdf.

———. "Performance Events in Early Christianity: New Testament Writings in an Oral Context." In *The Interface of Orality and Writing: Speaking, Seeing, Writing in the Shaping of New Genres*, edited by Annette Weissenrieder and Robert B. Coote, 166–201. Eugene, OR: Cascade, 2015.

Rodriguez, Rafael. *Oral Tradition and the New Testament: A Guide for the Perplexed*. New York: Bloomsbury, 2014.

———. "Reading and Hearing in Ancient Contexts." *Journal for the Study of the New Testament* 32.2 (2009) 151–78.

Rollston, Christopher A. "Scribal Curriculum During the First Temple Period: Epigraphic Hebrew and Biblical Evidence." In *Contextualizing Israel's Sacred Writings: Ancient Literacy, Orality, and Literary Production*, edited by Bryan B. Schmidt, 71–101. Atlanta: SBL, 2015.

Rushdoony, R. J. *The One and the Many*. Fairfax, VA: Thoburn Press, 1978.

Sanders, Seth L. "Empirical Models for Pentateuchal Criticism?" In *Contextualizing Israel's Sacred Writings: Ancient Literacy, Orality, and Literary Production*, edited by Bryan B. Schmidt, 281–304. Atlanta: SBL, 2015.

Sayers, Dorothy. *Letters to a Diminished Church*. United States: W, 2004.

Schiedewind, William M. "Orality and Literacy in Ancient Israel." *Religious Studies Review* 26.4 (2000) 327–32.

Schmidt, Brian B. "Introduction." In *Contextualizing Israel's Sacred Writings: Ancient Literacy, Orality, and Literary Production*, edited by Bryan B. Schmidt, 1–10. Atlanta: SBL, 2015.

———. "Memorializing Conflict: Toward an Iron Age 'Shadow' History of Israel's Earliest Literature." In *Contextualizing Israel's Sacred Writings: Ancient Literacy, Orality, and Literary Production*, edited by Bryan B. Schmidt, 103–32. Atlanta: SBL, 2015.

Schneider, William. "The Search for Wisdom in Native American Narratives and Classical Scholarship." *Oral Tradition* 18.2 (October 2003) 268–69.

Schweitzer, Albert. *The Quest of the Historical Jesus*. Mineola, NY: Dover, 2005.

Scott, William R. *A Simplified Guide to BHS*. 3rd ed. N. Richland Hills, TX: BIBAL, 1995.

Seifrid, Mark A. "Romans," In *Commentary on the New Testament Use of the Old Testament*, edited by G. K. Beale and D. A. Carson, 607–94. Grand Rapids: Baker Academic, 2007.

Sperber, Alexander, ed. *The Targum and the Hebrew Bible*. The Bible in Aramaic. Vol. IVB. Leiden: Brill, 1973.

Stoeltje, Beverly. "The Global and the Local with a Focus on Africa." *Oral Tradition* 18.1 (March 2003) 93–95.
Stuhlmueller, Carroll. "The Influence of Oral Tradition Upon Exegesis and the Senses of Scripture." *Catholic Biblical Quarterly* 20 (1958) 299–326.
Sweeney, Marvin A. "Habakkuk, Book of." In *Anchor Bible Dictionary*, edited by D. N. Freedman, vol. 3, 1–6. New York: Doubleday, 1992.
———. *Zephaniah: A Commentary*. Hermenia—A Critical and Historical Commentary on the Bible. Edited by Paul D. Hanson. Minneapolis: Fortress, 2003.
Tannen, Deborah. "The Oral/Literate Continuum in Discourse." In *Spoken and Written Language: Exploring Orality and Literacy*, edited by Deborah Tannen, 1–16. Norwood, NJ: ABLEX, 1982.
———. "Relative Focus on Involvement in Oral and Written Discourse." In *Literacy, Language, and Learning: The Nature and Consequences of Reading and Writing*, edited by David R. Olsen, 124–47. New York: Cambridge University Press, 1985.
Teffeteller, Annette. "Orality and the Politics of Scholarship." In *Politics of Orality*, edited by Craig Cooper, 67–86. Boston: Brill, 2007.
Tonkin, Eizabeth. "Investigating Oral Tradition." *JAH* 27 (1986) 203–13.
Torgerson, Heidi. "The Healing of the Bent Woman: A Narrative Interpretation of Luke 13:10–17." *Currents in Theology and Mission* 32.3 (June 2005) 176–86.
Tov, Emanuel. *The Greek Minor Prophets Scroll from Naḥal Ḥever (8ḤevXIIgr): (The Seiyal Collection I)*. DJD 8. Oxford: Clarendon, 1990.
———. *Textual Criticism of the Hebrew Bible*. 3rd ed. Minneapolis: Fortress Press, 2012.
Urbrock, William J. "Formula and Theme in the Song-Cycle of Job." In *Society of Biblical Literature, 1972 Proceedings*, 459–87. Missoula, MT: Scholars, 1972.
Van Seters, John. *Abraham in History and Tradition*. New Haven: Yale University Press, 1975.
Van Til, Cornelius. *The Defense of the Faith*. Edited by K. Scott Oliphint. 4th ed. Phillipsburg, NJ: P&R, 2008.
Vansina, Jan. *Oral Tradition as History*. Madison, WI: University of Wisconsin Press, 1985.
———. "Oral Tradition, Oral History: Achievements and Perspectives." In *Fonti Orali: Antropologia e Storia*, edited by B. Bernardi, C. Ponti, and A. Triulzi, 59–74. Milan: Angeli, 1978.
Vergani, Emidio. "An Introduction to Ceriani's Reprint of the Ambrosian Manuscript B 21 Inf. (Codex Ambrosianus 7a1)." In *A Facsimile Edition of the Peshitto Old Testament Based on Codex Ambrosianus (7a1)*, vii–xi. Piscataway, NJ: Gorgias Press, 2013.
Wallace, Daniel B. *Greek Grammar beyond the Basics*. Grand Rapids: Zondervan, 1996.
Waltke, Bruce K. "Oral Tradition." In *Inerrancy and Hermeneutics: A Tradition, a Challenge, a Debate*, edited by Harvie M. Conn, 117–35. Grand Rapids: Baker, 1988.
Watts, Rikk E. "Mark." In *Commentary on the New Testament Use of the Old Testament*, edited by G. K. Beale and D. A. Carson, 111–249. Grand Rapids: Baker Academic, 2007.
Weil, Gerhard E. "Foreword to the First Edition II." In *Biblia Hebraica Stuttgartensia*, edited by Karl Elliger and Wilhelm Rudolph, 5th rev. ed., v–xi. Stuttgart: Deutsche Bibelgesellschaft, 1997.

Wenham, Gordon J. "Sanctuary Symbolism in the Garden of Eden Story." In *Proceedings of the Ninth World Congress of Jewish Studies*, 19–26. Jerusalem: World Union of Jewish Studies, 1986.

West, T. M. "The Art of Biblical Performance: Biblical Performance Criticism and the Genre of the Biblical Narratives." Ph.D. diss., Vrije Universiteit Amsterdam, 2018.

Whallon, William. "Formulaic Poetry in the Old Testament." *Comparative Literature* 15 (1963) 1–14.

Wolf, Herbert M. "Judges." In *Expositor's Bible Commentary Volume 3*, edited by Frank E. Gaeblein, 373–506. Grand Rapids: Zondervan, 1992.

Wünch, Hans-Georg. "The Strong and the Fat Heart." *OTE* 30.1 (2017) 165–88.

Würthwein, Ernst. *The Text of the Old Testament: An Introduction to the Biblia Hebraica*. Rev. ed., translated by E. Rhodes. Grand Rapids: Eerdmans, 1996.

Wyrick, Stephen von. Comment on dissertation, "How Should the Reader Run: Implications of Orality and Textuality in the Transmission and Message of the Habakkuk Tradition as Seen in Important Witnesses to the Text," by Nick Acker, B. H. Carroll Theological Institute, 2022.

Yang, Inchol. "A Text Critical Analysis of the First Taunt Song in Habakkuk 2:5–8." *Canon and Culture* 12.2 (2018) 45–75.

Yoder, Perry B. "A-B Pairs and Oral Composition in Hebrew Poetry." *Vetus Testamentum* 21 (1971) 470–89.

Young, Ian. "The Original Problem: The Old Greek and the Masoretic Text of Daniel 5." In *Empirical Models Challenging Biblical Criticism*, edited by Raymond F. Person Jr. and Robert Rezetko, 271–301. Atlanta: SBL, 2016.

———. "The Stabilization of the Biblical Text in the Light of Qumran and Masada: A Challenge for Conventional Qumran Chronology?" *DSD* 9 (2002) 364–90.

Ziegler, Joseph, ed. *Duodecim Prophetae*. Vetus Testamentum Graecum. Vol. 8. Auctoritate Academiae Scientiarum Gottingensis editum. Göttingen: Vandenhoeck & Ruprecht, 1984.

Zoccali, Christopher. "'And So All Israel Will Be Saved': Competing Interpretations of Romans 11.26 in Pauline Scholarship," *JSNT* 30.3 (2008) 289–318.

www.ingramcontent.com/pod-product-compliance
Lightning Source LLC
Chambersburg PA
CBHW071234230426
43668CB00011B/1437